Of Parrots
and People

It is through error that man tries and rises.
It is through tragedy that he learns.
All the roads of learning begin in darkness and go out into the light.

—Hippocrates

To my muse, Mango,
    with more love than I can express.
      You started this journey, and you
        continue to inspire it.

      And with much appreciation to Rosie,
       who came when I most needed her.

      With gratitude and love to Zazu,
     a little parrot who had some
    big shoes to fill and has
done so well.

VIKING
Published by the Penguin Group
Penguin Group (USA) Inc., 375 Hudson Street, New York, New York 10014, U.S.A. • Penguin Group (Canada), 90 Eglinton Avenue East, Suite 700, Toronto, Ontario, Canada M4P 2Y3 (a division of Pearson Penguin Canada Inc.) • Penguin Books Ltd, 80 Strand, London WC2R 0RL, England • Penguin Ireland, 25 St. Stephen's Green, Dublin 2, Ireland (a division of Penguin Books Ltd) • Penguin Books Australia Ltd, 250 Camberwell Road, Camberwell, Victoria 3124, Australia (a division of Pearson Australia Group Pty Ltd) • Penguin Books India Pvt Ltd, 11 Community Centre, Panchsheel Park, New Delhi - 110 017, India • Penguin Group (NZ), 67 Apollo Drive, Rosedale, North Shore 0632, New Zealand (a division of Pearson New Zealand Ltd) • Penguin Books (South Africa) (Pty) Ltd, 24 Sturdee Avenue, Rosebank, Johannesburg 2196, South Africa

Penguin Books Ltd, Registered Offices: 80 Strand, London WC2R 0RL, England

First published in 2008 by Viking Penguin, a member of Penguin Group (USA) Inc.

10   9   8   7   6   5   4   3   2   1

Photograph credits appear on page 318

While the author has made every effort to provide accurate telephone numbers and Internet addresses at the time of publication, neither the publisher nor the author assumes any responsibility for errors, or for changes that occur after publication. Further, the publisher does not have any control over and does not assume any responsibility for author or third-party Web sites or their content.

LIBRARY OF CONGRESS CATALOGING IN PUBLICATION DATA
Tweti, Mira.
    Of parrots and people : the sometimes funny, always facinating, and often catastrophic collision of two intelligent species / Mira Tweti.
       p. cm.
    Includes index.
    ISBN 978-0-670-01969-4
1. Parrots—Miscellanea.   2. Human-animal relationships—Miscellanea.   I. Title.
SF473.P3T84 2009
636.6'865—dc22   2008022854

Printed in the United States of America
Set in Fournier

Of Parrots and People

The Sometimes Funny,

Always Fascinating,

and Often Catastrophic

Collision of Two

Intelligent Species

Mira Tweti

VIKING

Contents

Introduction

This book must begin with Mango, a rainbow lory and my decade-long muse. It was love at first sight when we met and moved in together. It would have been nice to have a muse that didn't bite, but we don't choose our muses; we are just lucky to find them.

Mango was the inspiration for this book and why I began writing about birds and other animals for newspapers and magazines, why I joined a bird club (and ended up becoming its president), and why I spent more than two years making a documentary film about pet birds. All this from one little eight-inch-long parrot covered in multicolored feathers (they didn't name them rainbows for nothing) that, unbeknownst to me when I bought him, had as much to say about life as I did.

Were it just for the love of a bird, I don't know that this domino effect in my life would have occurred. It happened also because under those feathers I discovered a being with an intelligence so keen it astounded me.

I was a cat person from childhood. Honeybunch, the grand dame of the neighborhood strays, held court in our New York City brownstone's backyard (mostly because my mother fed her and her friends). A black-and-white alley cat, she was impressively smart. She could open windows or turn on the water faucet for a drink. So I never expected the leap from cats to birds to be so dramatic; if anything, I expected much less from a parrot. I assumed the phrase "bird brain" was an insult for a reason. I only realized the scope of Mango's intelligence when he apologized for biting me. I let him out of his cage while I was preparing breakfast or dinner. Because his wings were clipped, he played on the floor and sometimes got underfoot. There was an unmistakable pained squawk when I accidentally nipped his foot or stepped on his tail feathers. I would quickly bring him up on my finger, kiss his beak, and say, "I'm sorry. I'm sorry. I'm so sorry." He liked the attention and developed a routine, feigning the pained squawk, as if he hadn't recovered, so I would apologize over and over. When enough absolution was made, he'd show his forgiveness by saying, "Give us a kiss" (the first English phrase he learned with "comprehension," an understanding of the meaning of his words), which would mark the end of the episode.

A few months later he nipped me on the finger. When I said "Ow!" he looked at me and in a sweet, caring voice said, "I'm sorry. I'm sorry. I'm soooo sorry!" After that Mango apologized whenever he did something wrong, or if he was about to. When I heard him saying, "I'm sorry. I'm sorry. I'm soooo sorry," in another room, I rushed in because he was about to do something he wasn't supposed to. Not once in all the years we lived together did he say he was sorry unless it was appropriate. He could not be induced to say it otherwise. If I said "I'm sorry" to elicit that response from him, he would assume I'd done something wrong and give me a forgiving look. It wouldn't occur to him to say "I'm sorry" unless he meant it because he had crossed from copying to comprehension. Over the next decade, Mango learned to say fifty things with comprehension and understood thirty-five more that he didn't verbalize.

With Mango what I initially thought was a pet turned out to be the most demanding relationship of my life. There's a saying in animal behavior science: "Never study an animal that's smarter than you." This definitely applies to parrots.

The boom in purchasing parrots as pets, which started in the 1960s and lasted until recently, generated unprecedented interest in understanding these enigmatic exotics. Researchers have found they are more like us than we ever dreamed. Parrots have remarkable brains and know how to use them to learn, to read, to do math problems, and to communicate with humans. This has led to some marvelous marriages of humans and birds.

I had one such relationship, and when Mango died in the winter of

2006, I grieved in a way I had never expected. I wondered whether I was unique and sought out others who had experienced the loss of a long-term parrot companion. Some of their experiences are shared in this book.

I also explored the huge, unexpected, and often terrible consequences of taking these complex creatures out of the wild and into our homes—consequences that have now become a crisis. Parrots are the world's most endangered group of birds. Thousands are being hunted to extinction for the legal and illegal pet trade, yet there are an estimated forty to sixty million pet birds in the United States alone, and a growing epidemic of unwanted parrots.

In 2003, I wrote an exposé for the *Los Angeles Times Magazine* titled "Plenty to Squawk About," which broke the national story of the terrible, but routine, practices of the legal pet bird trade. The article won a Genesis Award from the Humane Society of the United States for outstanding investigative journalism. But it utilized only a fraction of the investigative research I had done. Knowing how much was left unsaid compelled me to write this book.

This book not only celebrates parrots but also reveals how they think, how they live with us, and how they suffer because of us. I hope I have created a document that will change the way people think about parrots and positively affect the lives of these remarkable beings.

I hope you will come away as I have, awed by a new awareness of the avian world around us.

Of Parrots
and People

Chapter One

Bird Brains

After a movie let out, one patron ran over to another walking with a parrot on his shoulder. "Excuse me," he said, "but I must ask you about your bird. He's quite remarkable. He was making insightful comments throughout the film. I find that amazing!" "Yes, it is amazing," said the bird's owner, "since he didn't like the book very much."

In 1976, Irene Pepperberg, a research associate professor at Brandeis University and a research scientist at the Massachusetts Institute of Technology, applied for her first grant to study the intelligence of parrots.

It was met with disbelief.

"The National Institutes of Health panel came back basically asking me what I was smoking because nobody remotely thought birds could do anything like what I was proposing," says Pepperberg.

She ultimately received funding for her research, and today she continues to consistently prove wrong naysayers who underestimate parrot intelligence. She and her now-famous study subject, an African gray parrot named Alex, revolutionized what people thought about avian brains.

When Alex died suddenly at thirty-one in September 2007, thousands of condolences poured into the Alex Foundation, and the media heralded his legacy around the world. The *New York Times* ran two stories—a feature obituary, the first ever for a parrot, and an editorial that ended, "Ethically speaking, the value [of Pepperberg's research] lies in our surprise, our renewed awareness of how little we allow ourselves to expect from the animals around us." In the obituary she presented on ABC's *Good Morning America,* Diane Sawyer called Alex "Einstein," and said it was a loss to all of us that he had died. His last words, spoken as Pepperberg placed him into his cage the night he died, were, "You be good. See you tomorrow. I love you."

Alex was bought from a pet store as a young bird to prevent any claims that he was genetically altered or specially bred for intelligence. In the three decades she worked with Alex, Pepperberg taught him to speak with comprehension, and he was able to identify eighty objects and give their locations.

Alex didn't just know the objects he referred to; he was able to demonstrate critical thinking about objects that were similar to one another. When shown two different keys, he could compare their sizes, colors, shapes, and other characteristics. In some cases, Alex demonstrated complex understanding beyond what had been shown in primates. In addition to object and location labels, Alex learned the sounds of some of the alphabet and could identify them when written. Once Alex had those under his wing, Pepperberg started teaching him to read phonetically, using colored refrigerator letters. He would say "Shhh" for the letter combination SH, and "Sss" for the letter S. That was particularly impressive when you consider that our language was not his native tongue.

Alex could also count. Asked how many "blue blocks" were on a tray that had different numbers of colored wooden squares, balls, and triangles, Alex's brain went through the same processes as a human's: isolating the correct color, identifying the right shape, and figuring the number of them. He was counting, versus using instant visual recognition, as one does when looking at dice.

In exercises like these, Pepperberg said Alex's "margin of error tests out the same as humans," and only his impatience with classroom-type learning limited what he could learn. Pepperberg has worked with several more African grays in her lab, with similar results. Some learned faster than Alex did, and surpassed him in certain skills.

Pepperberg's life's work became the first continuous intensive and scientific parrot intelligence research project. It dispelled many of the myths that birds, and animals in general, are purely emotional or volitional, unable to reason using perception, memory, and judgment. Only recently has Pepperberg's work been substantiated by other studies showing the power of a bird's brain.

Over much of the last millennium, science intentionally or inadvertently legitimized cultural concepts that nonhuman animals were lower life forms. The combination of bad science and speciesism (racism toward nonhuman animals) firmed up the idea that animals were simply flesh-and-blood machines that could neither think nor feel pain. These ideas filtered down into common colloquialisms such as "birdbrained."

Over the last fifty years the established manifesto placing man at the top of the evolutionary ladder has been revised to acknowledge that there are lots of ladders, different kinds of intelligence, and parallel evolution with other species.

In his doctoral research, Harvard biologist Michael Schindlinger specialized in parrot dialects and insect communication. To him, the premise that humans alone are endowed with consciousness is obviously incorrect. "If you assume a discontinuity [in brain function between humans and other animals], then you've already made your faulty assumption," says Schindlinger. "Start with the assumption that what's good for one mind is probably good for another in terms of functionality, and revise your theory as new information comes in."

Pepperberg and Schindlinger are not alone in their thinking. Research studies are continually opening doors into the world of animal communication, to find it teeming with conversant beings.

Who would expect bees to talk to one another? It turns out they have plenty to say, and they maintain their reputation for stellar organizational skills by communicating in a well-defined, complex bee version of Morse code. Scientists have confirmed this ability by allowing a group of bees to track a food source as it was moved progressively farther from their hive.

The researchers painted dots on the backs of the bees that remained in the hive and watched as the first travelers returned and thumped out detailed directions to the food for the others to follow. With this information the hive bees flew directly to it, zigzagging along the same long trail on the ground as the first group of bees, then up vertically into the canopy, where they found the food atop a ladder tower. Researchers know it had to be the "Morse code" that tipped them off: a bee's smell and sight range is just twenty feet.

Other studies have shown that species such as elephants and giraffes can communicate with others of their kind from miles away, using infrasound frequencies below human hearing, and ants and caterpillars are in dialogue with one another (the latter thumps out signals to the former). Even fish communicate.

It might turn out that birds and humans have the most complex of all communication systems in the animal world.

Largely unnoticed by nonbirds, a vast, invisible network of avian communication exists all around us in cities, suburbs, and parks. Walk past a noisy, bird-filled tree, and you're hearing a coffee klatch of exchanges between conspecifics (members of a species, or a flock). Their chirping, squawking, and singing are not mindless utterances but meaning-laden sounds directed at a mate, a friend, or a flock. They can be simple messages such as, "The food's here on this branch," "I'm leaving now," or "Let's get back to the nest; it's getting dark," or a complicated enticement to a serious relationship.

Just as a Bostonian's dialect will differ from a southerner's, even birds that speak the same language will have different dialects, depending on where they live. These different accents enable birds to form and maintain flock systems and are a sign of sophisticated communication and complex social structures.

From 1962 until his death in 2000, world-renowned avian research scientist Luis Baptista, based at the Academy of Sciences in San Francisco, studied white-crowned sparrows. He found that birds on the northern side of the Golden Gate Bridge sang the same songs as their counterparts on the Fort Baker side, but in completely different dialects. He checked the white-crowned sparrows on the three islands in San Francisco Bay and mapped out different dialects in each group. Baptista maintained that, even blindfolded, he could tell which island he was on by the dialect of the birds in that area.

Baptista didn't just record the birds he studied; he spoke to them. Watching him do so in Golden Gate Park was a unique experience. He sang the white-crowned sparrow's mating call, and moments later, two male sparrows flew to the ground in front of him. With their tails high in the air, they showed aggressive postures by strutting back and forth and vociferously calling at him. Baptista translated their actions. He explained that the dominant male was telling him this was their home territory, and it was time for him to move out. They knew he was an interloper, Baptista believed, not because he was a giant human towering over them, but because he wasn't singing in the right dialect. The birds weren't about to lose their wives to a playboy in the neighborhood with some hoity-toity new dialect.

Baptista banded all the white-crowned sparrows around his office building on the academy grounds and got to know them as individuals. At the back of the building lived a female who sang in three different dialects. "She was so dominant she regularly beat up her husband," said Baptista. "Then she divorced him and married the guy next door, and he beat her up."

Baptista could never understand what she saw in her second husband. But he must have been pretty special in other ways, because they raised more offspring than any other couple in the park. Baptista guessed the male's aggressiveness was an indication of his fitness.

"There was another bird that was born in the conservatory of flowers who did some interesting things," he added. "He moved a half mile away, changed his dialect to match the dialects of his new neighbors, and got involved with two females and became a bigamist." A bird Baptista named Oedipus ran off with his mother and mated with her. Baptista explained that, as different as birds are from us, they often behave very much like us; the only way to learn this, however, is to get to know them personally.

It isn't only in communication that birds excel. They are complex through and through. For example, aside from humans, birds are the only other animals to invent tools they use on a daily basis. Some primates use objects they find, but none have actually created tools the way birds have. Crows and finches bend twigs to hook food out of places too deep for them to reach with their beaks, an ability that has been replicated in a laboratory. In repeated tests, New Caledonian crows provided with only straight pieces of metal wire spontaneously created hooked tools each time they needed to reach inaccessible food down a hole. Scientists studying them likened their tools to those of Paleolithic man.

Finches use their beaks as scissors and snippers to make hooked tools, and make barbed, serrated combs to rake the ground out of hard leaves, carrying them along to use again in different places. Crows are so smart that some of them make use of human technology in an ingenious form of nutcracking. In Japan several crows have been documented standing on the curb at a busy intersection holding nuts in their beaks until traffic stops. They then walk across the street with the crowd of pedestrians, pausing along the way to place the nuts next to the tires of stopped cars. After the departing cars crack the shells, the crows hop out and pick up the shelled nuts. If the cars miss the nuts the first time, the birds try again.

Some crows perch on overhanging power lines and drop nuts to be cracked. Recently, crows in California have been documented doing this as well.

Sophisticated behavior like this is typical of the complex problem solving birds engage in daily. "Clever businessmen," birds move through the world calculating the probability of finding food in one location over another, waiting or leaving based on what they decide, says Dr. Frank Gill, whom many consider the godfather of current ornithological science.

"All of life is a trade-off in time and energy," says Gill, senior vice president and director of science at the National Audubon Society, "and birds play this game at amazing levels and in ways one would never expect. It's game theory. Birds are living game theory every day."

Insights like Gill's into avian thinking are important to note because the intelligence of birds and other nonhuman animals is generally evaluated not on their own terms but on ours, using the criteria used to measure human intelligence. That is inherently hazardous, as proven by the immense problems researchers have encountered trying to quantify human intelligence with the same criteria.

For example, IQ tests were designed to measure innate intelligence, not learned information. Over the last century they have been used (and sometimes still are) as incontrovertible proof of the inferiority of some ethnic groups. These claims were finally debunked in the 1970s by developmental psychologists such as Dr. Robert Serpell at the University of Zambia. He showed that cultural differences between African children and those in the West, and different definitions of intelligence within cultures (which resulted in certain behaviors being encouraged over others), played a huge role in a person's test results.

Eventually researchers realized that they couldn't get accurate measurements of intelligence in a culture if they used a test devised outside that culture. It follows that humans can't expect to accurately measure the intelligence of another animal species without accurately understanding its language, culture, and behavioral cues.

Schindlinger gives a good example of this in a famous experiment whose goal was to breed smarter rats. The geneticists conducting the experiment thought they had bred a line of intelligent rats, which they called "maze bright" because they ran a maze faster than others, which they named "maze dull." They finally discovered that the maze-bright rats were blind. The rats had inadvertently been selected for blindness, not intelligence. They ran the maze so well because, unlike the sighted rats, they weren't distracted or stressed by geneticists standing over them with clipboards.

"We have to use great caution with the labels we apply to behaviors we see," says Schindlinger. "We don't know that we're dealing in a common framework. And that's true even in methods of communicating: when caterpillars are talking to ants, it's not an airborne sound, like our communication."

Just as it has been generally assumed that species whose behaviors don't mimic ours are not intelligent, it has been assumed that species with brains not designed like ours are naturally lacking in intelligence. But you can't judge a brain by its size, and birds prove that point in spades. Though it goes against commonly held wisdom, a big brain in itself does not guarantee intelligence (in fact, Neanderthals had bigger brains than we do), and a small brain doesn't automatically indicate a lack of it. Big brains were an evolutionary option, just like the migration of sea creatures to land to avoid the myriad predators in the water. And they were an option not exclusively offered to humans. In much the same way that we have generally assumed that birds have little intelligence because of the size of their brains, we have assumed that large, complex brains are the exclusive domain of humans.

Many other species could have had large brains, in fact, but didn't take that evolutionary option because they are expensive to maintain. Unlike other organs, the brain never sleeps; it drains energy like a gas-guzzling car with the engine running all the time. In areas where food is scarce, a big brain can put a species out of business. The added weight of a large brain, when speed and mobility are required to outrun predators or catch prey, is also a bad deal in evolutionary terms.

Brain size in relationship to body size is an important marker of intelligence, and in that regard bird brains are the same as human—6 percent of total body mass. In December 2002, a study published in the journal *Integrative and Comparative Biology* reported that parrots have larger brains relative to their body size than any other group of birds, and that several parrot species have relatively larger brains than comparably sized primates. Also crucial is the presence of the right kind of wiring to enable the brain to support intelligence.

According to evolutionary biologist Stephen Jay Gould, four million years ago it wasn't brain size or behavioral complexity that determined the fate of *Homo sapiens;* it was simply the ability to stand upright. Without that evolutionary perk, the human species could just as easily have ended up ecologically marginalized, like gorillas and chimpanzees, and would probably be extinct by now.

A good analogy for the relationship of brain size to intelligence can be found in the evolution of computers. In the 1960s, the average computer system took up an entire room. That was acceptable at the time, given the volume and complexity of information the machines were required to process, such as the calculations for sending men into space. But now computer systems as smart as those early ones can fit in the palm of a hand, and are getting smaller all the time.

The same idea applies to birds. Stellar examples of evolution, birds have efficient and highly intelligent brains that are very small, so they stay light for flight. Unlike the bulky and heavy cerebral cortex common to humans, birds have compact cortical areas that function in much the same way. The latest research shows that the intelligence areas of birds' brains are not much different from those of humans in function. But in form, theirs are like computer microchips—small with phenomenal capabilities. Parrots test out at the intelligence levels of three- to five-year-old children and routinely outperform primates in problem-solving tests.

In 2005, science finally caught up with reality. After seven years of research, an international consortium of twenty-nine scientists unanimously agreed to revise the nomenclature describing functional activity and structure of the brains of birds and, for the first time in Western society, gave birds their due. They based their decision on their findings that two areas of the brain—the claustrum and the amygdala, sources of the emotional systems in humans—are much larger in birds because they co-opted those areas to integrate information. Judging the book by its cover, scientists had previously cited those enlarged areas as proof that birds were primarily emotion-based and lacked intelligence. One of the consortium scientists, Georg Striedter of the University of California, Irvine, claims that this research has refuted many of the old views of avian and mammalian brain evolution and function.

This research further demonstrates that birds' brains are more sophisticated than previously imagined, but it's only logical: if the biodiversity of the world runs on survival of the fittest, then the longevity of birds, and their ability to thrive in all the terrains and temperatures around the globe, is in itself a testament to the perfection of their physical design. Most people don't realize how remarkable their lineage actually is.

It was long thought that birds evolved from reptiles or small dinosaurs from a common ancestor, but paleontological evidence shows that birds and dinosaurs are inextricably linked; some dinosaurs evolved into birds, while others had birdlike qualities. For example, the gigantic *Tyrannosaurus rex* had feathers, as did the voracious velociraptors.

Discoveries in Lionang, China, have uncovered remains of feathered dinosaurs that couldn't fly, such as the 130-million-year-old dromaeosaur, which was two-legged and predatory. Fossils show that it was covered from head to tail with downy fluff and primitive feathers. A scientist involved in the discovery has stated that it is "indisputable" that many nonavian dinosaurs had a featherlike covering. Since dromaeosaurs are older than birds, scientists believe feathers were probably developed to retain heat when the animals became warm-blooded and that flighted dinosaurs, i.e., birds, evolved directly from them.

Scientists now speculate that theropods—"bird footed" carnivorous dinosaurs, such as *T. rex*, which walked on two hind legs and lived between the Triassic and Cretaceous periods (230 million to 65 million years ago)—looked more like strange birds than giant lizards. Velociraptors, whose name means "speedy thief," were feared predators six feet tall that could run forty miles an hour on two hind legs. Many people became familiar with them from the film *Jurassic Park*. Because the feather findings are recent, the film depicted the velociraptors and *T. rex* in the traditional lizard skin. The movie's lead consultant, Jacques Gauthier, a professor at Yale University who specializes in vertebrate paleontology and reptile evolution, admits it was a mistake. "We got them wrong," he says. Still, it's hard to imagine humans being terrorized by a Terminator-like bird covered in fuzzy feathers.

One of the oldest bird fossils found in the United States was of a parrot, not unlike a lory, that dated to 65 million years BCE, also in the Cretaceous period. And there is even a group of dinosaurs called psittacosaurids, "parrot-beaked," that were small and lived earlier than ever imagined in 135 million BCE.

The question of whether birds were dinosaurs, or some dinosaurs were birds, has divided scientific camps. Those who believe the latter say dromaeosaurs, a type of therapod, represent a separate evolutionary line of flightless birds, like the ostriches of today—a theory fueled by the discovery of the first intact soft tissue remains in the bones of a seventy-million-year-old therapod, a *T. rex*, in Montana. Researchers found medullary tissue, a hormone-generated calcium deposit found only in present-day female birds during egg-laying cycles. It is not present in other dinosaur-related species, like crocodiles, that also lay eggs.

The modern birds whose tissue most resembles that of *T. rex* are ratites—flightless birds such as ostriches and emus. When the *T. rex* tissue sample was scanned with an electron microscope, it showed blood vessels that are virtually identical to those of modern ratites in form, location, and distribution.

Though the largest dinosaurs are extinct, many medium and smaller ones are not, Gauthier claims; because the ten thousand known bird species outnumber the four thousand known mammal species, we are still living in the age of dinosaurs. "Dinosaurs are flying around us all the time," he says.

New evidence also shows that dinosaurs behaved more like birds in nurturing and caring for their young than was previously thought. An interesting similarity can be found in modern alligators, a cousin of the dinosaurs. They not only lay their eggs in nests but also sing songs to their young still inside the egg, just as birds do. The young sing back to their parent and siblings through the eggshell, and their calls sound similar to birdsongs.

With three hundred million years of evolution behind them, it's no wonder the dinosaurs we now commonly call birds evolved to be so smart, so energy efficient, and such great athletes. They are considered models of evolution, and with good reason:

- The ability to fly is one of birds' most fascinating characteristics. Some years ago the National Institutes of Health spent millions of dollars on several bird physiology studies whose goal was to discover how migratory birds' light but resilient muscle fibers could withstand the rigors of yearly cross-continent flight. The answer remains undiscovered. However, we do know that bird brains are specially wired for flight, with features such as well-developed semicircular canals in the inner ear for balance and enlarged optic lobes for keen vision.

- Migrating birds get the energy equivalent of five hundred miles to a gallon of gas, and they can navigate thousands of miles flying through pitch-black skies using the earth's magnetic field and star systems. Their extraordinary internal compasses are like built-in GPS satellite technology.

- Birds have extraordinarily advanced spatial memories. Clark's nutcrackers cache seeds and nuts in up to ten thousand different places and retrieve more than 80 percent of them, even though they might be miles apart and covered in snow.

- Studies have demonstrated the remarkable abilities of rock pigeons (common pigeons), popularly thought to be unintelligent birds. Pigeons can recall more than seven hundred visual patterns, and are capable of tricking other birds to keep a food source to themselves. Pigeons can also be trained to discriminate the differences between paintings by Monet and Picasso, indicating visual cognitive functions similar to those of humans. During World Wars I and II they were used to carry messages from the frontlines to headquarters with information about enemy troop movements. Some, like Cher Amie and G.I. Joe, flew on scores of missions through heavy combat, saving the lives of thousands of Allied soldiers.

- Birds' beaks, simple in form and function, are fantastic tools. Light and maneuverable, they are as strong as a can opener because they are part of a bird's jawbone. One researcher credits birds with having colonized the world because they were armed with beaks. "There is no tool that reaches the efficiency of a beak," says parrot expert Dr. Carlos Yamashita.

Parrots demonstrate this well. Moluccan cockatoos have beaks capable of exerting five hundred pounds of pressure, and can reduce a broom handle to toothpicks in no time. Hyacinth macaws eat palm nuts, the hardest nuts in the world. Humans need a hammer to get one open, but these nuts are no match for a macaw's beak.

Beaks are covered in a sheath called the rhamphotheca, which is made of a calcium compound similar to our fingernails. The section closest to the bird's head contains veins, arteries, and so many nerve endings it is more sensitive than our fingertips. Beaks are also surprisingly accurate: professional aviculturalists tell stories of padlocks being picked open by parrots' beaks, forcing them to switch to combination locks. (Now the parrots are working on figuring out those.) Parrot tongues are also highly sensitive and contain bones that make them tremendously flexible and able to manipulate objects as if they were fingers.

- Of all vertebrates, birds have the best-developed color vision. Humans and primates have three cones in their eyes for recognizing red, green, and blue—but birds have a fourth cone for ultraviolet colors, broadening their spectrum of vision. Many bird species have ultraviolet-reflective plumage, so a bird can see color gradations in another bird's feathers that we can't. And a parrot can tell whether a piece of friut is ripe or not just by looking at it because the sun's ultraviolet markings show on its skin. Placement is also crucial. Birds' eyes are positioned on either side of their head so they take in an entire field of vision, allowing them to watch two events at the same time and process all the details in both.

Even something as simple as breathing is state-of-the-art in bird physiology. Unlike in human and other mammalian lungs, bird lungs don't mix old air with fresh. Clear air flows unidirectionally through open-ended parabronchi (the counterpart to alveoli in mammals). As clear air is inhaled stale is exhaled through a separate tube, with air sacs acting more like bellows than receptacles. This system provides a more efficient way to pull oxygen from the atmosphere. Avian lungs are so efficient that where humans struggle to breathe at high altitudes, bar-headed geese breathe easily as they fly over Mount Everest, five and a half miles in the air. (The cold doesn't bother them either, because a thick coat of feathers is warmer than fur.)

With thousands of uniquely different species, birds are also astounding in their diversity. Some people believe the universe comes together most perfectly in avian form. But the wonder and essence of birds is deeper than the sum of their parts, and that can't be scientifically measured, as demonstrated by Baptista and Gill's dedication to them. "I'm biased," says Gill. "I worship birds." He went on to describe an experience that epitomized the reason for his regard:

> If some day you're down in Antarctica, and you have a chance to sit on top of a hill next to a wandering albatross incubating an egg, which they do for many months through the winter, just look it in the eye and communicate with it.
>
> That bird exudes a wisdom I have never seen in the eyes of any human. He lives a long time. He works the oceans. He flies thousands of miles on a single foray. He views the world, his domain, in an extraordinary way. And it's there in his eyes. What it is I don't know, but it is huge.

We know surprisingly little about parrots, considering that they have long been the most popular birds humans have kept as pets, dating back to ancient times. One reason we are bereft of information is that parrots, unlike songbirds, which are generally content to sit and sing, have busy, involved lives and are always on the move. This makes them logistically difficult to study in the wild.

Another reason has to do not with the birds but with the agendas of their human researchers. Baptista said many of his doctoral candidates didn't want to do fieldwork on parrots. "Scientists like to be published in their lifetimes," he noted. "Parrots are long-lived birds, and so intelligent, it will take three lifetimes to publish something really significant that explains their communication and behavior in the wild."

Songbirds, which been studied fairly thoroughly, have been found to have ten to twenty different things they can say to one another—but parrots in the wild are estimated to have five hundred. "The real challenge now is communicating with them to understand what they're thinking about," says Gill.

Perhaps the most compelling reason for studying parrots is that they might offer us our best opportunity to understand the minds of other species, because they are so intelligent and can learn to speak to us in our own language.

Jack Bradbury is a professor of ornithology at Cornell University and the director of the Macaulay Library of Natural Sounds, which has the largest collection of animal sound recordings in the world. In studies conducted in the Brazilian Amazon, the Caribbean, and Australia, he and his associates have uncovered patterns in the seeming mimicry of parrots, finding that copying one another's calls aids the birds directly in communication.

In a flock, many birds can be talking loudly and simultaneously. Learning another bird's call and attaching it to the end of yours is a good way to tell a bird on a distant tree branch that you are addressing him directly. For example, if a parrot named Sam wanted to converse with one named Rebecca, he would start by exchanging calls with her. When they were both familiar with each other's call, he would send out his call with Rebecca's tagged on, sort of saying, "Hi, I'm Sam-'becca," so Rebecca would know he was addressing her.

Bradbury and his colleagues also found that parrots sometimes call to flocks passing overhead to alert them to food. But they are picky about when they call. The decision is based not only on the availability of food but also on who is flying by. Parrots discriminate, notifying birds they like and avoiding calling to flocks of birds they don't. These spontaneous, tailored, and directed communications, as well as illustrating the intelligence of parrots, might also further prove what some researchers believe: like us, parrots learned to speak for the purpose of communication, not just for food finding. "For sure, their repertoire is more complex than we know. But how do we prove it to ourselves? We haven't found the right methods. Now we're teaching them with experimental methods to resolve some types of complex problems," says Yamashita.

This is all borne out by Pepperberg's Alex, who learned language and used it as we do. "Alex and all other parrots have perfectly good species-specific communication systems—what you might want to call 'parrot language,'" Pepperberg said in an interview before Alex's death. "So trying to teach him to communicate with humans in English is paramount to trying to teach him a 'second' language." The difficulty in that can be appreciated if you consider trying to learn parrot, crow, or pigeon as a second language.

I was fortunate enough to film in Pepperberg's lab for my documentary on parrots. While the crew was setting up I witnessed a dialogue between Pepperberg and Alex that I still regret I didn't catch on tape.

As soon as he saw the camera tripod, Alex knew what was going on. "Want to go back," he said to Pepperberg, meaning he wanted to return to his cage. Pepperberg started making offers: "Just one hour," she said, pleading. Alex was nonplussed and turned to leave. Pepperberg reacted quickly. "And pizza," she added. He thought about it. "And shoulder," he countered, referring to his preferred perch. "Okay, one hour, pizza, and shoulder," replied Pepperberg, happy to seal the deal.

Pizzas were ordered, and Alex grudgingly started to answer Pepperberg's questions. At one point he said, "Want a nut." When Pepperberg gave him a peanut, he discarded it, saying, "Want a walnut."

Pepperberg and I have discussed this scenario since. She says she hadn't taught Alex about time (though she referred to it often in exercises with him, as in, "I'll give you a nut in a minute"). When she said an hour, I checked my watch. Later, when the taping was through, Alex turned to leave and couldn't be cajoled into coming back. It was an hour on the dot. We all had pizza. My crew, having watched Alex's negotiations, expected pizza for their time as well.

Perhaps the most remarkable example of Alex's command of language was the "banery" incident. Pepperberg taught Alex several fruit labels for cherries, bananas, and grapes, which he learned easily and used appropriately. As standard practice, Alex was taught to always say the correct label of an item after it was given to him. Pepperberg had also been coaching him for a long time to identify an apple by name, but could never get more than a "puh" sound out of him. She found this perplexing, given the more complicated words he quickly adopted.

One day when she got to the lab, Alex was saying, "Banery, banery," clearly and intentionally, as if it were something he wanted. She gave him several items, all of which he promptly discarded. Then, as a last resort, she gave him a piece of apple. When he took it, he repeated, "Banery." Confused, Pepperberg called a colleague who was a linguist and explained the situation. The linguist asked what other fruit labels were in his repertoire, and when Pepperberg told her, it became clear. Alex had ignored the seemingly arbitrary label of "apple" and instead created a logical name to identify it. Because it was white on the inside like a banana and red on the outside like a giant cherry, it became a "banery."

Alex was not alone in his abilities. Parrots overall have the capacity to learn as he did, but they can't just pick up the kind of language skills Alex acquired unless they are in an environment dedicated to learning. Otherwise, like toddlers, they pick up words by sound, but no more. Unfortunately, in most instances the human companion repeats the same few phrases without explanation, and the parrot mimics the sounds to get a positive reaction. When they are taught referential language (the meanings and definitions of the sounds being repeated to them) and learn to communicate using those meanings, parrots inevitably excel at it.

Parrots are willing students because they are highly social and need constant stimulation. I heard from many people about an African gray parrot named Morgan that lived not far from me in Beverly Hills, and had extraordinary capabilities. I contacted Richard Levine, Morgan's human companion, to see whether I could meet her for possible inclusion in my film.

"Yes," he said, "but only if she *wants* to meet you."

Morgan was napping, so Levine set a time for me to call back and speak with her directly on her personal speakerphone. When Morgan feels like having a chat, she presses her beak on one of two speed dial numbers to reach her groomer or Levine's longtime girlfriend, both of whom she adores.

Later that day I called back. Morgan was awake, so Levine told her she had a phone call, and she hit the speaker button on her phone.

"Hello," she said.

"Morgan, this is Mira," Levine said on the extension line. There was a long silence. I was already embarrassed for him. I felt sure Morgan couldn't have the slightest idea what he was saying. Regardless, I forged ahead.

"Hi, Morgan, I'm Mira. I'd like to meet you!" I said enthusiastically.

"Say hello to Mira," Levine urged, but still there was nothing.

Uncomfortable, I started to chatter. "It's okay," I said, not wanting to embarrass Levine or Morgan further. Just then Morgan chimed in. "Hello, Mira. This is Morgan." I was stunned: she had repeated my name after hearing it only a few times, she understood that a person she didn't know was speaking to her, and she knew how to use a telephone.

"Mira seems very nice, Morgan," Levine said, "and she would like to meet you and maybe film you. Is that okay?"

Another silence lasted a few moments while some or all of what he said sunk in, and then she responded: "Okay," she said. I couldn't get my crew together fast enough. When we arrived, she was watching the credits on her favorite TV show, *Happy Days,* and singing along with the theme song.

Levine, a Harvard MBA, led a highly active life with a demanding career that included a senior staff position in the Reagan White House. Several years earlier he had spent a year at home recovering from a serious illness. Housebound and unable to work, he had plenty of time on his hands, so he focused his attention on Morgan and her education.

The gray had already amassed a reasonably proficient vocabulary, but

Levine, who abhors bad grammar, even coming from a parrot, endeavored to teach her syntax. Morgan now speaks in complete, conversational, complex sentences with comprehension, just like Alex did.

Over the years on their daily neighborhood walks, Levine reminds Morgan about things like cars and dogs that are perilous to birds in case she ever ends up outdoors without him. "Dogs are bad for birds," he told her. In no time she could identify each dog they passed by breed and mimic their barks. She could also identify cars by model. "That's a Cadillac," she calls out as one zooms by.

Levine's strategy to persuade Morgan to stay away from dogs by familiarizing her with them has backfired. For some time she has been nagging him for a pet. "Morgan wants a puppy," she whines. "A beagle." Beagles are her favorite dogs. Levine tells her she can have one when she grows up, because he's sure she'll never grasp the concept. So far that answer has sufficed, though lately she's been getting impatient.

N'Kisi is a ten-year-old Congo African gray who lives in New York City with his human companion, artist Aimee Morgana. His name is an African word for "medicine spirit." Morgana calls him "Kisi" for short.

Morgana has been practicing a similar approach to Levine's. She works with Kisi at home in a casual, nonacademic manner, but she has taken it a step further: rather than teach Kisi specific things, she encourages him to learn everything. She treats Kisi like an inquisitive child and speaks to him like a friend. As she teaches him words or ideas, Morgana will explain them in context and then describe them referentially. She'll work on pronunciation and definition further if needed.

This technique is known as "sentence framing" when used by educators, though Morgana didn't know that when she implemented it. The method has enabled Kisi to learn sentence construction and grammar. Morgana hasn't encouraged Kisi to learn anything in particular, only what he wants, because she's more interested in his creativity and showing how his mind works.

Morgana has kept track of Kisi's vocabulary from the time she got him at five months old. In the first seven months, he learned 89 words. After two years, he had a vocabulary of 286. Now he has more than 1,000.

Morgana began recording Kisi and logging his utterances regularly at his third birthday. She averages 250 pages a year, including a typed, alphabetized list of his vocabulary, which ranges from "angel" to "yup." Morgana says she captures only about 30 percent of what he says, because he is so prolific she can't keep up. She has also documented 10,000 sentences, stories, and expressions that are Kisi originals, such as "TV toy" for video game and "yummy smoke" for cigarette.

"The plural of anecdote is data," Morgana says. "I'm doing field research in my living room."

Morgana is excited about what she considers Kisi's latest breakthrough, which revealed itself in a mistake. "He'll say, 'Jane flied in an airplane,' though he would never have heard a person say that," says Morgana, "He's saying, 'Okay, let me just put a *d* on the end of this word, because that's how it works usually.' That's big because he's aware of conjugation." Morgana says this shows Kisi understands language as a system, what linguists call "having" language.

Morgana interferes as little as possible with Kisi's behavior and is immune to criticism of his being a Clever Hans. (Hans was a horse that seemed to have a learned repertoire but really was picking up on subtle clues from his trainer, who rewarded him.) "There's no reward for Kisi, regardless of what he does," says Morgana. "He learns and I keep records with as little control as possible. My original idea was, 'Wouldn't it be great to talk with an animal?' I gave him dominance in the relationship. He decides what he wants to say when he wants to say it."

Kisi even composes haiku-like poems. This is a Kisi original:

> I talk to people.
> Birds out in the snow.
> I talk to the world.
> Outside the big water. [Big water is Kisi's word for *ocean*.]

Like Alex, Kisi has demonstrated complex reasoning based on previous information. When Jane Goodall heard about Kisi and Morgana, she wanted to meet them. In anticipation of her visit, Morgana told Kisi about Goodall's work and showed him photos of her in Africa with her Gombé chimpanzee study subjects. Goodall said that when she was introduced to Kisi, the first thing he said to her was, "Got a chimp?"

And, much as Alex invented the new word *banery* based on understanding other labels that applied to fruit (there were obviously other red and yellow items in his vocabulary that he ignored because they weren't fruit labels), Kisi conceptualized the idea of death from extrapolating from his reservoir of known things. Kisi was saddened after their parakeet, Pepper, died and repeatedly talked about her. At one point not long after Pepper's death, Morgana, who had been ill for a period, fell behind in changing the batteries in the birds' toys, and some stopped working. When she finally got a fresh supply, Kisi watched in fascination as Morgana replaced the batteries and the toys became active again. "He was really impressed," says Morgana. "He talked about batteries for quite a while after that."

When the battery in his toy piano finally ran out, Morgana had a video camera running. The tape shows Kisi trying to get her attention. "Needs a battery," he calls to Morgana repeatedly. She is busy with something in the kitchen and can't come. Kisi then checks the back of the piano where the batteries go, and with his beak feigns replacing them. When he is done, he says, "There. I put a battery!"

Right after the September 11, 2001, attacks, Morgana and Kisi watched outside their window as their block was lit with memorial candles. Morgana explained to Kisi that many people had died and that's why the candles were put there. A short time later Morgana arrived home to find that her pet lizard had died. She laid him out in a box with dried leaves and flowers while Kisi looked on.

"He's dead," she told him.

"Got a broken there," he told her. "Gotta put a battery."

"We can't put a battery in him," she replied.

Without missing a beat Kisi replied, "Gotta put a candle."

African grays like Alex and Kisi are so remarkable, there is a tendency to think grays have a monopoly on intelligence when it comes to parrots. As one knowledgeable pet store employee put it, "Grays are the computer nerds of the bird world." Their generally calm personalities make them ideal teaching candidates, but other parrots are equally smart, even little ones like parakeets. The winner of the best talking bird contest several years in a row at a leading British avicultural show was a budgerigar with a four-hundred-word vocabulary. Many I've run across are capable of speaking in sentences with comprehension.

A common pitfall of trying to understand parrots is underestimating them. They are not domesticated animals that humans have spent generations getting to know. They are not mammals, which makes them different in makeup from familiar companion animals such as cats and dogs and or even horses and rabbits. Yet an estimated forty to sixty million caged birds are kept as pets in the United States, and many millions more worldwide.

Chapter Two

Parrots and Parronts

MR. TWINKLE'S SONG

The grey of your breast puts the moonlight to shame
Your wings are the green of the new leaves in spring.
Your dear little beak is an apricot flame
And you are the heart of the song that I sing.
We're two different species, I know this is true,
But nevertheless I dream only of you.

—Antonia Stampfel, parrot lover

Of more than 10,000 species of birds, around 350 of them, in 85 genera, are of the order Psittaciformes. Commonly called parrots, they include lorikeets, cockatoos, macaws, conures, cockatiels, lovebirds, parakeets, keas, and kakapos. Parrots are easily identified by their hooked upper mandible. Their size ranges from the smallest, the pygmy parrot of the South Pacific, at three and one half inches, to the hyacinth macaw of Brazil, which runs three feet from head to tail. From the smallest to the largest, they have long been collected from their native forests to be kept in cages as pets.

Most feed on seeds and nuts, though lorikeets are nectar eaters, and the kea of New Zealand will eat carrion. Almost all nest in tree cavities, but monk parakeets build stick nests, and a few species nest on or in the ground. Parrots are native to the southern hemisphere and are primarily found in Australia, Africa, Mexico, across all of South America, and parts of Asia and Africa.

Parrots are an old race of birds. Fossil evidence has led scientists to believe the ancestors of today's parrots lived in the late Cretaceous period, about seventy million years ago.

The most complete parrot fossils and others that are verified to be parrots, have been found in Europe. One found in England dates to early Eocene, about fifty-five million years ago, though there are no parrot species indigenous there now.

Modern parrots have retained their prehensile feet—the last visible remnant of their prehistoric ancestry—though these look incongruous with their elegant plumage. (Like wearing flip-flops with an evening gown.) Their four long toes—arranged two in front and two in back, versus three in front and one in back on most birds—are known as zygodactal ("yokelike"). Designed to put a vise grip on tubular tree branches, they cause the birds to waddle back and forth when they cross a flat surface. Parrots' unique feet allow them to easily climb like monkeys, one foot over the other, up trees or living room curtains.

Parrots have been coveted as companion animals for millennia because of their intelligence, beauty, ability to talk, and willingness to form strong bonds with humans. Historically, they have been valued for their beauty and talents and were traded across continents as valuable exotics. A traditional African poem says that parrots speak "in a thousand tongues," and the Aruba tribesmen of Ghana, Africa, believe parrots taught humans how to speak. The Quechua and Shuar natives in Brazil believe that long-lived macaws carry their languages and will keep them alive when the tribes die out. Tibetan Buddhist translator Herbert Guenther wrote a gloss on Tibetan Buddhist patriarch Padmasambhava's reference to a parrot by saying, "Psychologically speaking, the parrot is a symbol of the Self that, unlike the ego, speaks the language of Being."

Artifacts of macaws have been found in archaeological digs of native American tribal sites in the far West. Macaws are portrayed in the art of these tribes, and their feathers were used in ceremonial headdresses dating back to 1000 CE.

Parrot images are found in pictographs on the walls of pharaohs' tombs. Affluent Greeks kept parrots as pets, and Aristotle's pet bird is thought to have been a parrot, since it was named Psittace, which could have been short for the Latin *Psittaciformes*. The Greeks ate parrots as a delicacy (as some indigenous people still do where the birds are found in the wild), though they reportedly don't taste very good.

No parrot species are naturally found in Europe, and the United States had only one, the Carolina parakeet, a large green bird with a yellow and orange head, whose range was restricted to the Southeast. Hunting and trapping wiped it out early in the twentieth century. When Christopher Columbus made landfall in the Caribbean, he was convinced he had made his way around the world to India, in part because his first greeting was from islanders who swam to his ships carrying parrots to trade. The birds were then known to come only from the Far East. Columbus's journals abounded with references to them: on October 21, 1492, he saw "flocks of parrots that darken the sun."

For hundreds of years there has been an ongoing demand among the wealthy in Europe and North America for parrots. The first American presidential pet was a parrot owned by Martha Washington. (Conflicting reports say George both loved and hated the bird.) In fact, more U.S. presidents have had birds than cats as pets. During the White House fire of 1812, Dolley Madison is said to have rescued the two things she felt were most important: a copy of the Declaration of Independence and her pet parrot. Andrew Jackson, Ulysses S. Grant, William McKinley, Theodore Roosevelt, and Calvin Coolidge all had parrots. McKinley appointed his parrot, named Washington Post, the official greeter at the White House. Thomas Jefferson had a mockingbird he loved so much it slept in bed with him every night after his wife died.

America's love affair with birds is still going—and growing. According to U.S. Fish and Wildlife Statistics, one in four Americans, sixty-six million people, are birders, creating a multibillion-dollar industry in accessories alone. The number of pet birds in the United States today is estimated at between forty and sixty million, following cats (seventy-seven million) and dogs (sixty-five million). The number of pet birds in the United States today is estimated by the people who would know best, the breeders themselves. It was put forth by National Avian Welfare Alliance, a group of twenty-nine national companion-bird-industry organizations and associations that includes the Pet Industry Joint Advisory Committee (PIJAC), a powerful industry lobbying group, and the largest national bird breeders organization, the American Federation of Aviculture. Birding is behind only walking and gardening as the most popular outdoor activity in the United States, and the fastest growing of the three.

Audubon defines a birder as "anyone who experiences nature through birds," and birders say they enjoy the experience because it connects them with the wild. Beyond those experiencing birds in the wild, millions of other people are having some pretty wild experiences with birds indoors. For more than two decades, beginning in the 1970s, exotic birds were the fastest-growing pet choice in the United States, and a new secret subculture of people engaging in passionate and eccentric behavior with birds was born.

Rebecca Fox, an avian behaviorist, said of companion parrots, "Better than thinking of it as living with a feathered kid, you should really think of it as living with an alien." Unfortunately, most humans whom parrots live with are unaware of how unique a being is sitting in their living room.

A significant study by Dutch scientists who focused on the personalities of wild birds found that each had stable and consistent individual personalities in the same degree as humans. Some were shy by nature, others gregarious. Other avian behaviorists have found parrots have qualities, such as a sense of humor, compassion, and loyalty, long thought to belong only to humans.

This doesn't surprise parrot owners, who know the birds are complex. They can be demanding, often have fractious personalities, hold a grudge, and have idiosyncracies. Owners find out the hard way if their parrot is a "toe nabber" who takes offense at exposed digits. The birds will chase feet across a floor, biting hard when they catch a runaway toe. Others feel the same about crumpled paper towels (you can lose a digit that way too), or are "hair surfers" eager to toss a freshly coiffed do into disarray. On the other hand, parrots are prone to giggle when their stomachs are tickled, they like to be stroked and kissed, and they will follow their human companions around the house. Even so, to their core parrots are still wild animals not designed to be tamed. Though they live in domestic situations, they are never fully domesticated and will always retain their wild natures. You can break a parrot's spirit by keeping it indoors, but the psychological damage is damning to the bird. They aren't mammals, like so many of the domesticated species bred as pets, and they are meant to spend most of their time off the ground. As a result, they are wired differently, both psychologically and physiologically, from familiar companion animals like cats, dogs, horses, and rabbits.

Life with a parrot brings daily challenges. They have high intelligence but the emotional maturity of a two-year-old child and require constant attention. They are generators of uncontained mess. To live with a parrot is to know parrot poop. Though the birds are smart enough to be toilet trained, some experts say that's ill-advised. The ability to fly gives birds fast metabolisms, and their feces must be expelled frequently or they can be toxic or even fatal. Toilet-trained parrots are taught to defecate on particular surfaces, like newspaper or paper toweling. Once they understand that pooping elsewhere is undesirable, some parrots won't relieve themselves at all if their poop-training surface is unavailable, which can lead to adverse health effects. While parrot diapers are available, not every parrot takes to wearing one. As a result, many parrot owners resort to donning some kind of poop jacket when they act like a human perch. The so-called Ca-Ca Cape with a "unique ca-ca catching cuff" is popular and can be bought online for under $25, but any shoulder cover will suffice.

Parrots also make a mess when they eat. For every piece of food that stays in a parrot's beak, ten end up on the floor of its cage (or your living room). In the wild, food grows on trees, so why worry about it? A parrot's beak is growing all the time, so the birds are always looking for something to chew on, both to wear it down and for the sheer fun of using it. In a home, they like to entertain themselves by engaging in avian demolition: breaking, cracking, or shredding everything from newspapers to kitchen cabinets. To a parrot, anything can be inviting. They are especially fond of turning furniture (i.e., trees in any form) into wood pulp.

Thanks to parrots' physiological and mental complexities, life with these birds is a series of sophisticated interactions, trials, tribulations, joys, pains, and endless challenges. To have a positive relationship with a parrot, "parronts" (parrot parents) must put as much into it as they wish to get out—and just as much as they would invest in another person. Unlike a dog's heart, which will bond with an owner quickly, a parrot's heart is not easy to win. They are discerning when it comes to affection. "Birds are unlike cats and dogs, which are more focused on pleasing us," says bird behaviorist Mattie Sue Athan. "Just because you feed a parrot doesn't mean it's going to like you."

According to bird behaviorist Chris Davis, parrots have a caste system where they see themselves as not just equal to humans but superior to them. In her home consultations, she finds the bird often has a favorite person in the household and regards everyone else as inferior. If a parrot favors the husband, it will be mean to the wife and treat the children as it does the dog.

When parrots do commit, their emotions run deep. Research on this behavior in birds has been done by raven expert Bernd Heinrich, who speculates that ravens can fall in love, but dogs, for example, can't, because internal rewards, not just external things like food and affection, are required for long-term bonding. Parrots are long-lived creatures. Once they bond to a human or avian companion, they form a monogamous, committed relationship that can last for a lifetime. Dr. Richard Farinato, director of captive wildlife programs for the Humane Society of the United States, has two companion parrots he's worked with for decades in the United States and overseas. "A parrot," he says, "is infinitely more bonded to you than your dog will ever be if you allow that relationship, because with the parrot, you're an equal. With the dog you're always the leader."

Parrot loyalty is legend. Stories abound of parrots picking the locks on their cages to escape, but flying off only after they opened several other locks to release their neighbors. There are stories of parrots that have stood by their owners in harrowing situations or fought to the death to protect them. One parrot attacked the assailant who killed his owner in a robbery attempt. The parrot died, but not before doing serious damage to the offender's face and hands. The culprit was arrested and charged with murder as a result of the DNA found on the bird's body. When he was apprehended, the killer told police he had never seen anything fight as hard as that parrot to save his owner.

> She was not quite what you would call refined. She was not quite what you would call unrefined. She was the kind of person that keeps a parrot.
>
> —Mark Twain

Bird people are a breed unto themselves. Eccentric parronts devote their lives to their "fids" (feathered kids). Many customize their homes to accommodate their birds. Mordecai, a scarlet macaw, has been living with his owner, Dave Botwin, a litigation consultant (who rescues sea corals on the side) for eighteen years. When Botwin got Mordecai as a fledgling, he bought the largest macaw cage available at the time—thirty-six by thirty by sixty inches tall—but Mort, as he's commonly called, grew out of it in no time. At full size he was more than thirty inches from head to tail, and his tail feathers broke on the cage bars every time he turned around. Botwin decided he had to do something.

Botwin had a custom cage measuring seven by five by four feet built for Mort. Doing the intelligent thing, he designed it to fit through the French doors on the balcony of his two-story home, leading into the office he shares with Mort.

Unfortunately, when the two short delivery men lifted the eight-hundred-pound cage onto the balcony, they found it couldn't be turned to get through the doors, and they couldn't get it down. The two men became trapped under it. Once they were rescued, Botwin made a decision: it was more important for Mordecai to have the bigger cage than to keep the balcony. The balcony came down, the cage was lowered in, and the balcony was rebuilt. Botwin says he doesn't regret any of it, and had he known he'd have to take off the balcony, he'd have built the cage twice as big.

Some parronts never want to be separated from their avian flock and will plan their vacations around them. For years, Phyllis Levine and Peter

Baggs traveled across the United States and to Canada in their RV. Once Peep, Baggs's cockatiel, was part of the family, he traveled with them, and they sometimes also brought along other cockatiels they were breeding. Peep would run back and forth across the dashboard as the RV sped down the road. Baggs put Peep's cage in the large space between the two front seats. Sometimes he put a paper bag on the side of his chair, and Peep would nest in it.

On one of their first trips, to Alberta, Canada, the couple wanted to drive home to Seal Beach, California, along the Pacific Coast via Washington State, but no veterinarian was on duty at the border, so they weren't allowed to cross back into the United States. They were rerouted twelve hundred miles east, to a port of entry through North Dakota that had a vet. "Peter said over and over, 'If they don't let me back in with Peep, I'm not coming back to the United States,'" says Levine. "He called the Canadian border veterinarian every time we stopped to make sure he would be there. When we finally got there, we climbed up the stairs past the cattle stalls with this little bird in a cage. He looked at Peep for a moment and said, 'Nice bird,' then stamped our papers."

The next time they went to Canada, Baggs parked the RV in a motor home park and took the ferry with Peep into Canada for the day. Once or twice a year Peep went with them to Catalina Island, where they all stayed in a motel.

Though traveling with a bird was a huge amount of work, the couple didn't mind. "They're not a burden," said Baggs. "The constraints they make are that you can't stay away for a whole day at a time, and you have to make arrangements, like leaving the generator running, leaving the air conditioner on, and parking in the shade. But that's no problem."

The couple usually traveled in September or October, timing their trips for when their birds weren't breeding. But Levine says there was always a cockatiel that decided to lay eggs at the last minute, so two years straight she took fifteen babies with them. "I adapted the couch in the RV to hand-feed. We would stop at a laundromat and wash everything, and it worked out fine."

Things have changed over the years. Baggs suffered a serious heart attack that caused global brain damage. He now lives in a convalescent home, and Levine visits daily. She sold the RV and hasn't spent a night away from home since it happened. "And anyway, now I have a cockatoo that gets carsick," she says.

She takes Peep to visit Baggs, but the two don't know each other anymore. Baggs is unsure who Peep is because of his brain injury. Peep has a hard time recognizing his old pal, who once had a scruffy beard and long hair but now is frail, clean shaven, and unreceptive. Levine says Peep, now fourteen years old, still misses Baggs. She whistles to him every night, like Baggs did, but it's not the same. "Pete called it his music lesson," she says. "It's like a bedtime story, but Peep shrieks because I don't whistle well like Peter did."

Before buying her first parrot, Frances Longmire of Los Angeles joined several online bird boards to research different breeds. She found that people in chat rooms dealing with specific species mimicked the personalities of the birds they represented. "There seemed to be a certain personality that goes with the different bird people," Longmire says. "The macaw people were tough and fought a lot and flamed each other all the time, and the eclectus people were kind of nerdy and clinical and very dignified. The African gray and cockatoo boards were my favorites. The latter seemed cuddly and outgoing, like their birds, and the former were funny, sweet, and bright 'cause grays are."

Over the last ten years since Longmire ventured onto the first bird boards, avian chats have mushroomed on the Internet. Chat rooms like Paradise Perch, BirdsnWays, and Avian Addicts, where parronts meet to share information, gossip, and commiserate on the joys and tribulations of living with their fids, are commonplace. Some are specific to a particular species (African grays, Amazons, pionus parrots); others are specific to common interests or parrot-related problems such as free flying, feather picking, screaming, and biting.

Christiana MacKnight is a former stripper and successful clothes designer. She has no problem turning heads as she walks down the street, but she has focused her attention on parrots over men, since having discovered that birds are loving and more reliable companions. And she doesn't doubt she's made the right choice.

MacKnight's faith in parrot relationships over human ones was reaffirmed when she was being affectionate with her constant companion Thor, a black palm cockatoo, on the Las Vegas strip. "This guy came over to me," says MacKnight, "and said, 'When was the last time you kissed a guy like that?' And that's how we started dating. Two years since I had a relationship with a man, now I'm in one for two months, and it's already not working out." On the other hand, her parrots are still true to her today.

Because of her history, MacKnight gets some unusual propositions. The Velvet Hammer, a burlesque group performing in Las Vegas, approached MacKnight about going onstage wearing a wood bikini and letting her parrot chew it off. She refused. "I don't want to be naked with my bird onstage," she says.

MacKnight talks over lunch at a restaurant near her new two-acre Sunland, California, home, which she bought so her fifteen parrots, mostly from rescue organizations, would have more room to roam. Thor is at the table, enjoying some pasta. "He likes peanut butter sandwiches, pasta, and vanilla sandwich cookies," she says. "He takes the top of the vanilla sandwich and scrapes vanilla with his beak and says 'Mmmm.'" His beak is designed for a particular food, the Pandanus palm nut, and is shaped to open it. "There's no competition for that food," says MacKnight, but in captivity black palms get a diet easier to manufacture.

Thor looks like a bird from Mars, with a face only a mother could love. He is large, weighing about a kilogram, and runs about eighteen inches from the tip of his black beak to the tip of his black tail. He has a jagged black crown, a red-skinned face and tongue, and a mouth that remains perpetually open. When he gets excited, the skin around his eyes gets redder. If he's nervous or intimidated, it goes almost white or pale pink. In their native New Guinea, these birds are called *raja*, "king" of the jungle.

"Only low-life poachers would think of taking a palm out of the jungle," she says.

Thor is a celebrity on the rare cockatoo Internet list where Mac-Knight first saw him. "He's big and beautiful. It was love at first sight," she says as she leans over and kisses him gently on the beak. "Oh, you're so precious," she whispers in his ear. Because they are hard to breed, black palms are rare and command one of the highest prices of any captive-bred parrot, running $18,000 apiece or more. MacKnight feels lucky to have gotten Thor for that price.

For MacKnight, parrots have become an addiction. "I'd have so much more money without them," she says. "It's not even what I spend. I could've saved $250 in commissions going in to work [at her store] on one Saturday, but I only want to hang out with the birds. I used to spend money on hair extensions and eye creams. Now I want to buy bird toys."

Becoming a parront has completely changed MacKnight's lifestyle. Previously she never rose before noon, and now she's up at 6:00 a.m. to feed the birds and clean cages. And having parrots has made her more outgoing. She says she could never ask a guy if he wanted a lap dance when she was a stripper, but now she'll knock on the car window of a perfect stranger with a parrot bumper sticker. MacKnight is also a member of five bird clubs and says that if there were more, she'd join those, too.

Her passion for black cockatoos has overtaken her. She has deposits on five black palm eggs so she'll have dibs when, and if, they hatch. "It's like playing futures on the stock market," she says of the potential $100,000 investment. Even though she has had dogs and cats, MacKnight is quick to confirm that birds aren't like any other pet. "Birds aren't like animals, they're like a person. I could never imagine paying $18,000 for a dog!"

Though happy with her parrot life, MacKnight sometimes wonders about her future. "Lately I've been thinking I can't do this forever," she says, "sleeping alone, waking up alone, and hanging out with birds all day. Now parrots are the only date I can get."

MacKnight is not alone in her devotion or her concern. Parronts find that if they give their bird respect commensurate with its intelligence, they must continually compromise their own lifestyles to provide their birds with the fullest lives possible. A dog or cat is pretty contented if it's well fed and cared for, and generally happy to be on its human's schedule. Parrots expect much more. They are exactly like children and need precisely the same amount of attention, care, and love.

When Mort, Dave Botwin's scarlet macaw, gets lonely for avian company, he has ways to make new friends. Most afternoons and evenings he likes to sit on the balcony, facing the yard. When other birds are around, he goes into his cage, scoops up small seeds in his beak, and scatters them on the balcony for the bluejays and doves. "When the birds come up and eat, he sits there and talks to them," says Botwin. "He says, 'Hello. Hi. What are you doing?' This goes on for hours. Since he was raised with dogs, he's figured out that dogs are great stupid animals to talk to, so he goes into his cage and pulls out bones and bits of meat left over in his food dishes, and he feeds them as well."

Given the active and stimulating lives they live in nature, parrots always oppose the predicament they face living in captivity. In the wild, they spend their entire lives within earshot of their flock or a mate, and they depend on their flock to learn. Isolating a parrot in a cage is the antithesis of its natural state. It is, plain and simple, avian abuse. The birds never get used to being alone all day, and in many cases being so either stunts their psychological growth or causes serious emotional problems. Even when they are allowed to breed in captivity, they aren't permitted to be responsible parents, finding food and nesting sites and raising their young. By cutting up their fruit and vegetables and doting on them, their owners further infantilize them. They are never allowed to mature and fend for themselves, and therefore never have a full spectrum of life experiences, with the responsibilities and maturity that brings. Without constant role modeling and challenges, they are stuck in an immature emotional state. Many birds start to painfully pull their feathers out one at a time. According to research studies, feather plucking is found in an estimated one of ten captive birds, which may also develop myriad other dysfunctional behaviors as a result of living in captivity.

Irene Pepperberg has been working on an enrichment program for caged birds after realizing that a lack of stimulation is a primary cause of distress for parrots living in homes. At MIT's Media Lab, she developed different kinds of software programs for parrots to use at will. With InterPet Explorer, a modified Web browser for parrots, a bird can use a joystick to listen to music, watch video, look at pictures, or play a game designed for them. Each category contains four choices. In the music category, for example, the parrot can choose to listen to rock, country, classical, or jazz. Pepperberg says that when Alex tested the browser, he liked it a lot at first and then seemed to get bored. Her students were concerned the system didn't work. When she queried them about how regularly they changed the content, Pepperberg says they were surprised by the question. "The students looked at me as though I was insane and replied, 'What do you mean?' And I said, 'How often do you want to hear Vivaldi's Cello concerto?' They reorganized the system to use four different channels of Internet radio, so Alex had something different whenever he clicked a choice. And Alex's interest shot back up."

> Why parrot owners are crazier than other pet owners I'll never know, but they are by far.
>
> —A longtime bird club member

In addition to 40 national bird associations and 510 Audubon chapters, there are hundreds of companion bird clubs across the country. These clubs are unique among pet owners. People love their cats and dogs, but they don't show up every month to meet and talk about them. The oldest club in North America for captive-bred birds is the Avicultural Society of America, founded in New York City in 1927. The club still meets regularly today.

Thousands of parrot lovers across the United States attend bird club meetings, and many bring their birds. They seek the camaraderie of like-minded people who share a meaningful relationship with a feathered being that most outsiders wouldn't understand. These clubs hold bird toy raffles and birdie buffets and bring in a Santa at Christmas so their parrots can ask for presents and be photographed with him. Some clubs have newsletters with names like *Newsbeak*, *Tweet Sheet*, *Squawk*, the *Beak Bugle*, and the *Hatchling*.

Phyllis Levine is not only a multiple bird owner; she also is a long-time member of multiple bird clubs. With all the work of feeding and caring for her flock of more than 250 parrots, plus her two jobs, Levine still makes time to attend eight bird clubs a month, including a pigeon club. "I just love them," she says. Levine averages forty miles driving each way to her club meetings.

Virtually every state has a companion bird club, and some, including California, New York, Florida, Virginia, Texas, and Washington, have many. Among the largest and most thriving in the United States is the Bird Clubs of Virginia (BCV), founded in 1985. BCV is a conglomerate of seven clubs around the state that operate independently but cooperatively; each takes a turn sponsoring the annual convention. Their main focus is avian education and support for research.

Not all bird clubs are doing well. When Steve Fitzsimmons and his wife Paula joined the Madison Area Cagebird Association of Wisconsin (MACAW), the club's attendance was so low that only two board members were coming to meetings, the president had resigned, and there was talk of ending the club, which had existed for a decade. Fitzsimmons saw value in educating people about parrots and committed himself to keeping the club going. Shortly thereafter he was elected president. But Fitzsimmons has been fighting an uphill battle to build membership, and it worries him. He cites national estimates of birds in U.S. households provided by the American Pet Products Manufacturers Association (which does a national study every two years) and bird breeders nationwide. Their statistics (which range from seventeen million to sixty million, respectively) put the number of birds in the Madison area alone at seventeen thousand to thirty thousand, but the club has only seventy-five members and just twenty show up for events. Fitzsimmons believes the large number of uninformed bird owners is the reason there are so many relinquished birds in this country. "I absolutely cringe," he says, "when people write or call me to say that after having their bird for ten years, they want to surrender it and its cage for a tax write-off." This isn't unusual. A parrot is expensive, and many owners who never connect with their bird, keep it confined, and never experience its personality or social abilities see their parrot only as a liability.

Many owners figure a bird club is the best place to relinquish a bird, so some clubs have been compelled to form adoption services to address the unending flow of parrots coming through their doors. Pat Baltozer has placed 131 birds during her three-year tenure as chairperson of the South Jersey Bird Club Parrot Adoption Program, which has existed for nine years. At first, club members, many of whom were bird breeders, refused to believe there were so many unwanted parrots. "The membership said they'd no sooner allow a parrot adoption to come in than a horse adoption, but things change," says Baltozer.

She has traveled five thousand miles in one year alone to pick up unwanted birds or to check on adopted birds in new homes. "It's mushroomed in the last five years. It's gone crazy," she says. "Bird club membership is down, but bird relinquishment isn't. There's less people in bird clubs and more birds in adoption."

Baltozer has instituted several requirements in order to find the best match for a bird. A four-page preadoption questionnaire is taken over the phone, the adopter must take a seminar on parrot care, and a home visit is done by Baltozer or one of the other committee members. She also checks personal references. One bird, an umbrella cockatoo named Floyd, went to a rabbi in northern New Jersey. "Floyd's happy now," says Baltozer. "He was taken to Hebrew class. He was dancing and taking the yarmulkes off the students' heads."

Because they are on the frontlines of companion parrot keeping, bird clubs are in large part responsible for the radicalization of average bird owners into avian rights activists and for the formation of the avian welfare movement.

Denise Kelly, a cofounder of the Avian Welfare Coalition (AWC), confirms this. "It was through my club that I started to realize what a problem was developing with people and parrots," she says. "That is something that always irks me about the breeder folks who claim that AWC is a bunch of radical ARs [animal rights activists] who don't know anything about birds and are out to take away their rights. In fact, we are all bird people with companion parrots at home who experienced many of the inherent problems firsthand and came to the same conclusion. We felt the animal welfare community was not addressing the problem of exotic birds. They gave it no attention."

Anna Dove is president and founder of the Companion Bird Club in New York City. Dove (whose personal e-mail and Web site are godisapigeon and www.pigeonreligion.org) took her surname in honor of her three companion doves, Lucie, Dahlia, and Daisie. All her birds—the doves, her two canaries, and three finches—fly free in her studio apartment on the Upper East Side of Manhattan. They have a cage but go in only for food. They sleep in two big trees in the apartment.

Dove, whose club has about a hundred members, says her agenda is to be progressive. The club meets more than most, with get-togethers five to six times a month. At least one meeting a month is designated as a "play day fly day" at the New York Theosophical Society, their main meeting hall. The birds that are flighted get to cruise at will around the six-thousand-square-foot hall. "The club is for the birds really, not for the people," Dover says. "The birds have a good time at the meeting. They have a chance to play and preen each other. This was all worth it because these birds probably never had so much fun."

Dove urges her members not to keep their birds in cages or clip their wings. She's received a lot of criticism for these radical ideas. "They don't want to hear it," says Dove. "I felt their birds' lives were so terrible that I had to say something. But now we're losing membership as a result. Maybe it'll come back up when people realize and say, 'Oh see, she was right all along.'"

Like Dove, many bird owners realize parrots are a lifetime commitment, and the question that finally plagues them is whether it's even appropriate to keep parrots that need constant environmental challenges and social interaction in captivity. It is a moral issue not easily resolved. "I'm a slave owner," said one parrot owner. "I'm a good slave owner, but that's what I am." The consensus among experts that most parrots in the United States aren't dying of old age but of human-related problems only adds to the moral dilemma. "You can trace all the problems pet parrots have to one thing—living in captivity," says Dr. Charles Munn, a global wildlife conservationist and the world's leading macaw expert.

Dr. Kim is a Chicago-based animal communicator and author of *Ask the Animals* and the CD *Songs to Make Dogs Happy*. She says she has had a heart "bridge" connection with animals since she was a child and started communicating with foxes, birds, and raccoons near her home. When communicating with a parrot, she appears to silently gaze at the bird, but internally she says she's receiving images from it. "Their intelligence comes from the same source ours does," she says. "Some use words I've never used before. They talk eloquently. They are spiritual beings. If they're allowed at our table, they can teach us plenty."

Kim says most of the birds she talks to are living dismal lives, and she has to steel her heart when she listens to them. "I seldom have a bird that says, 'I'm so happy,'" she says. "A bird's life is no life in most cases. They have nothing. They don't ask for a trip to Paris. All they want are tiny things like light for an hour a day, for their caretakers to not forget they have a bird. People don't realize how deep their feelings run. I negotiate for the birds. All I can do is chip away at their owners. If you respect something, you cannot abuse it." Whether you believe someone can communicate with animals or not, there is no question that Kim understands what they are experiencing, and she says she spends a good deal of time apologizing to the birds for their owners' behavior.

When parrots are allowed to live the fullest, freest, most enriched lives possible, they are happy and independent instead of needy and dysfunctional.

Hugh Choi, a personal trainer in New York City, has never clipped the wings on his two macaws, Otis and Gizmo. Instead, he has trained them to fly free. He releases them on the great lawn in Central Park, and they return when he calls them to go home. Both are superb flyers. Like hummingbirds, they can hover in midair, turn on a dime, and land and take off vertically. "It's like watching the Blue Angels air show," says Choi. "They fly in and out of each other's flight paths and alternate weaving up and down. They'll do circles together, then circles apart. It's very cool to watch."

Research on wild birds has shown that 30 percent of the time, birds fly for fun. Choi says that's obvious when he watches Otis and Gizmo. The birds are a favorite of parkgoers, even though Otis can be devilish, attacking little kids' shoelaces and the buttons on people's clothes. But this fun still requires vigilence. Even in a place as seemingly safe as Central Park, dangers lurk. The park is home to a growing population of red-tailed hawks (one was made famous by the PBS documentary *Pale Male*) that prey on other birds. On one outing a hawk chased Otis and Gizmo three times. "Redtails are not great at maneuvering. They have to work at it," says Choi. "Anytime they've come after my birds, they get outflown, but one did get dangerously close." Gizmo searched frantically for Choi to protect him, but he was almost out of sight. Gizmo let out loud calls to locate Choi, who responded in kind. Gizmo dashed back to the sound of Choi's voice as the hawk flew down to nab him. The hawk got hit by a Frisbee (Choi still doesn't know whether it was intentional or not), and Gizmo landed safely on Choi's shoulder. "People on the meadow erupted in applause," says Choi.

It's impossible to learn the social behaviors of a flock of parrots in the wild without years of close study. Even then the intricacies of the birds' social interactions are still elusive to researchers, since they spend most of their time high in the tree canopy, fly miles away on a moment's notice, and nest in dark tree holes. The best way to observe parrots' natural social interactions and understand the complexities of their interrelationships and emotional needs is at a large zoo exhibit. At the Lorikeet Landing exhibit of the Aquarium of the Pacific in Long Beach, California, 130 lory parrots, mostly vivacious rainbow lorikeets, have unparalleled freedom in a captive situation. They live flocked in a 5,200-square-foot aviary, free flying and doing all the things wild lories do but for the fact that food is provided. Squawking lories greet visitors by landing (and sometimes pooping) on their heads, arms, and shoulders.

Beci Carr is the wildlife biologist and aviculturalist who designed the exhibit and curates it. "The lories are in tune with what goes on," says Carr. "If one gets scared, they all react. If one starts bathing, they all will. And the others can tell if one is eating or bathing from their vocalization—it's amazing. If I put a food bowl out where only a few can see it, everyone heads over in a matter of seconds. That indicates to me that the birds' feeding calls are so attuned. They figure things out and learn together, and it shapes the flock dynamic."

Carr, who proves that even unwitting trained scientists can become obsessed parronts, has seen it all—acts of loyalty, betrayal, anger, and sadness among the flock members and in their interactions with human visitors.

One rainy evening in the middle of winter, when the aquarium was closing for the day, employees were ushering out the last few visitors, and the birds were settling down for the night. Carr had wall heaters installed under the overhanging roof of the Howdy Hut, a wooden and mesh structure in the middle of the aviary. Most of the flock was huddled on tree-limb perches around the heaters, basking in the warm orange glow. Some surrounded the rim of a large bowl filled with a fruit smoothie. They took turns drinking, like plastic dunking birds from the 1950s. Others were perched together at the far end of the aviary, fluffed up for warmth and settling in for sleep.

It was time for Carr to leave, but she was getting more anxious by the moment as she focused on Sneakers, a female lorikeet frantically looking for her boyfriend, Bill. Sneakers was locked outside the Howdy Hut, and Bill was inside, calling to her. She flew back and forth, looking for an opening, hanging upside down from the roof and on the mesh wall, trying to see him. Though it was late, wet, and Carr's newlywed husband, Chris (a marine biologist also employed at the aquarium), was waiting for her at home, Carr was determined to reunite this Romeo and Juliet of parrots. "They always sleep together. She keeps him warm," Carr said of Bill, who is bare-chested. When he was young, he fell and cracked his keel bone. Nike, his girlfriend at the time, literally henpecked him bare at the injured spot as it was healing, and the feathers never came back. Now he has Sneakers, who is devoted to him and sleeps nestled next to him every night. "She is his blanket," says Carr.

For the next twenty minutes, in the pouring rain, Carr tried to cajole the increasingly anxious Sneakers around to the front of the hut to the entrance, but it didn't work. At the last second Sneakers got spooked and headed to the roof again, continually calling to Bill through the mesh, their beaks now just inches apart. Reluctantly, Carr gave up. "Bill will have to sleep alone tonight," she said. "They'll be all right apart, but it's like being separated from your loved ones."

Chris has been separated from Carr many times because of the birds. "I know who's more important to her," he says. "If it starts raining at night, Beci will be sitting up in bed, rocking because she thinks the birds aren't okay. So we'll go in the car at two a.m. to put up tarps in the rain. Of course, as soon as they're up, it stops raining." Chris says his whole attitude about parrots changed once he got to know them through Carr. Through her, he was able to appreciate the birds in ways he hadn't previously, as individuals with distinct personalities, desires, and personal dramas.

Carr was the opposite; she took to the birds as soon as she met them. "They're like ten times a dog in learning ability," she says. "It humbles you to see them growing in intelligence, especially in a flock. And their personalities are so complex. People say, 'Do lories do this or that?' I say, 'Well, which one are you talking about?' because they're completely individual in personality."

When Carr was hired by the aquarium in June 2001, she arrived to find an empty lot. She built the exhibit up from the ground, and when it opened in September of that year, it had been transformed into the largest interactive lorikeet aviary in the world. Carr feels the birds helped to build her life as much as she did theirs, because she met her husband when she relocated to the aquarium. "Parrots brought Chris and I together," she says. "I was purposely hired to build and run the exhibit. It was dirt when I got here. Creating their life created our life."

On an average weekend day four thousand people, mostly children, pass through the exhibit. They watch the birds interact, squawking, preening, flying, and rolling around in the grass to play. Visitors are mostly unaware of the complex interrelationships, romances, spats, and friendships of the birds they see. The true goings-on at the aviary are what Carr lovingly calls *"Days of Our Lorikeets."* (It could also be called *"As the Aviary Turns."*)

Carr knows each of the birds individually. Among the flock are forty singles. "They're waiting for the right bird to come along," says Carr. Some aren't waiting; they're going after ones already spoken for. Take Corey, for example. He courts Tiny, Bubba's girlfriend, right in front of Bubba. Bubba is recuperating in a medical cage in the Howdy Hut. Tiny was keeping him company until Corey stationed himself on a perch outside their cage. Now Corey is pacing back and forth, eyeing Tiny, who is responding favorably to the new suitor. Bubba will likely not forgive or forget.

Real estate is at a premium in the exhibit. Birds with a good location defend it. Some enter into alliances to do so. Sapphire and Zeus are a couple who let Bob hang out on their turf. In return, he helps defend it against trespassers. The couple lays their eggs (all infertile so far) under a rock, which Bob also guards. "He defends them, but he's not allowed to sit on them. He'd be like the chick's uncle," says Carr.

Cheez was Beau's best friend. Then Beau had medical problems that kept him in the Howdy Hut for three months so meds could be administered. While he was out of commission, Cheez's girlfriend, Finch, left him, and he took up with Bugsy, Beau's love. The new couple took up residence where Beau could see them, just inches from the far corner of the

Howdy Hut. Every day Beau sat on the hut's floor in that corner, watching them, and every chance he could, he snuck out of the hut and started a fight with Cheez to get her back. When Beau was released, the three started hanging out together, but by then Cheez was with Bugsy. Beau is still single. According to Chris, Carr has ideas why. "She'll come home and talk about them by name and relationship," he says. "She'll say Beau's got a new girlfriend. He can't keep a girl. I think he's really bad in the sack." Parrots that breed will do so away from the flock, and return with their fledglings. They introduce them into the flock, which also oversees their education and protection.

Just as humans do, the flock has dysfunctional relationships, like that of Tangerine, a male Swainson's lorikeet, and his girlfriend Fritz, an Edward's lorikeet. Carr says they're a very codependent pair that screams if separated. Sometimes Fritz mixes with other birds, but Tangerine doesn't take well to his having other friends and yells at him like a jealous girlfriend.

The birds can also be ruthless. The flock ripped apart a perfect lorikeet after she got caught in a tree. "A bird caught in anything will be attacked," says Carr. The assumption is that a screaming bird will alert predators, so it's done to protect the flock. Often the aviary staff can't get there fast enough to help the bird before the flock ravages it.

Carr has a deep understanding of the birds' behavior, and her husband says no one knows them like she does. "She can look at one and say, 'He's not right; he's a sick bird.' When we watch them, she narrates in the first person. 'I'm going over here. No, that doesn't taste good. I'm going over here.'" But Carr says she's not reading into their behavior, just recognizing it. "It seems like anthropomorphizing, but I don't think that's the case," she says, "because we see it every day." For example, many of the birds know their names, even though Carr hasn't spent any time training them. Tulip says, "Hi, Tulip," when Carr addresses her, even if she's surrounded by a dozen other birds. Tulip won't respond when Carr addresses a bird next to her. "They have identity and awareness of themselves," she says. "They'll hear the name of the bird next to them as much as their own, but they know their own name and only respond to it, and they won't mimic the other bird's name."

Carr says that in many ways she has learned how to live her life by watching the birds live theirs. "They are humbling," she says. "They put you in your place in the world. They are these little tiny beings, but they are so much larger than all the things that one thinks are so important. They live the life that should be. Their focus and their life energy is spent only on the important things—having fun, love, babies, and eating. Society has made everything so much larger and complicated. The lorikeets make you think that's not what it's all about, and it's not."

> A little fool lies here
> Whom I held dear—
> A starling in the prime
> Of his brief time
> Whose doom it was to drain
> Death's bitter pain.
> Thinking of this, my heart
> Is riven apart.
> Oh reader! Shed a tear,
> You also, here.
> He was not naughty, quite,
> But gay and bright,
> And under all his brag
> A foolish wag.
> This no one can gainsay
> And I will lay
> That he is now on high...

In 1787, Wolfgang Amadeus Mozart wrote this poem as part of the eulogy for his pet starling.

Mozart bought the bird in 1784, and for three years it was his constant companion. He noted how it had impressed him by singing one of his piano concertos (which it learned in its previous situation). Mozart said the bird was an inspiration and attributed one of his compositions, "A Musical Joke" (K.522, second movement, Menuetto), to the bird's song.

When his starling died, Mozart was bereft. So important was his avian companion that he not only gave it a formal funeral but also enlisted veiled professional mourners to give the little bird the grand send-off he felt it deserved. The funeral had all the pomp and circumstance reserved for any revered human being. Many observers thought he was crazy, but then they weren't bird people.

All beloved companion animals bring grief to their humans when they pass, but birds, and parrots in particular, perhaps even more so. They live much longer than other animals, and their owners say they hold a place in their hearts more like a person than a pet.

Lorrie Mitchell got Carla, a double yellow-headed Amazon, when she was just five months old. "She was kind of an olive green with brown eyes, a yellow baseball cap, and dark spots on her beak and tongue and toenails—baby stuff," says Mitchell. When she grew up, Carla loved a crowd and would excitedly repeat her favorite phrase, "I'm a green chicken!" to adoring fans. She could also sing "Somewhere over the Rainbow." Mitchell, an elementary school teacher, often brought Carla to school to educate her students. But bigger things were in store for Carla. She was discovered by two record producers and signed to cut a single, aptly titled "I'm a Green Chicken." Her publicity stills show her in a studio, singing into a microphone, listening to her song through headphones, and, in typical Hollywood fashion, donning sunglasses at the contract signing.

When Carla died at eighteen, those who know Mitchell said it was harder for her than losing her husband of twenty-five years, who passed away some months later.

"People grieve, they mourn the loss [of a pet bird]," says psychologist Bonnie Wolkenstein. "Usually the longing continues for the rest of the life of the human being companion. You don't just go out and get another bird, because it was so intelligent and had such a unique personality. It's a one-of-a-kind type of thing. It's very similar to grieving for a person you've been a companion with."

Gay Bradshaw, Ph.D., is a psychologist and animal behavior researcher who has run grief groups for pet owners. "The group is very important because it is a legitimizing and validating force for the feelings and experience of the loss," says Bradshaw. She has group members engage in a number of rituals, like bringing in photos of their birds, lighting candles, telling stories, and doing other remembrances. "People do these things in human grief groups, but in some ways these rituals become even more important [with companion animal loss] because it helps validate the animal's existence and the humans acknowledge their emotions about them," she says.

Nonhuman relationships are still marginalized in our society, both in life and death. Bradshaw says grief counselors don't want to mix people grieving for their pets with those grieving for people because they fear it may be insulting to the latter. "I talked to one person who said, 'I think it would be very awkward for someone who lost a child to hear someone else weeping because their dog died.'" But Bradshaw disagrees. She believes that losing a longtime companion, whether parrot or human, is always devastating, and points out that the words people use to describe their loss in either case are basically the same, and their reactions to the loss are too.

Western society also doesn't condone long-term grieving, and it's particularly unacceptable for companion animals. "The core of our culture is the denial of death," says Bradshaw. "Death is like a shadow in our society. Life and death, humans and animals, light and dark. Animals and death are on the dark side. We're at an interesting cultural shift, moving from one paradigm, this mono-specific human-dominated one, to one that is more multispecies." She says grieving for a pet deconstructs the Judeo-Christian belief that animals are inferior: "That's why 'PETA' is worse than a swear word."

With long-term parrot-human relationships, it isn't necessarily the bird that dies first. Large parrots can live a hundred years or longer, outliving multiple caretakers. The loss of a companion can be as hard on the parrot as on the person. Los Angeles–based avian veterinarian Attila Molnar says he is seeing a lot of geriatric clients with young parrots and worries about the number of birds that will be put up for adoption when their owners pass away. Some avian sanctuaries do offer care for widowed parrots if their owners bequeath funds to support them after they die. But even if they're physically cared for, parrots may not psychologically recover, given that the memories of their loved ones appear to last as long as they do. Lori Rutledge, founder of Cockatoo Rescue in Stanwood, Washington, has watched many birds brought to her sanctuary cry incessantly for their owners' return and light up if they come to visit. "They never forget their humans," says Rutledge.

Dr. Jamie Gilardi, director of the World Parrot Trust (WPT), found this out when he sent Iris and Napoleon, a pair of endangered iris lorikeets (small green parrots with splashes of red and blue on their heads), to the Bronx Zoo some years ago. The birds were housed in their own exhibit in the zoo's Tropical Bird House, with hundreds of visitors a week passing through. Four years later Gilardi was at the zoo for a meeting and went to see how the pair were doing. They not only recognized his voice instantly (even though they had seen and heard tens of thousands of people since they last heard him speak), they raced out of their nest box and rushed over to the screen where he stood, yelling excitedly at his return. Gilardi says their screaming could be heard two exhibits down for several minutes after he left.

Theft is a tragic way to lose a parrot, but more and more people are faced with this painful experience. Large parrots are valuable, and their homes are easy to spot. The birds are so loud they can be heard far beyond their own walls. As a result, parrots have become the number-one stolen pet in the United States. There's even a racket to stealing parrots: thieves listen for a bird squawking, stake out the home, and break in when the owner is away. Drug addicts will cruise streets, listening for homes with birds, and sell the address in exchange for drugs. After the theft, the perpetrator sometimes watches for flyers offering a reward for the missing bird. They'll say they found the bird, or contact the owners and offer to sell their pet back to them. But most of the time the birds are sold to anyone who will buy them. It helps thieves that the laws for stolen companion animals are lax, making trafficking in birds at swap meets and street corners in low-income areas a lucrative business.

Unlike the parrot people who will do anything to have their stolen bird returned, many parrot owners—indications say most—don't care about their birds and don't grieve when they're gone. These owners never saw past their parrots' colorful feathers and didn't connect with the bird on an emotional level. When these owners realize parrots are live pooping machines, or that the bird acts out, screaming, biting, and destroying furniture, it's an easy decision for them to get rid of the problem.

Chapter Three

No Joy: The Crisis of Unwanted Birds

The biggest and best-kept secret about parrots is that they make excellent companions but terrible pets. They are intelligent, loyal, and loving. But the never-ending demands of a bird that is high maintenance by nature will wear anyone out. Add to that the screaming and squawking, wrecked furniture, and biting, and it is understandable why so many people don't keep parrots for long.

The image of parrots as quiet, docile, and self-contained—the equivalent of fish in a cage—has been promoted over decades, saturating all cultural media. In movies, a cockatoo will add statuesque exotic beauty to the background of a scene. Audiences think nothing of the fact that the bird is sitting on a perch, in a barren cage just big enough to fit around it, when the minimally acceptable size is at least four times larger and loaded with bird toys and other enrichments.

A bird in a cage, by any moral standard, should be an abhorrent sight. But society has tacitly accepted this long-standing practice, and it has distorted our view of the obvious: even the prettiest cage is no more a decorative item than are a slave's shackles. Regardless of appearance, the two serve a single purpose: bondage.

The illusion that a caged life is a decent life for a creature designed to fly is so pervasive, it was mindlessly promoted in a magazine as progressive as Oprah Winfrey's *O*. A full-page home decor layout in 2003 featured a Moroccan-style living room adorned with deep jewel-toned silk pillows and palm fronds. The description read: "A few exotic accents add to the enchantment: palms, brass trays, a bird in a gilded cage." The bird listed as just another accessory was shown in an otherwise empty Taj Mahal–shaped cage at the back of the room.

Even from its cage, a fun-loving bird could do damage to that room: empty seed husks and flung fruit generally do not go well with silk pillows. Once the bird is let out to play, as it should be for a few hours every day, those palm fronds are done for. Parrots have hooked nails that naturally pull threads from fine fabrics, and bird poop doesn't look great on them either. Plus, the numerous toys needed to enrich the bird's cage would ruin the room's decorating scheme. This kind of unfortunate portrayal keeps consumers on the wrong track when buying a bird, ignorant of the animal's needs and demands.

"People will give up a bird easier than a dog because they have been taught by the way we sell birds in this country that they are a decorative, ornamental item, like furniture," says Richard Farinato, director of captive wildlife programs for the Humane Society of the United States. "They are not considered a living thing that needs to be treated the same way as a dog."

When these decorative objects are unexpectedly unruly (which might as well be the dictionary definition of *parrot*), their owners try to suppress the birds' natural behaviors. They are hidden away in the garage, closet, or back room, or kept under cover because birds stay quiet in the dark (though this is a form of both emotional and physical abuse—birds should never have their cages covered, since they need constant air flow). Ziyal is a Moluccan cockatoo who suffered years of abuse by several owners. She was kept in a dark closet to stop her from continually screaming for attention. She was thrown against a wall after she bit her owner's hand, and more than once her toes were burned with a lighter to loosen them from the perch she clung to during her owner's tirades. When she was rescued, she suffered from a broken keel bone and was almost bare of feathers. From the terror, trauma, and lack of affection, she had systematically mutilated herself by plucking her feathers out and chewed a hole into her chest when they were gone. Ziyal is now living with a new loving family and with a boyfriend, another cockatoo named Rocky. This story had a happy ending; most don't.

Surprisingly, many people who make their pet birds' lives a misery are not typical animal abusers. Often they are regular people whose patience has been worn thin by their parrot's wild behaviors. The misconception that a parrot is tame because it was bred in captivity is one of the great illusions about this bird. Just as big cats raised from cubs still retain their wild instincts, even captive-bred, hand-raised parrots remain wild. For example, the majority of parrots, for their entire lives, will bite the hand that feeds them. It is not something that can be trained out of them completely.

The definition of animal welfare is the appropriate match of an animal to its surroundings. "Anytime there is a mismatch between the animal and the environment, then welfare is going to be compromised," says avian behaviorist Dr. Cheryl Meehan of Orange Wing Consulting, in Portland, Oregon. Many problem behaviors in parrots arise from their being in captivity. Stereotyped behaviors, like those of zoo animals repetitively pacing back and forth in their cages, are prevalent in caged parrots.

When their owners ground them by clipping their wings, parrots are further psychologically and physically debilitated. Great athletes, parrots become "perch potatoes" who do nothing all day but eat, sleep, and wait for their human flock members to return and give them attention. On birdie play gyms or T-stands they can only perch, or minimally climb. Even in big cages without proper enrichment, empty space is just that; there's nothing to do without engaging challenges. Many end up obese, with serious behavior problems. Just the nature of living indoors, with prolonged exposure to air-conditioning in summer and heating in winter, can make them sick or kill them.

Karen Davis, a prominent activist, chicken rescuer, and founder of United Poultry Concerns, explains a bird's perspective of captivity:

We think of their natural jungle environment as wild. To us it is unfriendly, inhospitable. We can't navigate it, the food is unfamiliar, and it has predators that terrify us. Life would be a struggle for us there. But the jungle is not wild to them; it is natural. Our urban jungle is wild to them. It is unfriendly and inhospitable. They can't navigate it; the food is unfamiliar. Life is a struggle for them here.

How little we know about any bird's needs and behavior is put into high relief by those species living with us for thousands of years, such as chickens. Many people are unaware that chickens are descendants of wild, exotic birds native to Indonesia. Hundreds of thousands of generations have been raised in captivity, but they still retain their ancient heritage and instincts.

For example, when Davis opens the back of her truck to let out the latest group of chickens rescued from poultry farms, they fly to the trees and perch just as they would in the wild, even though they were hatched in food-production facilities and have never even seen daylight. At night, she has to urge them down from the trees, their natural roost, to stay indoors because of local predators. Domestication has not bred out of them what millions of years of evolution and natural instincts bred in. Key West, Florida, is famous for its wild chickens, which roam freely around the streets and also perch high in trees at night.

Because parrots' needs are so vast and their owners' abilities (and often their inclination) to meet them usually so limited, several directors at avian welfare organizations concur that an estimated 75 percent of pet birds live a life of neglect or abuse. One parrot rescuer told me that most are "neglected to death."

"What we do is mess up the mind and/or body of the large parrot," says Brian Speer, former president of the Association of Avian Veterinarians and a veteran bird breeder. "They are psychotic and feather-picking, and they're not right. They don't die. Whereas the dogs that got the same degree of neglect, they're dead. With parrots, our mistakes do haunt us."

Welcome to the dark side of the world of companion parrots.

The Humane Society of the United States, which has been on the frontlines of animal welfare for more than fifty years, considers parrots wild animals and advocates against having them as pets. In his career-long experience caring for parrots privately and professionally (including sixteen years in zoos), Richard Farinato says the owners who are equipped to deal with large parrots like Amazons, cockatoos, or macaws are few and far between. "We don't say, 'Since a few people can deal with parrots, it's okay for people to have them; we just need to educate the rest of the population," says Farinato. "It hasn't worked yet and doesn't work with most [wild] animals. What we find is, if you've only got a small minority that can deal with these birds, you've got to get them out of the hands of the rest of these folks, or make it more difficult for them to get them, because they do suffer."

For seventeen years B.J., a scarlet macaw, was kept in a tiny cage with a single metal perch and no toys. When he was finally brought to a rescue facility, he had to be cut out of his cage; he had long since outgrown the small door. He had only gone through it once, when he was put inside. He suffered from bowed legs and curvature of the spine from a combination of malnutrition and cramped quarters. His reaction to years of round-the-clock confinement and isolation was, like Ziyal, to cut into himself a gaping wound that went down to his chest muscle.

"Feather picking, along with screaming and biting, are the most common behavioral problems in parrots for which people seek veterinary help," says Dr. Meehan. Feather plucking is estimated to occur in one out of ten pet parrots. But statistics indicate that only 15 percent of pet birds ever see a veterinarian, so the numbers might be much higher. It is not uncommon to hear of parrots being given antidepressants (Prozac was popular for parrots and people in the 1990s) and other drugs to control these dysfunctional behaviors.

Because feather plucking is never observed in wild parrots, it is considered an environmentally induced disorder. "They never pluck in the wild; what does that say?" asks Charles Munn, a leading conservationist and one of the world's experts on macaws. "I've seen hundreds of thousands of wild parrots, and I've never seen a plucked bird. Some can have a pretty good quality of life in captivity, but I think that it produces stresses on them in ways that are hard for us to understand."

The psychological impact of being deprived of a flock might also be inestimable. Like solitary confinement for a human, it is not something a bird ever gets used to. Aside from a short time during nesting season when a male bird is getting food for his mate and young offspring, a wild parrot is never alone. Parrots don't just need to be in proximity to others of their kind, they need constant interaction. In the wild, parrots spend a good part of their day preening and playing with one another and sleep nestled next to one another when they roost.

Not only are parrots kept like prison inmates, ignored and in isolation most of the time, but another troubling and little-known fact compounds the problem: there are no humane standards or minimum size requirements for pet bird cages. Sizes are completely arbitrary, and aim to contain the bird in the least amount of space.

Founded in 1896, the Prevue Hendryx company is the oldest birdcage manufacturer in the United States. When queried about cage sizes, Susan Barry, the company's sales coordinator, said the two general criteria to use when choosing a cage are that "the bird should be able to turn around and not get its head stuck in the bars."

Prevue's latest line, Featherstone Heights, won best new bird product awards in 2003 and 2004 at the American Pet Products Manufacturers Association's annual show. The cages are modeled after human houses. There's the Tudor, the Cape Cod, Cottage Home, the Brownstone (for city birds), and the Victorian (for more conservative birds). Accessories include recliner chairs that double as feeders, clothes racks, and chandelier toys with bells. The cages are immediately popular because they are designed for the humans who buy them, more than for the birds that will have to live in them.

One bird club member was shocked by a parakeet "starter cage" she saw for sale in a pet shop. She described it as half the size of her handbag. The very idea of a "starter cage" for a bird is all marketing. Once they've fledged, birds have reached their full size and need the same amount of space as an adult—as much as possible. The "starter" element is the low price point to induce the consumer to buy it. The problem is that most birds live their entire lives in the cage they were brought home in from the pet shop. "You wouldn't keep a porpoise in a bathtub," says one parrot owner, but the equivalent is done to birds all the time. A spokesperson for Reliance Cages, distributors of the starter cage, said the company had no idea about the size of their cages relative to the birds that will live in them. They buy them ready-made in China.

A study by Dr. Meehan has shown that 85 percent of parrots living in cages without toys or objects that stimulate and interest them display abnormal behaviors. When enrichments of physical complexity are introduced, such as specially designed toys with food hidden in them so birds have to forage to eat (as opposed to ordinary toys like bells, mirrors, or balls, which Dr. Meehan says are "useless" as enrichments), feather picking was prevented or reversed in birds that plucked. "When the facts are as striking as they are, you just need to lay them out," says Dr. Meehan. "Enrichment shouldn't be thought of as an add-on; it's a necessity. A lot of people say this is an insane amount of work to keep a parrot, but parrots are exceptional companions, and they require exceptional owners to make that relationship work. It's a huge commitment."

The irony is that many people will go out of their way for a dog that needs to be walked twice a day, but they won't take the same time with a parrot. James Serpell has been studying dog behavior for more than a dozen years, but his Ph.D. dissertation was on lorikeet parrots, which he spent time studying in the wild. His research on dogs has shown that despite their reputation for loyalty, the vast majority are promiscuous animals that will bond with a new owner and adapt to a new living arrangement at will. Serpell says that by contrast, parrots are models of fidelity.

But this is not apparent when the birds are deprived of basic psychological needs, and a catch-22 situation develops. The less attention and enrichment the parrot gets, the more it screams and bites. Birds deprived of attention for long periods can lose human socialization and revert to their wild nature, unable to be handled. The more the bird acts out this way, the less inclined the owner is to take the bird out of the cage, causing more screaming, biting, and psychological damage to the bird. Finally, the owner gets fed up and abandons the parrot.

As a result, a crisis of unwanted parrots has developed in the United States.

Because parrots are expensive, their owners aren't initially willing to give them away when they no longer want them. Selling them is not necessarily an alternative, since few buyers will pay for an older bird when they can get a baby for the same price. Soon owners realize there are more available birds than people to take them. They give up the idea of selling their parrots, and the birds begin the demoralizing and traumatizing cycle of being passed around to family and friends, wearing out their welcomes in one home after another until they end up in an avian rescue, or worse. Estimates are that the average parrot has seven homes in the first ten years of its life.

The American Pet Products Manufacturers Association's national survey of consumer behavior and trends in pet buying and pet care for 2003–4 showed that 35 percent of bird owners obtained their birds from someone they knew. Fewer than 10 percent of birds were bought from a "pet superstore" such as Petsmart or Petco, and about 20 percent were bought from a breeder or local pet shop. The survey also showed an 8 percent decline in the number of bird-owning households from the previous decade. Two thousand was the first year that birds were in decline as pets since 1988, when the survey started. This might indicate that word-of-mouth about the problems of keeping parrots has finally gotten out—but that won't affect the millions of birds already in the marketplace.

Twenty-five years ago, anyone would have been hard pressed to locate an avian rescue. Now there are hundreds. You can find one in most states a few hours in any direction, yet the public is mostly unaware they even exist. They are scattered all over the United States, from Anchorage, Alaska, where Parrot Education and Adoption Center gets calls daily from people who want to relinquish their birds; to Nashua, New Hampshire, where Fauna Rescue receives more than a hundred calls a month; to Minneapolis, Minnesota, home of Midwest Avian Adoption and Rescue Services (MAARS); and to Benson, Arizona, where the Oasis Sanctuary has been taking in birds for twenty years.

Not one of these locations is considered a hotbed of parrot breeding or selling activity, as Southern California, Florida, and Texas are. Yet they are filled to capacity with unwanted parrots of all ages and species. Dr. Fern Van Sant, an avian veterinarian in San Jose, California, said she was forced into avian rescue because parrots were being left in her office waiting room or on her doorstep.

Sandi Meinholz, the director of Fine Feathered Friends Sanctuary in Madison, Wisconsin, gets fifty e-mails a week from people wanting to surrender birds. Even with a new, larger facility, the sanctuary can't keep up with the influx. "It seems like if I adopt out one bird, we get in seven more the next day," says Meinholz. "It's very disturbing." Many rescuers say they predicted five years ago that they would be at maximum capacity now, and they are.

From the 1970s through the 1990s, the United States underwent a bird boom during which birds were the fastest-growing pet choice in the country, and the vast majority, about 75 percent, were parrots. The Pet Industry Joint Advisory Council estimated that in 1991 there were fourteen million caged birds in the country, and by 1996 the number had shot up to forty million. In 2005, a consortium of industry experts concurred that an estimate of sixty-five million pet birds (not including breeder birds and those used for exhibition or research) would not be too high. These numbers combine the wild birds that were trapped outside the United States and imported for the pet trade (which is the direct cause of their populations being diminished in the wild) and the boost in domestic captive bird breeding in the United States after wild birds were no longer allowed into the country in 1992.

The Gabriel Foundation, an avian rescue and sanctuary in Carbondale, Colorado, has as its motto a quote from Antoine de Saint Exupéry's *Little Prince:* "Many have forgotten this truth, but you must not forget it. You remain responsible, forever, for what you have tamed." But Julie Murad, the foundation's founder, says, "People don't keep their birds. It's like light-years. We see the stars, but we're seeing the light from years before. It's the same with unwanted birds. They embarked on the path to homelessness years ago."

Sybil Erden started Oasis Sanctuary in 1985 as a permanent home for unwanted birds. In 1997, she incorporated, got nonprofit status, and became the first avian rescue on record with the Internal Revenue Service. Erden said she is now getting twice as many calls as she had over the previous five years. Then she was averaging a call a day; now it's more than a thousand a year.

MAARS started out as many rescues do as an extension of a bird club, the Minnesota Companion Bird Association. At first unwanted birds were exclusively adopted within the club. When the membership became saturated with parrots and more kept coming in, MAARS became a separate adoption arm. A nonprofit rescue organization since 1991 (though it still gets volunteer help from the club), the rescue is filled with more than three hundred parrots and has a waiting list. Many arrive unhealthy, and in filthy cages. MAARS director Eileen McCarthy takes in about two birds a month and is now getting calls from people threatening to throw their birds out a window if she doesn't take them. "People surrendering their birds," she says, "always say the same thing: 'If I knew then what I know now, I'd never have bought it in the first place.'" In 2003, PetSmart Charities funded the National Parrot Relinquishment Research Project, a survey to determine how many organizations were taking in unwanted birds and how many. Individuals and organizations rescuing birds across the country sent in 779 completed surveys. But the total number of birds rescued was just 5,391. Many experts say that figure is extremely low, and doesn't reflect the actual number of unwanted birds. (One reason is that it doesn't take into consideration the birds on waiting lists to get into filled shelters, and those being turning away.)

Before the survey began, Jamie Gilardi, director of the World Parrot Trust, said, "They'll never find them," predicting the low numbers of birds reflected in the findings. Gilardi believes the problem is as serious as the avian rescuers say, but that most unwanted birds are off the radar of surveys like this one because they are placed into private homes or other facilities, such as zoos, in addition to avian rescues. Dr. Meehan admits the survey does not determine how many unwanted birds are in the United States today. Julie Murad, director of the Gabriel Foundation, says she knew some rescue officials who refused to fill out the questionnaire for various reasons (including that her foundation was involved, and Petsmart was sponsoring the survey). Meehan cautions that it is a pilot study based only on those who responded, met the study's requirements, and provided usable responses on the forty-five-question, seven-page questionnaire. The American Pet Products Manufacturers Association's 2003–4 survey, which had only 290 usable returns for bird owners, showed that fewer than 1 percent of all birds obtained came from an animal shelter or humane society.

If the statistic about the number of times parrots change homes is accurate, a good portion of the boom birds are still in the hand-me-down pipeline and haven't hit the streets yet, making it likely that in the next ten years, a tsunami of parrots will descend upon avian rescues or be released into cities and towns across the country, placing this problem squarely in the public's awareness.

Unlike with dogs or cats, overpopulation in birds is not the result of mating run rampant. Dogs and cats mate at will without the need for human assistance (which is why getting them spayed and neutered is so important). Breeding exotic birds is complicated, and often difficult to do in captivity. To succeed in producing offspring, nest boxes must be provided, the right birds must be paired up, and they have to be the proper ages. Plus, even if eggs are laid, they can be removed at any time, preventing reproduction. The birds themselves are not responsible for making their conditions worse.

McCarthy makes the point that overpopulation is based not on the number of unwanted parrots but on the number of available placements available for them. "There are not hundreds of thousands of good homes for parrots, not even one hundred thousand," says McCarthy, "so it really doesn't matter how big the number is of unwanted birds. We know it's big and we know it's going to get bigger, and nobody's prepared to handle what we have now. So how are we possibly going to be able to handle it coming down the pike? That is really the bottom-line issue. The more they keep selling birds as ideal companions for the new millennium, the more will end up in shelters. It's just cause and effect."

Barbara Fitzgerald is senior vice president for store operations at PetSmart, which promotes the fact that it does not sell dogs or cats because of the large numbers that wind up homeless, and are eventually euthanized. The company says it has helped more than one million dogs and cats get adopted. Fitzgerald said the company would stop selling parrots and hold adoption days if the PetSmart Charities survey revealed a problem with overpopulation. "I will tell you because of the legacy of this company, that we will do the right thing based on the information that we see," she said. "As a company, any pet that doesn't get placed and remain in a loving home troubles us."

In 2006, after the PetSmart study was completed and Petco came to an agreement with PETA (People for the Ethical Treatment of Animals) to stop carrying large parrots, I queried PetSmart again to see if they were planning to follow suit. "We take the viewpoint that large birds make good and appropriate family members," said Jennifer Pflugfelder, the company's communications spokesperson. "We continue to see them as we have before."

PetSmart is not alone. The bird-breeding industry equally denies there is an overpopulation problem, or even that there are serious behavior problems with birds in captivity that would push owners to relinquish them. At the 2004 convention of the American Federation of Aviculture (AFA), a veteran breeder gave a talk titled "The Myth of the Maladjusted Pet Parrot." AFA president Benny Gallaway said in an interview that if there were any unwanted birds, they wouldn't be homeless, because breeders would happily take them for breeding situations.

Many birds do end up in breeding facilities when their owners don't have another choice, or don't realize the fundamental problem with putting a homeless bird in a situation where it will potentially be producing more of the same. Plus, placing birds with behavioral issues into breeding situations is courting disaster, says Rebecca Fox of the Psittacine Research Project at the University of California, Davis. Fox points out that there is a strong genetic component to personality. In general, when animals are bred for pets, those with personality traits desirable for living with humans are bred, and those with undesirable traits are not.

"The traditional parrot story is, a bird that's too aggressive to be kept in a pet situation is put into breeding," says Fox. "I just find it a little bit disturbing that that's the first thing that people think of to do with an aggressive bird in a lot of cases."

But respected bird breeders like Dick Schroeder, who is also a columnist for *Bird Talk* magazine, make the point that since the Wild Bird Conservation Act stopped the import of birds for commercial trade in 1992, some parrot species are becoming rare in aviculture. He says the fact that rescues are not allowing breeders access to birds will be a problem down the line when some species become unavailable in the United States.

"With a few exceptions, there is a greater diversity of parrot species in private aviculture than there is in zoos," says Schroeder. "Some species of parrot are already hard to find, such as the Goldie's lorikeet or Goffin's cockatoo. They are in such short supply, we will soon hit a genetic dead end, and there won't be any left."

Schroeder has a waiting list for mynah birds that sell for eight hundred dollars apiece. But rather than selling the few babies hatched this season, he is keeping them for breeding stock because these birds have become hard to find. He adds that the problem is compounded by the fact that bird breeders become paranoid about making their inventories known for a host of reasons, including zoning infractions for keeping too many birds. They don't share information with other breeders, leaving a void in accounting for the types and number of species of parrots being bred nationwide.

Cockatoos are a prime example of how problematic some species are as pets. They might be the single noisiest parrot species in captivity, squawking unprovoked for long periods at a time. One rescuer, Sabra Brea, has a Web site (www.mytoos.com) where the sound of two screaming cockatoos loads as soon as you access the site. She urges all potential cockatoo buyers to turn up the volume and imagine the noise echoing through their homes. "They're the most advertised baby birds because they're so cuddly, but they grow up to be screaming maniacs that mutilate themselves," says Brea.

Other avian rescues agree and add that cockatoos, especially larger ones, are the most relinquished bird. One rescue got six calls to take cockatoos in one weekend. "One of our staffers gets so upset," says Murad of the Gabriel Foundation. "She says, 'What's this? The Gabriel Cockatoo Sanctuary?'" McCarthy and others say they could fill their spaces with male cockatoos alone. "They are not adoptable because they are unpredictable," says McCarthy. "Once they are sexually aroused, they will get aggressive and attack. No one can handle them." But breeders are still churning them out like fluffy candy to unwitting consumers.

Parrots that don't act out often have it worse because they suffer in silence. They live cagebound, easily ignored and neglected, and never get rescued. "The Senegals, the little, sweet conures, some of the smaller, quieter macaws, and a lot of Amazons will just sit there and endure," says Murad. "They languish and are in terrible, terrible shape because they are quieter birds."

Rose and Frank Levine's Parrots First rescue is in a modest two-bedroom apartment in the Palms section of Los Angeles, which is also their base of operations. They estimate they have placed more than eighty birds since they started rescuing birds nine years ago.

On this day Frank is reticent about being interviewed. "We don't have too many birds right now, just seven," he says. Further questions reveal seven are on the premises and another twenty are in foster homes, waiting to be adopted.

Pepper, a thirty-year-old umbrella cockatoo, greets visitors with open wings. "Hello," she says, standing on the back of the Levines' sofa. She's a beautiful bird. All smiles. She is also missing most of the feathers on her back and chest from plucking. The Levines have had her for four years. She had been a pet to a young girl who loved her. They were inseparable until the girl went away to college. She left Pepper behind with her mother and aunt, who would chase the bird with a broom to get her back in her cage. "Nice people, you'd like them," says Frank. "You'd never know they'd treat a bird like this." At first the Levines intended to find another home for Pepper, but Rose feared some of her behaviors would lead people to hurt her again. Then the Levines fell in love with her, and now she is one of their "keepers." Rose interrupts the tour to stop Pepper from eating the window.

In the kitchen all the baseboards are gone, and one of the cabinets looks like someone took a chainsaw to it.

There's a tiny featherless lovebird in a cage on the dining table. Frank calls him Little Dude. Even this bird has pulled out all its feathers. No one knows his story. The Levines assume he was neglected. Little Dude has a sweet spirit, and even featherless, he's a charmer as he hops on Rose's finger. It's unusual because lovebirds don't usually live up to their name; they can be nasty little nippers. Little Dude can fly, but it's not safe for him to zip around the living room. "The birds all watch him with their beaks open, ready to gobble him up," says Rose. They'd probably leave him alone in the wild, but in captivity, where they have little space, they become very territorial.

Stevie, an Amazon, is trying to get to the wires of Frank's new entertainment center. He follows Frank around the house, saying, "Frank, Frank." Frank and Rose are a little afraid of him because he has a terrible bite. It might be he's still angry about being given away to strangers and misses his owner. Stevie lived and was loved in the same home for twenty-two years. When his caretaker went in for heart surgery, the man's wife immediately called the Levines to take Stevie. "She couldn't get him here fast enough; she showed up at seven a.m., two hours early," says Frank. "And you'd think the guy would want this animal he loved while he was recuperating. The wife even said her husband missed Stevie, but she didn't care. She just wanted him 'out, out, out.'" Avian rescuers have a saying: "There are no bad birds, just bad humans."

Costa, a green-winged macaw, is twenty years old. He squawks every time someone walks past the Levines' first-floor window and will go crazy if he sees a handcart. His owner put him in a box on a handcart and wheeled him out to get rid of him. He hadn't been touched by anyone for years when Rose and Frank got him. His owner moved him from his perch to his cage with a stick. It took almost a year of nurturing before Costa trusted Frank. But now he lets Frank pet him easily.

Baby, Costa's girlfriend, is a twenty-seven-year-old blue and gold macaw who had a good life with a doting owner. He made her a room out of an enclosed patio, with plenty of perches and lots of enrichments so she could fly and play all day while he was at work. One day he came home and found her sitting on the living room sofa, happy to see him. She had eaten through the patio door. He fixed it and added a doggie door so she could have the run of the house.

When Baby's owner died, she stayed next to him, guarding his body, for two days. She fought off animal control agents to stay by his side. Rose says Baby was so depressed by the loss that she had stopped eating. She was skin and bones when they got her. They had to catch her in a towel and force-feed her several times a day for a month. She also had to contend with being caged for the first time in her life. "She looked stunned when we put her in a cage," says Rose. "She couldn't figure out what it was." Every day after they got her, Baby would sit by the window, crying, "Papa."

Costa helped Baby get over her grief. He would bring her toys and say, "Hi Birdie," his name for her. Though they are about the same size, they would never be a couple in the wild; they're two different species. But here they snuggle and preen each other. "He loves her, and she loves him," says Rose.

Costa is very protective of Baby. He shows her all the loyalty he never got in his life—especially now, since she has been laying eggs. One night

Rose came into the living room when Baby was in the middle of an egg-laying session and particularly vulnerable. Costa quickly covered Baby with a newspaper to protect her. Now Baby is sitting in the corner of the room, out of sight. Costa is bringing her some food in his beak. She's not hungry, but he's a doting mate and won't take no for an answer.

Rose tells of a man who e-mailed them to come get Mia, his blue and gold macaw. She had spent most of the last two years at a boarding facility. "He wouldn't even go upstairs to say good-bye to her," says Rose. Later he called to see how the bird was doing. Rose spoke honestly. She told him how traumatized the bird was and what bad shape she was in. The man said he felt bad hearing that. "Good," said Rose, "you should." "He wanted me to tell him what he did was okay," says Rose, "but it wasn't okay."

"We don't try to make the humans feel good," says Frank, "that's not our job. Not after what they've done to their birds."

The Levines get anywhere from a few relinquishment calls a week to several in a day. Frank says it's getting worse every year. One day they took in eleven birds, all from different owners. Because of the mounting veterinary bills, they started charging an adoption fee. "We don't make a dime, but there's been plenty out-of-pocket," says Frank. "We just want to help these little guys."

Recently Rose and Frank found out that their apartment building was being sold. They don't know where they'll go. They can't afford to buy a house, and it's very difficult to find someone who will lease to them with all their birds. This is a chronic problem for avian rescues, which go under all the time from the dual burden of too many birds and too little money. When they do, finding homes for large numbers of homeless birds all at once is daunting. Sometimes they are placed in local animal shelters, which are generally not set up to care for them. MAARS's Eileen McCarthy and Marc Johnson, founder of Boston's Foster Parrots rescue, once drove from Minneapolis and Boston, respectively, to rescue 120 parrots from a rescue that went belly-up in Maryland. They then drove the birds to Texas to be placed at another facility that had space to accommodate them.

Sabra Brea converted her south Florida home into Sabra's Parrot Rescue eighteen years ago. She has sustained it by using an inheritance from her mother and taking a second mortgage on her house. All the money from the mortgage goes to cover veterinarian bills. "There's little funding in any kind of rescue, but with birds it's zero," says Brea. "It's on a par with dog and cat neglect, abuse, and abandonment, but no one knows about it. We do it on a wing and a prayer."

Avian rescues miss out on funding and support because of, as Brea points out, a lack of awareness and because organizations and foundations set up to support cat and dog shelters think parrots are wild animals and won't allocate funds to them. But the ones that fund wild animal rescues say parrots are companion animals and won't support them either.

As some rescues do, Brea has made the choice not to adopt out. Once a bird comes in, it has a permanent home. This makes it all the harder to get donations from supporters. Most rescues canvass their list of patrons when new birds come in, but Sabra and her husband rarely do. Together they care for the dozen scarlet, green-winged, and blue and gold macaws that are their resident flock. All were badly abused or neglected and require a huge investment of time and energy. The couple is retired, but even with unlimited time, it is all they can do to keep up.

Brea says caring for the birds is like having twelve toddlers in the house, all screaming day and night. She and her husband never go anywhere because they're exhausted after cleaning cages, feeding the birds, administering their medication, and cleaning up after them all day. "They take all our energy," says Brea. She believes parrots need more attention in captivity than any human can provide. Recently she was at the dentist when the technician, knowing Brea had parrots, said she wanted to get one that talked. Even with a mouth full of metal implements, Brea warned her off the idea. "You get a parrot for what you can do for it, not what it can do for you," she told her.

Now sixty-five, Brea worries about her birds' future, even though she's made arrangements for when she and her husband can no longer care for them. She also worries about birds in other rescues whose caretakers won't outlive them and don't have the means to arrange for their care after they are gone. Many rescuers are middle-aged or older; people in their twenties and thirties are reluctant to take on this work.

"I know a seventy-year-old woman with a rescue in her home who will leave her house and the means to care for her birds to anyone good and responsible, but no one wants to do it," says Brea. "Young people, which are what is needed to properly take over this huge responsibility, aren't motivated or evolved enough yet to make the commitment to do this."

Twelve birds keep two people busy full time at Sabra's Parrot Rescue, so the very idea of 280 parrots loose in a house is incomprehensible. But that is the situation at Foster Parrots.

The rescue is in a residential neighborhood about twenty miles south of Boston in Rockland, Massachusetts. It has remained there unhindered because founder Marc Johnson is blessed with ideal neighbors, says one of his longtime staffers, Tami Myers. "One's elderly and can't hear; the other has screaming kids," she says. "Sound-wise, compared to the kids, the birds are nothing at all."

Myers is in her early thirties and has an effervescent personality. She looks pert in a short pink sweater, faded jeans, and a braided ponytail. She drives a Dodge Caravan covered all over, windows included, with bumper stickers and posters like "Thanksgiving is murder on turkeys," "There's a holocaust on your plate," "Petco Kills Birds," "Don't Breed, Don't Buy, Adopt," and "If you love animals called pets, why would you dissect animals called specimens?" The back window is almost entirely covered with a PETA poster urging, "Boycott Petco, don't buy into cruelty to animals," along with enlarged photos of dead and neglected Petco birds—not a pleasant sight for those driving behind her in morning rush hour just after they've finished breakfast.

"I had to take a bunch down," she says, "I couldn't see out the windows. It was getting dangerous driving." The posters have caused her problems in other ways. "All the windows were broken in," she says. The van is used all the time for animal rights rallies, rescues, and to shuttle wounded dogs and other animals to the vet. It looks and smells it, but cosmetics are the least of Myers's concerns.

Sometimes the Foster Parrots volunteers show up, other times they don't, says Myers; "On a bad day it's just the two of us." In addition to working at Foster Parrots, Myers started an avian rescue, the Angry Parrot, in her home. It came about accidentally, as most avian rescues do. She began a bird-boarding service called Beak Retreat to make extra money and to give parrots a parrot-friendly place to stay when their owners were out of town. But people started leaving their birds with her permanently. "It backfired," says Myers. "They'd say, 'He's better off with you,' and not come to pick them up." Now she has fifty-four birds and a business card that features a parrot mascot in a cape, sword, and mask. "The Pet Trade Bites and We're Biting Back!" the card states. "Join us in ending live animal retail sales."

Foster Parrots has a standing requirement that anyone who wants to adopt a bird must volunteer at the rescue first. How long depends on Johnson's assessment of the person and the bird they want (one with a history of abuse or special needs would take more time to adopt). Johnson is trying to forestall future relinquishments by familiarizing people with the responsibilities of caring for a parrot. And, he figures, if they're not willing to work for the bird, they shouldn't have it.

Myers says nearly all the birds at Foster Parrots are free flighted, allowed to keep flight feathers and roam freely around their surroundings. The ones who aren't are the troublemakers, like the caiques. These small, brightly colored birds have big personalities and are notorious for being little tough guys, the Jimmy Cagneys of the parrot world. "They are like gang members," says Myers. "The four of them get out of their cage and start looking for trouble." There are other troublemaking birds, and all are allowed out when someone is around to supervise their shenanigans.

In addition to parrots, Johnson has taken in a rooster named Victoria who was bought as a pink-dyed chick, then moulted white. "He would fall asleep in your lap as you stroked his face," says Myers. "They probably thought they'd have a pink chicken forever, and when he turned out to be a white rooster, they didn't want him anymore." Now fully grown, Victoria rules the backyard, shepherding eleven chickens and trying to do the same with thirty-five ducks, geese, and other water and land fowl that reside there.

As Myers and I drive up to Foster Parrots one freezing winter afternoon, Johnson, a friendly bear of a guy, stands on the porch of his Victorian-style house in a T-shirt, talking on the phone. It's freezing outside, but a parrot relinquishment call brought him outside—the only place he can hear through the squawking. The woman he's speaking with has five cockatiels. She and her boyfriend are splitting up. The boyfriend doesn't want the birds, and she's about to be homeless. Johnson agrees to take them.

He's especially busy on this day. He just returned from a three-day conference for sanctuaries and came back to several hundred e-mails.

"That was one of a million calls," he says. "Normally I tell them to ditch the boyfriend and keep the birds, but they were already breaking up."

Inside the house it looks like an avian hippie commune. Parrots are everywhere. At first glance the living room, which has no furniture, looks surprisingly empty until one notices the thirteen large macaws glaring down from hanging perches.

The floor is covered with large sheets of rolled paper, the kind you find on a restaurant table with a cup of crayons. The paper covers the floors throughout the house and barn so the birds can poop at will. Then it's just rolled up and replaced.

In the next room, the former dining room, a table stands against one wall. Birds fill the rest of the space. Johnson provides a roster when I return home; there were too many birds in my notes to keep track of, and I wanted to accurately report what I saw. The list is broken down by parrots and where they are in residence throughout the house:

Office: four
Bedroom: ten

Small bird room (upstairs house): thirteen

Downstairs house

Living room: thirteen macaws

Dining room: five cockatoos, one African gray, three Amazons

Great room: six cockatoos

Breakfast room: five cockatoos

Breezeway between house and barn: five cockatoos

Upstairs barn: Nine conures, four African grays, six macaws, twelve Amazons

Downstairs barn: dozens of conures, two eclectus, six Amazons, one alexandrine, fifteen lovebirds, three mini macaws, four caiques, three quakers

Outdoor aviary: seventy small birds, including two canary-wing parakeets, two grass parakeets, and dozens of cockatiels and parakeets

Second outdoor aviary: two Amazons, one African gray

Yard (three-quarters of an acre): eleven ducks, five geese, twelve chickens

Total house area: three thousand, two hundred square feet

Total birds: two hundred and eighty

Karen Lee is in her early forties. She has worked at Foster Parrots for five years. When we meet, she is cleaning food bowls in the kitchen. She wipes her wet hand to shake mine. Johnson and Lee are Foster Parrots' only full-time employees (Myers is part time), and their wages are minimal. "I live without health care," says Johnson. Lee says she can afford to work here because her husband has a paying job.

Upstairs are scarlet macaws, African grays, and more Amazons. Charlie, a cherry-headed conure, was attacked by a rat in his former home and is missing his left leg. Then his other leg broke. He wasn't given medical attention, so it set in a useless position. His owner was going to flush him down the toilet until someone said they knew a place he could bring him.

"I have no furniture," says Johnson. "Everything is eaten by the birds." He lists what he has left: a bed and night table, a table in the kitchen, and some chairs. And they have beak marks in them, too.

In the barn is an open space filled with mixed species of parrots, thirty-two in all, flying around the room or on perches suspended from the ceiling. It's a frenzy of activity, like a parrot Times Square, and each species has staked a territorial claim to a section of the room.

In a room in the upstairs of the barn are Amazons and other birds that have come out of tragic situations. Some have plucked their feathers; others are antisocial and can't mix with the other birds for physical or behavioral reasons.

One Amazon backs away when anyone nears her cage. She is from Mexico and was blinded with a hot poker when she was caught to make her easier to handle for the trappers, and to keep her a docile pet. The scars on the balls of her eyes are still visible. Johnson says that if anyone tries to pet her, she will take off their hand. Because of the way her scars healed, she isn't sightless, but she is still terrified of people.

The lives of all of these birds changed overnight when they arrived at Foster Parrots. Some were rescued out of dire situations. The sadness in their eyes is like that of a child too wise for its years. Others had been in decent homes when all of a sudden, without time to process what was happening to them, they found themselves in a new environment crowded with more birds than they had seen in their lives.

Each day the birds, who wake up at sunrise, go through twelve gallons of filtered water and fifty pounds of seeds, nuts, and dried fruit. They eat another thirty to forty pounds of fresh vegetables and fruit a week. After they're fed, the cleaning starts. "We put out eleven large garbage cans a week," says Johnson.

When care for the birds is done, there are hundreds of e-mails to answer, veterinarian appointments, escaped-bird calls, checkups on adopted birds, and all the administrative work.

Like Tami Myers, Johnson also got into this by accident. He had studied pottery-making in England and had a studio in the trendy area of Hampshire Street between Harvard and MIT in Cambridge, Massachusetts. The shingle outside read, "Interplanetary Potter." He specialized in dinnerware and casserole dishes.

One day he decided he wanted to have a pet and scoured the newspaper classifieds for a bird. He found a blue and gold macaw for six hundred dollars. He counted up all his money and spare change and came up with four hundred dollars. He called the guy and made an offer. "Okay," the seller said, "come and get him." That first bird was Wally, who is still with him. When Johnson arrived, he was offered a second bird for free, a conure who was Wally's friend. "I figured the more the merrier," says Johnson.

He says people could hear the squawking birds from the street outside his studio. "People would come in and say, 'I have a friend who doesn't want his bird. Can you take him?' I would say, 'Sure.' I thought the birds were great, but I knew something was wrong when people were just giving away two-thousand-dollar birds and one-thousand-dollar cages."

Soon birds started coming in faster and faster, and each year was worse than the one before. "People would come for the pottery class, and we'd have to move birds off the wheels and shelves just to clear enough space for the students to work," says Johnson. "They were surrounded by parrots."

When he moved into the house in Rockland, the barn was to be his studio. It never happened. Now, with more birds than ever, they can barely keep up, and Johnson says he, Lee, and Myers cry just thinking about all they have to do. "Everyone has a good reason to give up their bird," he says, "but you don't give up your children just because your own needs change." Even with as many birds as the rescue takes, Johnson still turns down hundreds of birds a year because they don't have space to accommodate them.

Along with Myers, Johnson has become a vocal opponent of the pet trade and the avian breeding community and its organizations, like the American Federation of Aviculture.

"The rhetoric of the AFA and the pet bird industry is an alarmist one," says Johnson. "In a lot of cases, you could take their published articles, replace the word *bird* with *gun*, and use it as NRA [National Rifle Association] literature. It's the same propaganda. They're against government control and regulation. And they're not really out to protect the birds' interests at all. They're out to protect the aviculturalists. That's what these organizations are all about. One breeder told me breeding birds is no different than making toasters or pickup trucks."

Johnson has been threatened by breeders saying they'd break all his windows in the middle of winter to release the birds so they would freeze or starve to death. "It was scary for a while," he says. "I slept with a baseball bat next to my bed."

Johnson, Myers, and Lee do their best to reach out to the community and raise awareness of the plight of parrots. When Johnson speaks at schools he always brings two parrots, one in good feather and one that has plucked its feathers, to show what happens when parrots aren't taken care of properly. He hopes to discourage young consumers from wanting one as a pet. Says Lee,

> Parents get pets for their children to teach them to be responsible and respect life, but it ends up teaching them the opposite. When the child doesn't take care of the pet properly, it dies or the parents get rid of it. If it's a goldfish, they flush it down the toilet. The lessons the kid learns are that animals are disposable.
>
> At Wal-Mart, if you buy a cage and all the accessories, you get the parakeet for free. If people are throwing away a parrot they spent thousands of dollars on, what chance does an animal have that is given away for free? None.

Johnson thinks the only solution is a national sanctuary for unwanted parrots. In 2006, he began working on forming one in his area.

In a remarkably symbiotic relationship between people and parrots, recovering veterans and rescued birds are finding serenity at Serenity Park, an avian sanctuary and work therapy program at the Veterans Administration Medical Center in West Los Angeles, California. The sanctuary is part of New Directions, a therapeutic community that provides rehabilitation to homeless and chemically dependent veterans, and now to homeless parrots as well.

It was almost by accident that Lorin Lindner, the sanctuary's founder and then clinical director of New Directions, discovered the psychological benefits parrots could bring to her patients and the reciprocal results of those relationships for the birds.

Lindner, who has been involved with avian rescue and welfare issues for many years, cofounded the Earth Angel avian sanctuary with avian rescuer Jeannie White in Ojai, California, in 1997. When Lindner took on the post at New Directions in 1999, she placed her own two rescued cockatoos at Earth Angel so they wouldn't suffer when she was away for the long hours the job required.

"I never missed a weekend in five years," she says of her regular trips north from her home in Los Angeles to visit and care for the birds.

Lindner started bringing some of her patients to Ojai to give them a break from the VA grounds and a chance to interact with nature, and to help at the rescue. She found that the veterans were being transformed by working with the birds. "These were tough guys, marines," says Lindner. "One named Willie said, 'I don't want nothin' to do with no birds.' Then one of the cockatoos climbed up onto his lap and put her head down. She looked up at him and said, 'Hello, I love you,' and Willie fell in love."

In addition to substance abuse and chronic medical problems, many of the vets suffer from disorders like mental illness and posttraumatic stress disorder (PTSD). "[They] often need to make a gradual transition reintegrating back into the workforce," says Lindner. "Working in a relatively stress-free environment for a specified period of time is imperative for them."

Lindner realized that the therapy goals she had been working toward with these men, such as empathy building, sensitivity training, anger management, and compassion, were more easily accomplished by engaging the rescued birds as their teachers. "The birds really help these guys get out of themselves," she says. "Some had lost their wife or family. The light had gone from their face. The parrots bring out a pure emotion of love. You see it in their eyes when they are with the birds."

The same healing was occurring with the birds, many of which also suffered from PTSD. Time with the veterans helped the wounded reestablish trusting bonds with humans.

Lindner got the idea to make that experience a form of therapy. She solicited the Veterans Administration for some of the unused land on the grounds for her sanctuary. The VA was willing to take a chance on her idea and agreed to let her build the sanctuary under the umbrella of the New Directions' existing work-therapy program, on a dilapidated and broken asphalt basketball court that hadn't been used in years. She and a host of volunteers, including an architect who provided his time and designs for free, transformed the formerly barren slab into an urban avian oasis. The result was the first rescue on government property in the United States. Lindner says it was built with "love from the ground up."

In 2007, when the sanctuary officially opened, there were sixteen avian residents—appropriately, a military macaw named Porky; a blue-and-gold named Sherman; three Amazons, Joey, Ruby (a male), and Magdalena ("Maggie"), who is minus a tail; a Lindner's cockatoo, Sammy; and nine Indian ringnecks confiscated by customs officers from a smuggler. Lindner is planning to bring more birds into the spacious aviaries, which are surrounded by trees and loaded with enrichments like water misters, toys, live bamboo for the birds to chew, and fruit and millet branches strategically placed along rope and tree branch perches for the birds to forage.

Veteran Stanley Smith, now in the program for seven months, is recovering from alcohol and drug abuse at New Directions after living on the streets of Los Angeles. He grew up on a farm and trained dogs as sentries to guard B-52 bombers in Vietnam from 1961 to 1966. He has also had a parakeet and an Amazon as pets. When he became eligible for work therapy, he requested work at Serenity Park.

"It's good therapy," he says. "You can tell a dog to come here and it'll come, but a bird won't just because you want it to. It will teach you patience, empathy, and sympathy. Doing this work serves a dual purpose. I'm taking care of my problem and enjoying it, too!"

At the opening ceremony of Serenity Park, environmentalist and author Andrew Beath spoke about healing trauma that comes from violence. "This is a violent time," he said. "Vets experience it, and so do parrots. The only way to make deep and lasting change is by love."

But Serenity Park is a unique situation that houses just a handful of parrots. While it is a powerful model, there is no knowing whether it could be replicated to accommodate the already alarming number of unwanted parrots, which is growing every year. "What the Humane Society [of the United States] has discovered is that about 6.5 percent of all the cats and dogs living in a home right now will end up in a shelter for no other reason than they're not wanted anymore," says Erden. "And of those, 60 percent are going to be euthanized every year. Let's assume there are only twenty million birds in the United States. If we use the statistics for dogs and cats, there are going to be hundreds of thousands of birds every year that are homeless and slated for death one way or another."

The number of relinquished birds is already overwhelming. "I don't think it's overstating it to say that it's a crisis," says Stephanie Shain, of the Humane Society's Companion Animal Outreach Program. "It is a huge issue, and the rescue groups are overburdened, but local animal shelters are also seeing the effects."

The word *sanctuary* sounds lovely, but in the case of unwanted birds it usually amounts to a bird isolated in a cage in an institution. Even if it is a well-lit and clean place where people care, the bird may stay there in a cage for five, ten, or thirty years or more, or until it dies.

"The answer is not the sanctuary situation, where you end up warehousing birds for God knows how long," says Farinato. "If the bird is placed where it will have a good quality of life for the rest of its life, that's one thing. It's an ethical value, it's a moral value, and it's a value of life. I don't believe that life should be kept at all costs. There has to be a quality of life, and I think that's integral to the regalness of a parrot."

Farinato has openly advocated euthanasia, and a majority of avian rescues randomly polled for this book agree that it might be the inevitable and humane solution to the problem. But it will be a terrible irony if parrots, in increasingly short supply in the wild, are killed en masse in captivity because of overpopulation because they're the latest unwanted pets.

Chapter Four

Naturalized Psittacines:
America's Avian Immigrants

In *Land Birds Bird Guide, Song and Insectivorous Birds East of the Rockies,* a small birding book published in 1909, the very first bird described is the Carolina Paroquet. "At the time of this writing, the bird is only known to be living in the interior of Florida and possibly Oklahoma, though its range had been all of the southern states," wrote Chester A. Reed, the book's author. "They were once abundant throughout the southern states but are now nearly extinct."

Just eleven years later, the only parrots native to the United States were gone.

Though called a parakeet because it had a long tail, at twelve and a half inches in length this bird was not small. It was mostly green, with an orange forehead, a yellow collar, and green wings highlighted with a brush of yellow along the forewing. Ornithologist Alexander Wilson said these birds were as beautiful to behold as any exotic parrot: "While Parrots and Paroquets from foreign countries abound in almost every street of our large cities, and become such great favorites, no attention seems to have been paid to our own, which, in elegance of figure, and beauty of plumage, is certainly superior to many of them."

The Carolina parakeet was confirmed as the only parrot indigenous to the United States. (The thick-billed parrot from northwestern Mexico resided in Arizona, but it has not been proven that it nested or bred there.) The Carolina parakeet was found as far north as Connecticut and as far west as Illinois.

Their demise began with the arrival of settlers, who converted the birds' habitat into farmland. In addition to liking wild nuts and berries, the parakeets were fond of new planted items like corn and apples. The Carolinas, like the smaller monk parakeets, were considered agricultural pests, and were often shot out of the sky before they ever touched a crop.

This practice is not unusual. It still occurs in Australia, where farmers shoot Moluccan cockatoos (some estimates say as many as hundreds of thousands of a year) when they encroach on crops. During nesting season, male cockatoos search for food for their families and are shot out of the sky. Hours later, when the males haven't returned, their mates fly in search of them, sending out loud calls. There are numerous reports of the females, finding their dead mates on the ground, nudging them with their beaks and urging them to fly away. It's a tragic loss for the remaining birds because cockatoos bond for life.

In nineteenth-century America, some Carolina parakeets were killed for their feathers, which were used in ladies' hats, and thousands were shot for sport. Alexander Wilson and fellow ornithologist John James Audubon shot the birds together. They were relatively easy to kill because they loyally returned to the body of a dead or injured flockmate, as Wilson describes in his journals, published in 1840:

> I had an opportunity of observing some very particular traits of their character: Having shot down a number, some of which were only wounded, the whole flock swept repeatedly around their prostrate companions, and again settled on a low tree, within twenty yards of the spot where I stood. At each successive discharge, showers of them fell, yet the affection of the survivors seemed rather to increase; for, after a few circuits around the place, they again alighted near me, looking down on their slaughtered companions with such manifest symptoms of sympathy and concern, as entirely disarmed me.

Carolina parakeets thrived in North America for thousands of years but were wiped out by humans in just fifty. By the 1880s, wild flocks were rarely seen, and the last one in captivity died at the Cincinnati Zoo in

1905. Fifteen years later thirty were seen flying in Florida, the southern-most part of their range. It was the last time any were seen.

Today, wild parrots once again fly in North America.

On any given day, sounds of the jungle can be heard around Los Ange-les—from the beach areas of Venice, the Pacific Palisades, and Malibu to trees in residential Mar Vista, West Hollywood's Plummer Park, or the downtown Civic Center. Many city residents can't miss their boisterous neighbors: the wild flocks of little yellow-chevroned parakeets, large scar-let macaws from South America, cockatoos from Indonesia and Australia, lilac- and red-crowned parrots from Mexico, red-masked parakeets, and others. Flying low, their mega-decibel squawks are unmistakable.

Naturalized psittacines in California received national attention from the book and film *Wild Parrots of Telegraph Hill,* about a flock of cherry-headed conures in that San Francisco neighborhood. Mark Bittner, who at the time was broke and homeless, had a temporary roof over his head while house-sitting, and started feeding the birds. Many were thought to be wild-caught parrots that had been released by owners who no longer wanted them, or escapees now navigating the wilds of the city. Bittner and the parrots formed a meaningful relationship as each struggled to survive living as outcasts in society.

Bittner's experience is not an isolated occurrence. Ornithologists Bill Pranty of the Archbold Biological Station in Florida and Kimball Garrett of the Los Angeles Natural History Museum estimate that thirty thousand parrots fly free from Connecticut to Florida and from Texas to California. Other estimates say more than thirty-five thousand parrots, in nineteen breeding species, live in Florida alone, making the United States home to the most diverse population of exotic parrots in the world.

California, which never had naturally occurring parrots, now has at least ten breeding species, numbering about five thousand birds, in thirty areas from San Francisco to San Diego.

It is illegal to release non-native birds in the United States, but many parrot owners who no longer want their birds set them loose, especially in climates as hospitable as those in Southern California, Florida, or Texas. They figure the birds can fly and have a good chance at survival because they are wild animals, but that isn't always the case. Hand-raised parrots have never had parrot parents to teach them the skills needed to live outdoors, and in all cases the birds are dependent on a flock.

Parrots are intelligent and ingenious, but when released in a city, they are strangers in a strange land. To survive, they must be resourceful and able to make friends wherever they can find them. In the Mar Vista neighborhood of Los Angeles, a large Moluccan cockatoo, a bird covered in downy white feathers from head to toe, keeps company with a murder of crows. This giant powder puff of a bird is often sighted sitting on a telephone line among a dozen crows or flying in their midst as if he were one of them. The crows seemed to think he is, too, even with the obvious color contrast and the fact that the cockatoo towers over them and is twice their girth.

No one knows how feral flocks formed or where the birds originally came from, and there is no way to trace their introduction to the areas where they are now found. Garrett, Pranty, and others who have done long-term studies are convinced that simultaneous releases of large numbers of parrots make up the thriving flocks.

There are stories of garages and trucks full of illegal parrots being released in large numbers when law enforcement is hot on a smuggler's trail. And in Southern California, there is an urban legend about a truck that overturned this side of the Mexican border, releasing hundreds of little green parrots (conures or Amazons). That is a possible scenario, though feral parrot aficionados in every state have a similar overturned-truck story.

"People say storms released the birds from pet stores," says Garrett, "and there is the story of a fire in a big bird nursery in the San Gabriel Valley. Everyone I've talked to in that area says that happened, so it probably did. But they all want it to be the creation myth of parrots here."

Garrett says it's more than likely there were also scores of individual releases of birds that all found or formed flocks, but hard data are impossible to obtain.

Whatever their origin, in the residential areas of Southern California the parrots found a plethora of food and habitat, in addition to great weather, at almost every turn. New housing developments landscaped with exotic fruit or flowering plants have displaced native bird and plant species, but these cultivated landscapes actually supply the parrot escapees with food from their native habitats.

Nonnative bird species have long caused problems by usurping the food and habitat of native species in the United States and around the world, but parrots don't. They are nonnative fauna that depend on nonnative flora and the kindness of strangers with bird feeders. "The parrots didn't bulldoze the native habitats," says Garrett. "They're just taking advantage of what has replaced them."

About twenty miles east of downtown Los Angeles in the San Gabriel Valley lies Temple City, home to the largest flock of red-crowned parrots in California. Small numbers of them have been spotted in this area since the late 1950s. Now about a thousand of these large Christmas-colored birds—green bodies and a distinctive deep red patch on the forehead— roost along the telephone lines near Live Oak Park in the city center. Another fifteen hundred are found in nearby Arcadia and Pasadena. There might be as many red-crowned parrots living in Southern California as in their native range in northeastern Mexico, where they are endangered.

About four hundred lilac-crowned Amazons also frequent Temple City. Slightly smaller, with a patch of lilac on their crowns, these are endemic to western Mexico. There they are separated from the red-crowned parrots by mountains and uninhabitable habitat, but in Temple City, both meet and mingle in the same trees.

More than 80 percent of the red-crowned parrots' habitat in the lowlands of the state of Tamaulipas, Mexico, has been lost to clearing. Lilac-crowned Amazons, which seem to have a naturally low reproductive rate in the wild (studies show wild populations had successful hatchings less than 42 percent of the time), have disappeared from more than a third of their native range because of poaching for the pet trade. Years ago the Mexican government banned the capture of both species, but trapping continues to seriously threaten the birds.

The Mexican border is only two hours from Temple City, so some speculate the Amazons flew to the city on their own. But Garrett says they are found along the Gulf of Mexico and would have zero chance of getting to California without help. It is more likely they were kept captive in Mexican border cities, somehow escaped or were released, and flew north into the United States.

As a rule, feral parrots are found primarily in urban and suburban areas, where there are few predators, rather than rural ones. "Parrots don't need quiet habitat," says conservationist Charles Munn. "They live in cities with a million people. What they need are food and places to nest."

Several cities around the world have thriving wild parrot populations, both native and nonnative. They include Barcelona, Spain; Sydney, Australia (where the birds climb into people's kitchen windows for meals); Caracas, Venezuela; and Campo Grande, Brazil.

Parrots can fly long distances, but they are almost always found in localized flocks, roosting and nesting in the same general area night after night. A flock of yellow-chevroned parakeets, mostly lime green parrots twice the size of an ordinary parakeet, calls the Civic Center in downtown Los Angeles home. Each morning, like commuters going to work, they fly ten miles to the Pasadena area, where they spend the day foraging for food. Then they commute back before sunset to roost.

Small black-hooded parakeets started out along the Pacific Palisades and the nearby neighborhood of Brentwood and then expanded their range, working their way up the Pacific Coast. "Our urban areas are patchily distributed," says Garrett. "If Camp Pendleton is taken offline and San Diego, Orange County, and Los Angeles all merge as one big sprawling metropolis, then we'd probably have parrots all the way across."

Until fairly recently, Los Angeles was the largest farming county in the United States. Even when suburban homes replaced the farmland, some crop trees remained, such as orange, avocado, persimmon, and walnut, all of which parrots love to eat. The first homes built in the 1940s and 1950s had spacious yards and large shade trees planted along the streets. Now well aged, the trees have developed cavities (from woodpeckers, rotted limbs, and other sources) that are ideal nesting spots for parrots.

Competition with native birds for nest cavities could be a problem, though Garrett says that even in that regard the impact of parrots is minuscule compared to that of another nonnative—and invasive—species, the European starling, which now numbers more than two hundred million in North America. There are tens of millions of them in California alone. Thirty thousand parrots pale in comparison. And because parrots are so slow at breeding, it's unlikely they'll ever pose a problem.

To put these numbers in further perspective, continentwide and including migratory species, there are estimated to be several billion birds living across the eight million square miles of the United States. So these parrots are a tiny population in comparison to most bird species.

Garrett and I drive up and down the residential streets of Temple City for half an hour, staring through the windshield at the sky, trying to sight the arriving flocks flying in to roost for the night, but there is not a single one in sight.

Then, like parrot car alarms all going off at once, there is a cacophony of squawking Amazons. We try to suss the direction they're coming from, but it's impossible because they are flying in from all directions to a central group of myoporum trees where they cheerily snack on the bitter berries, their last meal of the day.

"I always worry when I bring people here that there won't be any birds, but they rarely disappoint," says Garrett.

We track the tree, and the birds, no farther than eight feet away, play, preen, and feed their young, oblivious to us gawking at them through cameras and binoculars.

Garrett is now in his late forties, with a graying mustache and goatee, the proverbial bird-watching binoculars ever present. Of medium build and rugged looking in a sleeveless shirt and jeans, Garrett is soft-spoken and quick to smile. He is considered a guru among Southern California birders, and more than one begged to come along when they heard he was giving a private tour.

Garrett began bird-watching as a kid in the 1960s, keeping tabs on local birds in his neighborhood. When he started working at the Natural History Museum in 1982, his commute from West Los Angeles downtown to the museum took him past flocks of mitred parakeets. "The birds are only found in South America," he says. "Starting in the early eighties, they showed up here. With birds around here, you know what they are; you just learn more about them. No one knew what they were. You'd talk to hard-core bird-watchers who knew the markings on the fourth primary feather of a bird, and they would say, 'Oh, yeah, those green things.'"

Once the birding community figured out the birds were transplants, they weren't all that interested in them. "My feeling was, 'Well, they're here. Aren't we keeping tabs on what's here?'" says Garrett. "Sort of out of self-defense I started keeping track of the parrots." He tried to popularize them by writing articles on his findings. It has been slow going. Most birders still aren't very keen on the mitred parrots, though now the yearly Audubon bird counts include them.

Garrett is naturally reserved, but when he talks about the parrots, it's clear he admires them a great deal. "They're as interesting as all birds, but they are less predictable and they do have more personality, for want of a better word," he says. "They engage in very complex behaviors, and the way they interact, it's like language."

Today, the birds blend in with the trees so well that they are most easily tracked by their calls. About thirty are now eating little red myoporum berries, which are as non-native as they are (the tree is naturally found in New Zealand) and are not popular with many other bird species in the area.

As the sun sets, the birds start to arrive in droves. A parrot party, which Garrett calls "happy hour," ensues as the birds land one after another. The latecomers join the fray and greet the others loudly and intentionally. Then they engage in animated conversation, as if sharing notes on the day's foraging successes. The volume rises until it's a wall of sound.

The birds move from branch to branch, littering the ground with discarded fruit. Some of their calls are distinct, like the begging of young birds soliciting food from their parents. Several fly off to a persimmon tree in a backyard and gorge on the unripe fruit there. Even with human observers just eight feet away, they aren't distracted from their feast.

A live oak is one of their last fast-food stops on the way to roost. Like the persimmons, its acorns are unripe and deathly bitter, but the parrots love them. There is no competition from native species for this fruit. "You don't normally see other birds eating these," says Garrett.

City-dwelling parrots are more than mere neighborhood attractions. They have as much to offer researchers as they do breeders. Mature parrots are hard to catch. They are also very good at removing bands and other devices affixed by researchers who want to study them. Because they're not territorial, they move around a lot and shift their roosting sites. Given all these factors, Garrett believes avian researchers can learn more about parrot behavior and biology by studying urban flocks than by studying wild parrots in their native ranges. "It's a hell of a lot of work to get any kind of information on them in areas as vast as the Amazon," he says. "Here you could study them on a bicycle."

When the sun sets, the birds are lined up on nearby phone lines. They are invisible in the dark, and just as quiet.

It is not always a carefree life for naturalized parrots in the United States. Because they are listed as an invasive species, they are federally unprotected, and anyone can shoot, trap, or poison them without recourse. They are also the targets of cats. While the larger Amazons might be able to fend them off, many smaller species will become some of the four million birds (mostly native songbirds) killed every day by house cats in North America alone.

One parrot species not seen flying wild in California is the monk parakeet, also known as the quaker parrot, banned by the state as an agricultural pest, though there has never been any clear evidence that they pose that problem. Legal in forty-one states, they are still bred and sold as pets.

Monks are mostly mint green with a gray hood and underbelly and some blue on their wings. About twelve inches long and pudgy, these quintessentially adorable parrots were very popular as pets, but many didn't last in homes; their small frames belied their loud voices. Now monks are the most numerous parrot species living feral in the United States, with wild flocks in Chicago, New York, Connecticut, Florida, Texas, and Washington. As Pranty puts it, "A lot of people bought them because of the novelty of owning a parrot, but they are extremely and obnoxiously loud. There's no question hundreds of these things were let out because their owners just couldn't take the birds anymore and didn't want to kill them."

There are four recognized subspecies of monk parakeet, which are naturally found in lowland subtropical areas in Bolivia, Paraguay, Uruguay, southern Brazil, and Patagonia in Argentina. They are native to temperate and subtropical climates, but some of their range extends to areas that experience freezing weather through the winter. Because they are adapted to the cold, monks are regularly seen happily cruising around icy Chicago in winter while the wind is whipping off Lake Michigan and the human residents are bundled up against the cold.

Doug Anderson, lovingly known by his Chicago neighbors as "the Birdman of Hyde Park," is a former president of the local Audubon Society. He has been enjoying and monitoring the monk population there since 1977, when he saw the first monk parakeets on the grounds of the Lincoln Park Zoo. He waited for them to make their way to Hyde Park. They did so in 1980 and now number about 250, with nests in fifteen of the park's ash trees. All told, there are estimated to be a thousand monks (though Anderson says it could be many more) living checkerboarded across Chicago.

Anderson has researched the origins of the wild flocks and subscribes to a popular theory that two thousand birds were accidentally released from crates at John F. Kennedy Airport in New York City in 1967, some of which found their way to Chicago. He also believes that lone birds let go by unhappy owners easily find their wild kin because their nests are visible in trees, and they travel long distances in large, noisy flocks. "They're tremendous flyers," he says. "I've often admired how fast they can fly. They can find other monks, and they do."

Chicagoans were happy when the monks arrived, and during the 1980s they found an ardent admirer and strong ally in Chicago's well-loved mayor, Harold Washington. "Some monks had a large nest in a tree across from the residence of Mayor Washington," says Anderson. "He said he loved to look at them and he would never lose an election as long as the birds were taken care of there. There was always a police squad car under that tree. The standing joke was that the police were there to protect the parakeets and not the mayor." But when the mayor died in 1987, the parrots lost their protector.

Across the United States monk flocks have been the target of harassment campaigns by authorities. From the late 1970s through the 1980s the U.S. Department of Agriculture, with help from the National Audubon Society, went to war against the parrots with an eradication campaign that virtually wiped out monks across the East Coast. The campaign hit a brick wall when it came to Chicago.

To fight off the Agriculture Department, Anderson formed the Harold Washington Memorial Parrot Defense Fund. Some of the fund's supporters coined themselves the "parrot troopers." Two thousand Chicagoans signed a petition supporting the monks. The fund had plans to get a court injunction against the eradication program and demanded the government provide evidence in public hearings proving the birds were a threat to the farmers of Illinois.

The Agriculture Department backed off when asked for proof that the birds compete with native species or that they are a threat to cornfields or other agriculture.

According to Anderson, the monk population in Chicago is not growing exponentially, as some predicted it would, and he is happy the birds have made a comeback on the East Coast. "I felt strongly about letting them be," he says. "I say this is a wonderful new addition to our fauna in the country, and they're beautiful to look at." They are also easy to locate because they build large stick nests—one of only six parrot species to do so. Their nests are not just functional; their design is an architectural feat. The nests are so well constructed that they are waterproof and can withstand the strongest winds. They keep the monk families warm because group living generates heat. A group of birds will collaborate, collecting twigs and then industriously tailoring them by chewing the ends until they are the precise size needed for a particular spot. The end result is a compartmentalized, multistoried condo that can be small enough to house just two families, each in their own apartment, or as huge as a Volkswagen Beetle, weighing hundreds of pounds and housing a flock.

Their nests have also caused them problems.

Most of the hundred or so monk nests in New York City are found in Brooklyn. They can be seen on the stone-arched entrance of Greenwood Cemetery, on the tall lights on the Brooklyn College campus athletic field, and on the power lines along nearby Flatbush Avenue.

Eleanor Miele, a Brooklyn College professor of elementary science and environmental education, became interested in the monks when she saw some nesting right outside her office window. She and her graduate students began studying those living on campus. Miele's parakeet project has provided continuous study of their behavior since 1997.

Miele, as have many in the area, has come to admire their talents—a remarkable long-term memory and advanced social networks. Like most parrots, they like to mimic and have learned the calls of the crows and gulls in the area. They find a bounty to eat in this barren area—crab apples, acorns, dandelion seeds, field greens, clover, and whatever people put out in bird feeders. The latter is estimated to account for 80 percent of their diet, further substantiating the fact that they are not agricultural pests. Furthermore they leave most native plants for the birds that need them. Monks are wary of humans but are willing to venture closer to those that feed them.

Miele says she has seen a hundred monks grazing at one time. "There are starlings, pigeons, sparrows here," says Miele. "None of them are native. The monks interface nicely with the ecosystem." In part because of Miele's research, the college decided to protect any monks living on campus.

But because of their large and intricate nests, monks are not faring so well in the world outside academia.

Consolidated Edison, the energy company that services New York City, systematically removes the nests from its power lines, even in midwinter, when the birds can freeze to death without the communal warmth of their nests.

"When I came out and saw Con Ed destroying nests, I went crazy," says Janelle Barabash, a longtime neighborhood resident who lives around the corner from the Brooklyn College campus. "Why destroy something relatively harmless like these parrots? I love these parrots. They make great neighbors. We have three nests on our block. Their noises never bother me, and it is a wonderful reminder that we share the world with other creatures."

Barabash decided to take action to save the birds' lives, starting a crusade called Save Our Wild Parrots. She recruited strangers by shaking their hands and saying, "You love the parrots, don't you?" The neighborhood came out in support of the birds and flooded local legislators with calls and letters. The campaign got media coverage, and the birds became a cause célèbre. Con Ed didn't fare as well, garnering considerable bad publicity.

Con Edison spokesperson Chris Olert defends the company's actions, saying the parakeet nests threaten electrical reliability throughout the city. In the summer of 2003, there were six fires at birds' nests on poles in Brooklyn, and 4,472 customers lost electrical power when a monk nest caught fire on the utility's equipment.

"What if a lung machine or other health aid was interrupted because of the parrots?" Olert asked, adding that if the monk population is not kept in check, it could increase by 30 percent a year. But he also admitted that the birds have been nesting on Con Ed power lines since the late 1980s, and to date there have been no injuries to humans from fires the nests might have caused.

"It's bullshit," says Regina Cussell, who runs a parrot sanctuary in southern Florida where monks nest nearby. "Squirrels are running up and chewing the lines, and the quakers [monks] take the blame for it." Cussell says that if the birds were really the cause of power outages and fires, there would be many more incidents, given the number of nests on power lines around the country.

Olert cites another concern, that of disease transmission, because the parakeets can be infected with lice or chlamydia. But avian veterinarian Tracy Bennett says Olert's concerns are unfounded. Pigeons also have chlamydia at a very high rate, she notes, and few, if any, people are infected by the millions of pigeons in the United States. And lice are very specialized. Human head lice can't live in pubic areas (and vice versa), and bird mites and lice are specialized to live in feathers and cannot migrate to mammals. "All wild birds like pigeons, crows, raptors, et cetera, can have mites and lice and often do," says Bennett. "So again, worrying about monks is silly."

In Connecticut, an estimated one thousand monks live in a dozen towns, many along the coast. The first wild monks appeared there in the 1970s, when they were sold as pets. But they are incredibly noisy, and many owners released them to be rid of them. These former pets, along with groups of monks escaping breeding facilities or pet stores, likely founded today's wild flocks. As part of the Agriculture Department's eradication campaign, the laws were changed, and the birds are now listed as an invasive species, which means they are unprotected (so they can be eradicated) and cannot be owned, sold, bred, or transported. The parakeets in Connecticut make their nests in trees, but several have commandeered electrical power structures for that purpose. United Illuminating (UI), which has 320,000 customers in southern Connecticut, removed nests as a matter of course. For two years, the utility waged a battle against the birds and the many customers that championed them. As with the Brooklyn monks, the parrots became a cause célèbre.

UI spokesperson Albert Carbone said the company had nothing against the birds themselves; the nests, considered a fire hazard, were the problem.

In the summer of 2005, UI instituted a campaign to eradicate the monks in West Haven, Milford, Bridgeport, and Stratford. The company's methods were called "black shirt" by some shocked residents. Instead of removing nests during the day—when the parrots were out foraging, their nests mostly empty, and the birds could find another place to roost for the night—the UI workers came after dark, when the birds were sure to be inside taking refuge from the cold, and local residents were less likely to see the company at work.

On Thanksgiving Eve that year, UI's trucks arrived in New Haven to find residents out in protest. One was arrested for trying to stop the workers by jumping on a company truck (the charges were later dismissed). Cherry pickers hoisted UI workers up to the nests, where they netted the terrified birds as they tried to escape.

For two years, Marc Johnson of Foster Parrots outside Boston commuted to Connecticut to support the parrots' cause, capturing the electric company's actions on video. "They caught as many as they could," says Johnson, "and they did it intentionally in winter. They were hoping the ones that got away would die of exposure. It was terrible."

Carbone admitted that the company's tactics were designed to trap the birds and have them killed.

That day, 179 monks were caught and turned over to the Agriculture Department, which killed them in carbon dioxide gas chambers. UI said the eradication project, including the training of employees and removing the nests, cost $125,000. The animal advocacy group Friends of Animals figured the cost to taxpayers and UI customers was $698 per parrot.

The *Connecticut Post* covered the story extensively, calling UI's actions "an extermination campaign." Friends of Animals called the birds

"Connecticut's littlest immigrants" and said of UI's actions, "The mal-treatment of monk parakeets was nothing more than a grotesque sanitation exercise, an exhibition of flagrant disrespect for birds and the sensibilities of the community."

Throughout southern Connecticut, residents turned off their holiday lights in memory of the captured parrots and in support of the surviving birds. Finally, faced with this outpouring of support and the bad press generated about UI's actions, local legislators got involved, and a bill was proposed to change the birds' status from illegal aliens (i.e., invasive species) to naturalized psittacines, giving them some protection under state law. As of this writing, the bill hasn't passed the Connecticut legislature.

UI admits that only a small percentage of electrical outages, eight to twelve a year, are caused by monk nests, compared to squirrels, which climb and chew on the power lines, causing an estimated one hundred outages a year. But even squirrels cause only about 9 percent of the total damage; 90 percent is the result of storms, falling trees, or other natural problems the company can't control. "We can control the nests," says Carbone.

Still, it's a never-ending ordeal for parrot and power company. Monks have proved to be industrious birds. As soon as their nests are removed, they go right to work rebuilding them. Carbone says that of the twenty-five nests the company removed, twenty-two were rebuilt in a few months.

New York and Connecticut are not the only states experiencing a clash between monks and utility companies. The situation in southern Florida makes the others pale in comparison. Florida Power and Light (FPL) estimates that two thousand nests and twenty thousand monks are spread out over eighty thousand miles of its power lines.

The utility tried to solve its parakeet problems diplomatically when local residents showed concern for the birds. FPL spokesperson Winifred Perkins, who has lived in Florida for twenty-five years, says that after Hurricane Andrew in 1992 there was an explosion of monks on FPL's power lines because the storm had knocked down so many of the large trees the birds were nesting in. FPL sought guidance from bird-control experts, including the environmental science company Pandion Systems. Dr. Michael Avery at Pandion says that toxic chemical repellents, such as Starlicide, for starlings, are routinely used on problem birds. The repellents didn't work on the monks because the dying birds would send out an alarm call to warn away the rest of the flock. Over the last four years, FPL has spent upward of $500,000 on research and development to come up with creative but humane solutions to the problem. The company tried several scare tactics, including effigies of owls and hawks. It also tried sweeping a red laser light on a pointer along the monks' nests. "The birds would see it coming and freak out," says Avery. This might have had some effect over time, says Perkins, but it was too labor-intensive (it had to be manually manipulated) to be a feasible deterrent.

FPL also tested a large multispindled device that resembled the spokes of a bicycle. It was intended to prevent the birds from building their nests in the first place. But the parrots used it as a foundation for their nests and wove their sticks all around it. Another attempt was to play a loud, constant noise near the nests to harass the birds, but again they were unfazed. The company also tried installing a device adjacent to the nest openings that emitted a chemical irritant in the hopes the birds would abandon their nests and build elsewhere. Instead, the birds reengineered the opening of the nest to another side and closed the hole closest to the irritant.

Over the years, FPL has also spent millions of dollars to deter other species of birds. The most common and effective method is the Xena cone, a heavy, opaque black plastic cone that goes over parts of the transmission or distribution system so birds don't nest. It also prevents their droppings from hitting the lines and shorting them out.

But the monks got around this formidable and proven deterrent as well.

"It's pretty simple and very successful at keeping raptors, like osprey and hawks, from doing that," says Perkins. "These monk parakeets have figured out a way to get under it. They make their nest under this dark black cone where it's extremely hot in the summer, and they're as happy as can be."

Overall, none of the deterrents FPL tried have worked; the birds have figured out ways to get around them all. In the process, Michael Avery of Pandion has come to admire the monks, and Perkins says she is impressed with the small birds' tenacity, and their ability to thrive in places as dangerous as the utility's substations: "These birds are very smart. We've had people that have gone into substations trying to collect the birds to sell them, and we've had deaths or people badly burned. It's highly dangerous inside a substation. These birds manage to live amongst the most dangerous equipment and somehow most of the time nothing happens. It's just amazing that so many of these birds can happily, cheerfully, and safely live in this kind of environment because literally two steps in the wrong direction and they'll be cooked."

Just as a hurricane increased the monks' presence on electric lines, hurricanes diminished it. The number of monks near the Florida coast has dropped dramatically due to eight hurricanes that hit the Florida coast in 2005, as have FPL's fears of major monk population growth in the next decade.

To protect the parakeets from persecution, Marc Johnson, the avian rescuer, got involved with local pro-monk-parakeet neighborhood groups in New Jersey and Connecticut. He helped them fight the electric companies, but realizing that the monks' champions could not deter them forever, he took on the task of designing an alternative nesting site, coming up with a forty-foot platform pole made of wood, chicken wire, and PVC tubing that residents could build in their backyards. He tested it in his Massachusetts backyard on some of the monks in his rescue. Proving that if you build it, they will come, the birds moved in and started decorating it with sticks.

Johnson knew he was on to something. Several Connecticut residents volunteered their yards, and platforms went up in Lordship, Stratford, and New Haven. It took time for the wild monks to accept the new idea, but on Christmas Eve, four months to the day after the first platform was installed, a pair moved in. Now many monk families live securely on private property.

"The platform showed that you can change their habit of nesting only on power lines, which is one of the excuses used for killing them. We proved the electric company wrong," says Johnson, who believes the only way to save the parrots is to "privatize" them by building the nesting poles on private property.

The homeowners say they love having the birds around. "Parrots are welcome here," says Michele Slowik of Stratford. "Their friends come and visit and they're very noisy, but by five or six at night they're snuggling and you don't hear them again until the morning. They don't bother anyone, and they are adorable."

Ornithologists, biologists, and some respected birders make the case that monk parakeets are the natural successor to the Carolina parakeet and should be allowed to fill their niche. Interestingly, there are reports that the Carolina parakeet also made stick nests and was similar to the monk in appearance and habits.

On November 21, 2005, *Connecticut Post* columnist Charles Walsh championed the birds when he wrote, "After all, the monk parakeet story is, in a way, the story of America. A warm-climate creature is carried to this country against its will, then freed, left to fend for itself in a hostile environment. Instead of crumbling under hardships, the bird perseveres. Indeed, it thrives. If animals were eligible for the Horatio Alger award, the monk parakeet would have had one years ago."

Chapter Five

From the Wild Life to Captive Breeders: The Legal Parrot Trade in the United States

The greatness of a nation can be judged by the way its animals are treated.
—Mohandas Gandhi

The last several decades of captive parrot breeding in the United States mark the first time humans have so extensively bred and raised an undomesticated species of such complexity. The consequences of the rapid growth of the parrot industry have been dire both for the millions of imported birds and for those bred in captivity.

In the 1920s, young German émigré Max Stern brought singing canaries from the Hartz Mountains in Germany to sell in New York City. He named his company after the birds' mountain range and single-handedly popularized bird-keeping in the United States.

The government didn't become involved in the importing of birds until later that decade. Between 1929 and 1930, eight hundred people in a dozen countries were afflicted with psittacosis (chlamydiosis), commonly called "parrot fever," a respiratory virus that can infect humans. It was transmitted by a large importation of infected parrots that were shipped from Argentina to Europe and the United States for the Christmas season. To combat the disease, quarantine laws in 1930 drastically curtailed the importation and sale of parrots in the United States.

Parrots from exotic locales became available and coveted again after World War II, when air travel became commercialized and they could be more easily transported. The more people saw them, the more wanted them, and the demand for exotic birds grew exponentially. In the postwar United States, they became a symbol of the American dream—a Shangri-la, a perfect country, where you could find anything you wanted. You didn't need to travel to exotic places to have exotic creatures; they would come to you. Not a second thought was given to the harrowing methods used to obtain, contain, and transport the birds.

In the 1950s, bird-loving hobbyists began backyard breeding. States such as Texas, Florida, Oklahoma, and California had ideal weather for breeding parakeets, and many people, especially retirees, did so to supplement their incomes. Most started with a pair or two and expanded their flocks as they gained some success.

Parakeet and finch species were most popular because they were colorful, small, and easy to handle, bred well, and were inexpensive to the consumer. Over the next twenty years, backyard breeders put millions of these birds into the marketplace through national chain stores such as Woolworth's. Many baby boomers remember having a parakeet as a child, and that's not surprising: by the mid-1960s, more than five and a half million Americans had one.

In the early 1970s, the United States saw an outbreak of velogenic viscerotropic Newcastle disease, also known as exotic Newcastle disease. The most virulent strain of that avian disease, it is especially dangerous to poultry, with a 95 percent mortality rate. For two years, the pet bird trade was heavily affected as millions of birds—those once wild or bred in captivity, companion and poultry—died from the disease or were "depopulated" by the U.S. Department of Agriculture to end the outbreak. An estimated twelve million birds were killed in California alone.

Toucans, ringnecks, and mynah birds were banned in the United States until 1974, when an Agriculture Department quarantine system was established in cities across the country to ensure that only healthy birds were imported. The changes triggered a resurgence in the popularity of pet birds that may be abating only now.

When the United States enacted the Wild Bird Conservation Act

(WBCA) in 1992, it closed its borders to most of the 450,000 wild birds brought in yearly as a way to protect endangered wild bird populations from being depleted by U.S. demand. Enactment of the WBCA further fueled the growth in domestically bred parrots, large and small. Now that local breeders could control the populations, the birds were plentiful, the species varied, and they were less expensive to the consumer.

California quickly became, and remains, the pet bird breeding capital of the United States. Florida is number two, and Texas and other southern states are producing more birds every year. At least ten thousand bird breeders in the United States (some estimate double that number) produce as many as two million birds each year. One of the largest breeders is Magnolia Bird Farm in Riverside, California. The company has more than one thousand cages of breeding birds on its ranch. It sells five to eight thousand birds a week and more than seventy thousand pounds of bird food a month from its two stores.

Without established breeding practices, breeders from the 1950s to the present figured things out (or made them up) as they went along, often at their flocks' expense. Even today, only the rare hobbyist or professional breeder has any formal education in avian science or animal husbandry, and most had limited contact with parrots before they started breeding them for money. Parrot expert Dr. Yves de Soye, a former executive of the renowned Canary Islands breeding facility, Loro Park, described parrot breeding in the United States as "more religion than science."

The extensive information we have on breeding other species of birds, such as chickens, is not applicable to parrots. The differences between the two species are apparent as soon as hatchlings are born. Chickens are born covered in down and able to see, walk, and eat on their own. Parrots, like human infants, are born helpless, and remain dependent on their parents and flock for months or years, until they are fully fledged and can fend for themselves.

Also unlike domesticated fowl, exotic psittacines have unique physiologies, behaviors, and highly specialized diets that evolved over millions of years in isolated ecosystems, and which avian science still does not fully understand.

Even so, most parrot breeders arranged their facilities like poultry farms and treated their birds like livestock. Millions of wild parrots brought stateside before 1992 have been living out a bleak existence as captive breeders. Never to flock, fly, or freely roam trees again, they are paired off in barren cages and often warehoused without sunlight. "Even in our penal system we let prisoners out of their cells," says Lori Rutledge, a former bird broker in Washington State.

The practices harm the breeding process itself. It can take six years or more for a large parrot, such as a macaw, to mature, and ten to thirteen for it to begin reproducing. In the wild, fertility rates run about 90 to 95 percent. Breeders say they can wait for years for a mature pair of birds in captivity to produce offspring, and as few as 40 percent will do so in a given year. Some never do.

Still, breeders have no moral issues about leaving their birds locked up with only bare necessities such as food, a perch, and a nest box for a decade while they wait. Parrot expert Carlos Yamashita says this is why parrots tend to craziness in captivity. "The most important years of their life—their teenage years, where they are most open to learning and have a social life—are taken from them. Imagine if until you married, the best years of your life were taken away?"

Breeding is all the more complicated because parrots, like humans, need to choose their own mates. "You may have a male and a female, but you don't have a pair," says Yamashita. "You have two individual birds who may or may not bond to each other." Smaller parrots are often "line bred." The male is paired with many females that are often related to him and not allowed a long-term bond with any one mate, as would naturally occur if they were left alone. Conversely, breeders will routinely separate happily mated parrots if they don't breed quickly enough. The loss of a mate can traumatize the birds, sometimes for life.

Another common practice is keeping parrots in the dark for months and even years at a time. Breeders believe that without any outside stimulation, parrots will be forced to spend more time having sex. "Taking sunlight away from birds is idiotic," says avian veterinarian Tracy Bennett of Seattle. "Their whole breeding schedule is based on following the sun!" Even when not intentionally deprived of light, nearly all breeding parrots in northern climates are kept in enclosures during winter months with indirect light, or live indoors under artificial light, further hampering their reproductive cycles.

Studies have supported the assertions of veterinarians and parrot experts that such long-established fundamental avicultural practices are in error. At the University of California, Davis, the Psittacine Research Project found that pairing birds in cages devoid of enrichments inhibits them from breeding. Avian behavior consultant Dr. Cheryl Meehan, who performed several parrot studies at UC Davis, said of their findings, "When older birds who hadn't bred over three to four breeding cycles were given baths, foraging enrichments, branches, the ability to fly and mingle with each other in a common space or retreat to their own cages at will, and most importantly, were allowed to choose their own mates, seventy-five percent laid eggs. If you're looking at it from a business perspective, this kind of enrichment might be useful to initiate breeding."

In the last two decades, pet bird breeding has burgeoned from a cottage business into a multimillion-dollar industry dominated by parrot production facilities. These "factory farms" contain hundreds or thousands of young birds processed on assembly-line schedules with no individual attention or socialization.

PetSmart is the largest pet store chain in the United States, with about nine hundred stores. Most of its birds come from a large bird breeder and distributor, Preferred Birds, a Milton, Florida–based facility owned by Kaytee Pet Products, a Wisconsin-based bird seed company. Ross Pittman, manager of sales and procurement for Preferred Birds, denies there are "factory farms," though he admits shipping more than one hundred thousand birds a year to pet stores around the country. He says parrots, which are shipped unweaned, are only a small percentage of the total. But one avian rescuer who discussed supplying PetSmart with adoptable pet birds, from finches to parrots, was told that the three thousand birds a year she offered would not be enough to supply even three of its stores. Do the math: PetSmart is handling more than nine hundred thousand birds a year.

One of the risks in breeding so many birds of different species in one place is the chance that disease may spread among the whole population. In December 2007 and into early 2008, PetSmart had to pull over seven hundred birds from nine hundred stores because of an outbreak of psittacosis, a highly communicable bacteria that affects the respiratory system and is contagious to birds and humans, causing flulike symptoms in the latter and high mortality rates if untreated. The birds had all come from Preferred Birds. Parrots can be "silent carriers," not manifesting diseases if their immune system isn't compromised by stress. Avian veterinarian Dr. Rob Marshall described some of the likely causes for birds to manifest and "shed" the infection: "Shedding can be activated by stress factors, including relocation, shipping, crowding, chilling, and breeding. At high risk are birds that are kept in overcrowded conditions, including pet stores, breeding facilities and multibird households—especially if new birds are added without following proper quarantine procedures." Of course, these are the precise conditions all of PetSmart's birds are subjected to as a matter of course from the time they hatch.

This point was driven home by graphic footage a PETA undercover investigator shot during a two-month employment stint at Rainbow World Exotics (RWE) in Waco, Texas. RWE, a major supplier of PetSmart, breeds tens of thousands of animals for them, including birds, hamsters, gerbils, and other small mammals, at several breeding sites. PETA was tipped off to the situation at RWE by a whistleblower on staff at a PetSmart store who witnessed animals consistently coming from RWE "not well, too young and dying."

The investigation revealed that animals were dumped into trash cans while still alive, or left to die suffering from illness, broken bones, or deformities. While Petco was famous for putting live animals in their freezers to euthanize them, PetSmart employees would relegate sick and injured animals to the store's back room and leave them there until they died.

One such was a young Goffin's cockatoo who couldn't digest food, who the PETA investigator named Angel. She is documented as being held in the back room of RWE without medical attention for thirty-six days while she starved to death. It is a chilling scene of a baby bird emitting incessant anguished cries for food, or screaming for attention while RWE employees and its owner, Jack Graham, behaved with shocking indifference to her pleas. Finally, on the last day, she is seen sitting at the bottom of the cage, swaying and moaning in pain, her head slumped because she is too weak to lift it or to shake off the flies that land on her small, emaciated body. PETA's undercover investigator alerted Graham and other staff members numerous times to Angel's condition, but none helped her. When the investigator asked Graham to get the bird medical attention, he laughed and said he knew more than any vet and there was nothing wrong with the bird. He also wouldn't let her have the bird to nurse at home, claiming other employees would say animals were sick just to take them home, and he also didn't want rumors to get out that they had sick animals at RWE. "They didn't have to keep her in prolonged suffering, screaming nonstop over the course of weeks and weeks. The investigator said she'll never ever get those sounds out of her head," says PETA vice president Daphna Nachminovitch of the Cruelty Investigations Department. "But there was such utter disregard for humane dignity, she wasn't considereed important enough to euthanize."

PetSmart responded on their Web site to PETA's charges, saying, "PetSmart requires each vendor to have an attending veterinarian, and Rainbow has a veterinarian that is responsible for overseeing the medical needs of the pets." They also said they that their inspections of the facility were positive, and they didn't see anything wrong. PetSmart is investigating RWE now, but in the meantime they are standing by the company. Nachminovitch says that's because they'll lose money if they cut loose RWE, a big supplier of animals to their stores.

The week of January 21, 2008, PETA released information on the investigation, and the *Today* show aired some of PETA's undercover footage. Within hours two hundred letters had been written to PetSmart from PETA's site. Less than twenty-four hours later, there were ten thousand.

As of this writing, PETA is filing a formal complaint with the U.S. Department of Agriculture (USDA) and a criminal complaint against RWE with County Attorney Andy J. McMullen in Hamilton, Texas.

The volume of business is high, but that doesn't necessarily mean breeders are making huge profits, which presents further problems for the birds. Twenty years ago blue and gold macaws sold for $1,200 wholesale. Today, with more people breeding, they wholesale for $650 and retail for $1,300 to $1,500. Now breeders have to produce more birds to make the same income they did two decades earlier. Many don't have the room to expand, so they keep as many birds as they can in the smallest possible cages. Avian veterinarian Dr. Scott McDonald, based in Westchester, Illinois, has several thousand companion bird breeders as clients. Six months a year for the last fifteen years he has traveled from state to state, making house calls on the facilities. "I see too many birds in cages that are too small," he says. "There's poor planning. There are definitely a lot of aviaries that are too crowded. More than fifty percent are probably too crowded."

When the horrors of puppy mills were exposed, the public was outraged. News footage showed dogs confined in cages without physical human contact or enrichment, repetitively bred by breeders who took their puppies prematurely and sold them unweaned. Though more prevalent than most people realized, puppy mills are still a small percentage of the dog breeding facilities in the country. By comparison, virtually all parrot breeding facilities are parrot mills.

In the book *Raising Pet Birds for Profit*, longtime production breeder James McDonald estimates he's sold more than one million parakeets. His book's chapters include "Putting Your Parakeets to Work" and "Working Your Nestboxes." He increased profits by increasing the production of each pair of birds. "If the conditions are right, they will lay one clutch right after another all year long," he wrote.

In a bad year, wild breeding birds might suffer the loss of eggs or young to storms or predators. Under these circumstances, nature kicks in to allow parrot hens to lay more eggs in the same season to compensate. For captive breeding birds, every year became a bad year when their owners discovered this ability.

"Double-clutching" involves bird breeders pulling the eggs and inducing the females to produce more. But unlike a chicken's egg production, it is an ordeal for a female parrot to produce and lay a single egg. Some large parrots now lay up to twenty-four eggs a year—ten times what they would in the wild. Overproduction results in malnutrition, broken bones, and worn-out reproductive organs in females. "I've seen cockatoo hens bred almost to death," says Bennett.

This kind of production breeding is now prevalent nationwide. One breeder estimated that 80 to 90 percent of all pet birds are production bred. Many in animal welfare consider this trend the "poultrification of parrots."

In captive breeding situations, large parrots are not allowed to raise even one chick or see one of their young fledge. In the wild both the male and female parrots spend the months after the birth of a chick caring for the young bird, and allowing the female's body to recuperate. They naturally breed seasonally. With no chicks to raise or enrichments in their cages to hold their interest, in off months they can grow aggressive from frustration, which can leave them mutilating themselves or fighting with their mates. The psychological abuse of isolation and boredom is compounded by the trauma of watching their newly hatched young stolen from them year after year. Of one hundred young produced by a fifty-year-old breeding pair, it is likely that not one will have laid eyes on its parents before it was taken by the breeder.

Unweaned, unfeathered, and blind, parrot nestlings are removed while their parents attack, biting and clawing the interlopers. Many breeders wear protective gear when they enter the aviaries to take the chicks. Others remove the hatchlings or fertilized eggs through a special hatch behind the nest box while the parents are out. Breeders report that the parents scream and search for their lost young for days afterward, and it is not uncommon for bird breeders to be attacked several weeks later by a mourning father, feathers puffed up in continuing anger at sight of the treacherous human.

Bird broker turned parrot rescuer Lori Rutledge of Cockatoo Rescue in Stanwood, Washington, once complimented a local breeder who kept his birds in large outdoor cages. "I said to him, 'Your birds must absolutely love you for giving them this much space, fresh air, and sunshine.' He said, 'They hate me. They think I am the devil. I take their babies. You should hear them scream.'"

Over the years many breeders have developed firmly held ideas, akin to old wives' tales, about parrot breeding. Few have any formal education in animal husbandry, ornithology, biology, or the disciplines and training required to raise exotic birds with specialized needs in a way that doesn't compromise their physical and psychological welfare. None are peer reviewed, and because birds are not regulated, the governmental agencies that might be required to monitor them, such as the U.S. Department of Agriculture (USDA) or U.S. Fish and Wildlife Service, do not. In fact, American parrot breeders have made up most of their methods as they went along, and then written them in stone as the best practices. Little, if any, of what they do to their parrots is based on actual research about the birds' needs and behavior in the wild. Bird breeders justify their methods by saying that they are parrot experts who understand the needs and behaviors of their birds and should determine their care without outside interference.

For example, a parrot breeder of forty years based in Santa Monica, California, said he kept his birds in small cages and in the dark for years at a time because they bred better that way. He tried giving them more space early on, but then they only played all day. Matt Perry, founder of the Project Perry parrot rescue in Virginia, attended a liquidation auction for Beech's, a well-known five-hundred-parrot breeding facility in North Carolina. Beech's had been a field research farm for Kaytee Pet Products, a leading bird food and toys manufacturer. The site was remote, so no one could hear the screams of the parrots or know what their living conditions were like. The birds were housed in small cages, closed off from one another, in scores of unheated, broken-down old trailers around the property. Perry brought bird toys for what he knew had to be sensory-deprived parrots, but was admonished not to place them in their cages. "They're only breeders," he was told by the owners; they didn't need them. They had numerous species, many of which required specialized diets, but they were all being fed the same food. Inside the office, bookkeeping records were kept in part with notes tacked to a corkboard that described the birds as "Cocatoo," "singal," "mulcan." Beech's had five hundred parrots, and couldn't even spell their names.

Another way breeders might justify their actions is by saying parent birds don't really care about their babies, that they have to remove the chicks because the parents are irresponsible, often breaking eggs or damaging young. And because their nests are preyed upon in the wild, the parents expect to lose their young anyway.

Former breeder Carla Freed, of Wichita, Kansas, strongly disagrees. "We now have evidence to disprove the idea that they don't care about their chicks and [to show] that it's very difficult for them to lay a lot of eggs," she says.

Freed is referring to more than five thousand hours of videotaped footage documenting previously unknown breeding behavior from inside nest boxes at various stages of egg laying, incubation, hatching, or caring for the young. Freed and her ex-husband, Joe, installed miniature cameras inside the nest boxes of their twenty-five breeding pairs of rare Bodini Amazons, native to Guyana, to monitor their behavior and help avoid egg-loss problems. What Freed saw on the tapes persuaded her to get out of breeding and on the road to educating aviculturalists by showing them how wrong they've been about their birds.

Even the first footage of a parrot laying eggs was a revelation, showing how traumatic and painful labor and egg laying is for the hen. "She grunted and strained, and in the end she was exhausted," says Freed. "We began to get more footage. These were healthy hens, and they weren't just popping eggs out. Despite what some aviculturists like to say, for the majority of these birds it's labor."

Freed shows the footage at avicultural conventions and bird clubs, where it makes a dramatic impact on audiences. She narrates the clips, pointing out the complex relationships among the males, females, and chicks.

Counter to the conventional wisdom of breeders, Freed found the hen turned the eggs frequently—about twelve times an hour. The male also moved them with his beak and licked them to examine them. (Males even try to incubate, but are usually inept.) Another clip shows that hens practice regurgitating to a feather or other object in the nestbox in preparation for feeding their young.

Freed found that the males do play a large part from the start, and in the case of healthy pairs that were well bonded and nondysfunctional, the interaction of males and females with the eggs further strengthened the pair bond. Once the chicks hatched, the males fed the babies and had an active role in their rearing. Freed recorded that males were in the nest box almost two thousand times over the four-week period until her husband removed the babies. The males brought food to the females and babies, and the females often fed the males to practice feeding (a natural behavior that, like flying, needs honing to perfect) and further strengthen their bond. In several pairs the males fed the chicks more frequently than did the females. Freed's footage demonstrated dynamic and complex family relationships among parrots that bird breeders had previously not suspected.

According to Freed, problems like the parents stepping on eggs or not feeding their babies properly is part of a natural learning curve. "They are just like teenage parents with their first baby, figuring out how to raise it," she says. "But these parents have to do everything in the dark of a nest box. Can you imagine if humans had to raise babies in the dark?"

Bird breeders don't allow for mistakes because they don't want the expense of lost young. When parent birds make an error, their chicks are taken from them immediately. "Sometimes they step on babies, but in every instance where there was a problem and we played the tape back, we found there was a logical reason for it," says Freed.

She tells the story of a hen that appeared to have killed her chick. After examining the tape, however, Freed found that the egg had been damaged by a dent that let air into the egg and killed the chick. The hen saw the hole and knew what it could mean, but she sat on the egg for another three days anyway, trying to give the almost-hatched chick a chance at survival. When she finally gave up, she sat stooped over the egg, emitting long, low guttural cries as she ate it to dispose of it.

There is so much peripheral noise from the other birds in the room that without the microphone in the nest box, it would have been impossible to hear the hen from the outside. This is why many breeders rarely know what is going on in their nest boxes.

"After days of sitting on this dead chick, she pulls the egg out and eats it and she's vocalizing," says Freed. "It's heart-wrenching. It is one of the most moving pieces of tape I've got. I have some big-time production breeders in my audiences who say that birds don't feel. After we showed that footage, one of them came to me and said, 'Was that bird crying? We stayed up all night arguing about it.' And I said, 'That's what I want you to do.'"

After spending weeks in pair bonding, with mutual preening, feeding, and nest-building behavior, followed by the trial and tribulation of egg laying and weeks or months of nurturing chicks day and night, the birds undergo the sudden and catastrophic loss of their chicks. With no flock to commiserate with, and no ability to fly away and engage in natural, enriching behaviors like foraging for food and bathing, the breeding birds are left trapped with nothing in a barren metal cage, their former warm nest now empty, coping with the overwhelming and incomprehensible psychological toll of their young being taken away from them. Freed says her husband would pull the babies from their nest boxes because she couldn't bear to do it. As soon as they laid eggs veteran hens knew what was coming when they saw Joe nearby. To protect their eggs, they wouldn't move off them. It is called sitting tightly. By the time the young had hatched it was worse. "Pulling babies is awful," says Freed. "You can't take them in a way that's nonconfrontational. Joe would have to fight off the bird."

Once the video was installed, the Freeds would watch the monitors, and when neither parent was inside the nest box, Joe would quickly remove the young. Carla Freed puts on a tape that shows this moment. The nest box is dark, the babies asleep. Then high-pitched alarm calls are heard from the parents outside. The back of the nest box opens, and the camera records Joe's face, peering inside. His hand quickly scoops up the baby birds; the parents rush in, screaming, as he closes the hatch. Frantically and repetitively, they search for their young, inside and out of the box. In the box, they scratch desperately with their beaks and feet, pushing the sawdust away in all corners. "This goes on for days," says Freed, sobbing. "They look for their babies and call for them for days."

The next clip shows the same scene much later. The nest box is in a shambles from the searching. The hen, drained and exhausted, lies down. The male goes over and starts preening her slowly. "It's hard to watch," says Freed. "I've wrestled hard with it over the last three years. I could never do it again," she says of parrot breeding. But a majority of breeders can, and continue to do it breeding season after breeding season without thought for the birds they say they love. Bird breeders say they must take unweaned birds from their parents because hand-fed babies make better pets, and they have to be taken young to be human-friendly.

As a doctoral student at the Psittacine Research Project, Rebecca Fox conducted studies in which baby birds were raised by their parents but handled by humans for twenty minutes a day once they were several weeks old, when they had become cognitive. Fox found that these babies were as tame as birds taken early from their parents and hand-fed. "It is absolutely not true that baby parrots need to be hand-fed or hand-weaned by people to make good pets," says Fox. "One of my very favorite myths is that if you want a parrot to really bond to you, you've got to hand-feed it."

But it's not cost-effective for breeders to handle young parrots like this, says Pittman of the PetSmart chain's distributor and breeder. "I can feed ninety babies in an hour. It takes about five to six seconds [each]. How can you give individual attention to ninety babies and have them co-parented?"

In addition to the removal of unweaned chicks, other common practices in the pet bird trade, such as beak mutilation, have come under scrutiny over the last few years.

Male cockatoos in captivity can be violent to their cell mates. "We talk about killer cockatoos and males that are hell on wheels to females," says Richard Farinato, director of captive wildlife at the Humane Society of the United States. "You take a bird that's not used to any confinement whatsoever. You shut it up in a three-by-five-by-eight-foot cage, and you don't expect it to become frustrated and stressed and kill its mate? You take the same bird, you put it into an aviary that's one hundred by one hundred by two hundred [feet], and it's a different bird. That is indicative of the wildness of these animals."

Some breeders cure the problem of confinement aggression by mutilating their birds' beaks. The male's beak is surgically split down the middle, making him unable to harm a female. It also makes it difficult for him to eat for the rest of his life. "It would not have passed peer review because of the ethical and moral issues involved with it," says Dr. Brian Speer, former president of the American Veterinary Association. "But it went out in a nonreview magazine. And then the proverbial feces hit the fan."

Later in the same interview, Speer added, "In some extremely rare circumstances, I believe the technique does potentially have a place." This comment is surprising because it shows that even a highly respected veterinarian still thinks maiming is a useful tool, even though the practice has been stopped (or is no longer openly done, as some animal welfare activists allege) because of the terrible violation to the bird.

Graphic photos were taken of Alexander, a once wild male Ducorps cockatoo that was operated on this way. According to Connie Pavlinac, Alexander's eventual owner, who took the images, it was likely done for no reason at all. Alexander had never shown aggression to another bird, but another cockatoo of the same species in the same facility had killed its mate. The owners decided to split the mandibles of all of the birds, as a preventive measure. "Other alternatives were never tried," says Pavlinac.

Another common practice is surgical sexing, an invasive surgical procedure to determine a bird's gender that's still done even though the sex can be determined easily and noninvasively by examining DNA from a feather or a small blood sample. Many breeders have the procedure done, even though it traumatizes the parrot and can result in injury, infection, or death, explaining that they want to know whether the parrot's reproductive organs are in good shape. But Scott McDonald, who has made a career of surgical sexing on breeder birds, reports that only a minuscule percentage of parrots have any physical abnormalities.

Avian veterinarian McDonald does the procedure full time as he circulates through more than a dozen states in the South, Midwest, and West, performing it in people's kitchens or setting up shop for a few days at a local pet store. Since he specializes in remote areas where there are not a lot of bird vets, he says, he's seeing fifty birds at a time, without benefit of a veterinary facility. But other avian veterinarians in the states he practices in say that what he does is inexcusable and against state laws. Two years ago McDonald was banned from practicing in South Carolina, and since then seven Washington State veterinarians have tried to get him banned there and in Oregon, alleging that he regularly breaks a laundry list of laws, including that the procedure be done only in surgical suites, not in residential kitchens; that he doesn't sterilize his equipment properly; and that he uses gas anesthesia using the assistance of nonmedical people, which violates regulations of the Occupational Safety and Health Administration. Sterilizing an endoscope, the device used in surgical sexing, takes twenty minutes in glutaraldehyde, a noxious antiseptic, and another five minutes soaking in a sterile saline solution before it is ready to use again. McDonald does the procedure on thirty to fifty parrots a day, making it impossible for him to take that kind of time sterilizing.

He doesn't argue with that allegation, but contends his work is "antiseptic." The veterinarians who oppose his methods say that isn't so either. McDonald says he works in kitchens and other nonsurgical conditions because he has sought but been unable to find a proper mobile medical unit.

The main reason parrot breeders use McDonald, aside from his making house calls, which vets will do as a matter of course to treat large numbers of birds, is price. His services are cheap. He charges as little as $5 per bird, a fraction of what a reputable veterinaran would charge, and that's a big incentive to bird breeders who are always looking for ways to cut costs. Parrot breeding is not a good way to get rich, as many optimists have found out the hard way. It is a seven-day-week, twenty-four-hour-a-day job, regardless of how many birds are bred. Of the many breeders I have spoken with over the years, only one ever took regular vacations.

Cut-rate veterinary procedures are not the only shortcuts hard-pressed breeders resort to. To avoid time-intensive and profit-killing hand-feeding using a syringe, some breeders force-feed, shoving food down a baby bird's throat with a tube—the same practice used to fatten geese for foie gras, which has come under scrutiny in recent years. Not only is this rough on the birds emotionally, it also carries a high risk of harm: the tubes can easily damage the babies' fragile membranes, or the birds can aspirate the food and choke.

Breeders also cut the time spent on feeding by not doing so at night. "Breeders have no excuse anymore to say the parents don't feed crying babies at night," says Freed, who discovered otherwise through her monitoring. "We know the male comes into the nest box at night to feed the female, which nobody ever thought. He goes in and out during the night. It's just because they [breeders] don't want to get up in the middle of the night to feed them."

Breeders will also "force wean" a young bird, forcing it to eat on its own or starve. They also put the babies on deprivation schedules, feeding them fewer times a day to get them into pet shops faster.

Phoebe Greene Linden of Santa Barbara Bird Farm, a pioneer in using gentle and nurturing early handling practices to ensure healthy, well-adjusted adult birds, created the techniques of Abundance Weaning. Her reputation is solid, and her experiences breeding birds have been extensively published, disseminated, and discussed in avicultural circles for fifteen years. Her baby birds were finger-fed warm, wet, and nutritious food akin to the way their parrot parents would feed them with their tongues and beaks. The baby parrots were not on a rigid feeding schedule and were never allowed to go hungry. In an article on the subject, Linden wrote, "Birds weaned on deprivation schedules no longer trust humans to feed them.... Birds who distrust humans often develop into biters. If you want a really loud adult bird that screams incessantly with little or no provocation, start to 'train' your bird early via deprivation weaning."

Wholesale, an unweaned African gray goes for $450; weaned it is $800 to $900 or more. Breeders make less money selling unweaned birds, but they don't have the burden of months-long care for the babies and can make room for more in their incubators and nurseries. And retail stores like the profit margin. It's a good deal all around, except for the parrots. "It's never been about the birds," says Freed. "It's always been about the money."

For the baby birds, being stolen from their parents and fed by human hands is just the beginning of an arduous and perilous journey for which millions of years of evolution to fly and forage has not prepared them.

Parrot chicks in the wild nest calmly in a dark tree hole for months, cared for only by their parents, who lovingly feed, preen, nurture, and communicate with them. Baby birds sleep next to their siblings and under the warm body and beating heart of their mother. In the rush to market, production-bred birds are fed by different people; handled, moved, loaded on trucks or planes; and then kept in bright glass cases under fluorescent lights until they are sold. In a talk at the 2004 American Federation of Aviculture convention in San Francisco, veteran breeder Howard Voren, who says he has hand-raised twenty thousand parrots in the last twenty years, said:

Between the ages of four and six weeks of age...is the particular time period that it's best to ship the bird. At this stage of development, it's a natural occurrence for it to spend time in a darkened, enclosed area and being placed into and traveling in a shipping crate creates very little or no stress.... It has yet to acquire prejudices. Prejudice about just how warm the hand-feeding formula is; about what type of feeding instruments are used; about how it's physically manipulated prior to and during the hand-feeding process;...and about its environment. It is at this stage of development that they are the most adaptable without stress.

Phoebe Linden of Santa Barbara Bird Farm strongly disagrees with this logic. While young birds would be in the dark, they would also be contained safely and solidly inside the trunk of a tree. She says they can process the upheaval only as "their nest has been obliterated, their habitat destroyed." Linden believes there is no excuse for people who are not yet practicing good weaning skills.

Francis Battista of the Kanab, Utah–based Best Friends Animal Sanctuary, the largest dog and cat rescue facility in the United States, wrote about this situation in the organization's magazine:

Bird mills crank out thousands of parrots at a time.... Point of sale is typically a low-overhead, lightly staffed, self-service pet or pet supply store.... Syringe feeding, which continues until they're old enough to eat on their own, is usually done by a rotating staff of well-meaning, low-wage, undertrained, high school-age "associates." The birds are then sold as "hand-reared" or "hand-raised," evoking the image of a kindhearted surrogate parent lovingly feeding them. In reality, the unsuspecting buyer is purchasing an emotionally deprived creature whose most intimate contact has been with a plastic syringe. This is not hand-rearing. It's poultry farming.

Developmental psychology and neurobiology shows that the lack of a relationship between an infant and a caretaker of the same species can alter brain and behavior patterns, says psychologist and animal researcher Gay Bradshaw. Replacing a parent bird with a human can cause psychological and physiological problems. This can lead to posttraumatic stress disorder and an array of symptoms associated with "relational trauma," such as feather picking, depression, hyperaggression, and abnormal screaming.

A moral component to this is all but ignored: Is breeding these birds in captivity ethical in the first place? Greg Glendell, a parrot consultant based in the United Kingdom, writes and lectures on this subject. He says it cannot be justified, either by breeders, who are compounding the cruelty by breeding more birds as rising numbers are dumped in rescues, or by buyers, who are in no position to commit to a bird for the next sixty years or longer.

"All we have to do is ask the obvious question: Who gains from producing baby parrots?" says Glendell. "What does any parrot get out of this? This stuff is not complicated: the function of the parrot trade is bucks, and damn the birds."

As the bird business has grown over the years, a subsystem of distributors, bird brokers, and wholesalers has developed. These middlemen take the young birds and move them into pet stores or sell them to other wholesalers or breeders around the country. Baby birds can travel several times from one state to another before they ever reach a pet store.

Though there are good pet stores, with owners and staff qualified and inclined to nurture and feed young birds properly, many birds sold into retail outlets end up in terrible situations. "There is certainly a filthy underbelly to American aviculture," says Linden. "It exists, it's thriving; unfortunately, it spreads disease, heartache, and sorrow."

Walk into any large chain pet store, and you will see why the pet industry is a $30 billion business. You can buy oatmeal dog shampoo, perches with suction cups (so you can shower with your bird), and battery-operated, sonar-activated water fountains so your pet always has a fresh-flowing drink.

Petco, launched in 1965, earned $1.8 billion in 2005. PetSmart, started in 1987, made $3.8 billion in the same period. The two chains are growing at roughly the same rate, sixty stores each per year, and both now have about nine hundred outlets apiece. Both companies sell a variety of small birds, including finches, parakeets, and cockatiels. PetSmart still sells large parrots such as cockatoos, macaws, and African grays.

The advocacy group PETA documents complaints about the two chains from customers and employees. Petco leads, with about one thousand grievances since 1999. (PETA became a shareholder in the company so it could obtain inside information on its practices.) PetSmart has had a much smaller number of complaints since 2001, covering similar issues: problems with birds, overcrowding, filthy cages, untreated sick animals, and employees who don't care or are unqualified. But perhaps the thorniest issue is the selling of unweaned birds.

"We're getting birds we believe that are almost at the point of being able to feed exclusively on their own and don't see the hand-feeding as a burden for us or for the customer," says Barbara Fitzgerald, senior vice president for store operations at PetSmart.

The experiences of those working for large pet stores suggests otherwise, however. Lisa Bell worked for five years as a bird specialist and assistant manager at Petco stores in northern California. She says breeders would give the store a schedule for feedings. "If a bird came in on two feedings a day, [the breeders] would say, 'In another three weeks it should be weaned.' I found typically it needed four or five feedings a day. Usually it was another two months instead of another two weeks." Though it was against company policy, Bell took unweaned birds home overnight to feed them so they wouldn't be hungry until the store reopened in the morning.

This type of situation was common at Petco. At another store on Long Island, New York, former employee Dominique Coppola said that if the girl in charge of birds didn't show up, the baby birds wouldn't get fed at all, something that happened often. Coppola said employees were told to put the hungry babies in the back so customers wouldn't hear them crying.

Kathy Buckler, a bird breeder from Round Rock, Texas, tried to intervene on behalf of a young bird at the mercy of uncaring chain store employees, but to no avail. "They starved that baby to death," says Buckler, referring to a caique parrot she saw at her local Petco store. Buckler discovered the young parrot in extreme distress. "It was screaming from hunger for days," she says, "but the breeder told them it was on two feedings a day, and that's all the food it was getting." Police later found the bird dead in the store's freezer.

Many complaints about Petco from current and former employees across the country recount the same alarming practice: workers being ordered to put sick animals in the store freezer to kill them rather than have them humanely euthanized, as is the law. "You can check any store at any time and get an accurate count of what has died by just looking in the freezer," said a former district manager for the chain.

One Petco employee in northern California recalled an assistant manager who made a joke of putting animals in their store freezer. "Lizards and snakes die quickly because they are cold-blooded," he said, "but those damn hamsters: you can check on them after an hour, and they are still walking around." Store and district managers were unwilling to risk their quarterly bonuses by taking sick animals to a veterinarian, this employee said. Money spent from the store's allotment reduced the amount they would get. The employee recalled the store manager saying, "I don't care how you kill them, as long as it saves my bonus." And an assistant manager reportedly said, "Why spend twenty dollars to euthanize a two-dollar, ninety-nine-cent mouse? Just throw it in the freezer." The same is routinely done to birds.

Petco admitted to minor infractions, but claimed that they had never condoned the actions of those managers. The only problem with that retort is that animals were being put in the freezer to kill them at other Petco stores across the United States.

In 2002, San Francisco city attorney Daniel Herrera sued Petco to stop selling live animals in the Bay Area. The suit cited scores of animal deaths due to cruel and illegal treatment and the fact that the company repeatedly ignored warnings and citations over three years from the San Francisco

Animal Care and Control Department. Vicky Guldbech, a captain in the department, wrote many citations against Petco that were used as evidence in the case. "We have pictures of a freezer packed with animals that would blow your mind," says Guldbech. "There were boxes of animals lined up inside the door. It was disgusting."

Guldbech, who has seen as many as fifty dead birds in a Petco store freezer, said employees could have easily gotten emergency euthanasia for the animals at any one of three local establishments, including a nearby hospital operated by the American Society for the Prevention of Cruelty to Animals. "Their low-wage, poorly trained employees are not capable of handling exotic animals," said John Shanley, spokesperson for the city attorney's office.

More complaints against Petco came in once the lawsuit was filed, and in 2005 the company settled the suit with a payment of $50,000 and eighteen months of enforceable injunctions that included mandatory medical care for all companion animals, a review of the San Francisco stores by an independent veterinarian, and specialized training for all new employees, to be reviewed by the city's animal control department. The next year Petco came to an agreement with PETA, who agreed to stop harassing the chain in exchange for Petco stopping the sales of large parrots. The agreement was considered a major victory for parrots in the pet trade.

There is no reason to think smaller stores, with fewer employees to complain and less customer scrutiny, are doing a better job handling young birds. "It's a sale; it's gone. They don't have a conscience," one breeder said of the lack of scruples in the business.

When young parrots are sold unweaned to unsuspecting customers, they can end up with a myriad of problems, including high veterinary bills. (If you thought it was expensive to take your dog or cat to the doctor, try taking an exotic bird to an avian specialist.) Getting the temperature just right for hand-feeding formulas is almost an art. If it's not warm enough, it can harden and foster bacteria in the crop area, where food is stored while it's being digested. If it's too warm, it can *literally* burn a hole through the crop: "People have called me and cried their heart out because they have just burned a crop on an eight-week-old umbrella cockatoo because nobody told them to get a thermometer," says Linden of new owners inexperienced with hand-feeding.

Fifteen states have laws restricting the sale of unweaned kittens or puppies, protecting the basic right of a young animal to stay with its mother until it would naturally separate from her. In California, a pet dealer cannot possess a dog under eight weeks old, and in eight other states you can't transport a kitten or puppy without its dam until it is eight weeks of age.

Given the fragility of baby birds, the months it takes to wean them, the complexity of feeding them, and the length of time they would naturally stay with their parents, one would assume even more encompassing laws protected baby parrots. But until 2003, when California passed the so-called Baby Bird Bill to prevent the sale of unweaned birds in pet shops, there was none.

Parrots and other companion birds have remained under the radar of U.S. legislators, as have the bird industry's practices. This is how professional aviculturists want it, and they have fought hard to keep it this way. According to the Animal Protection Institute, which monitors local and national animal welfare regulations of this kind, only five states— Colorado, Florida, Georgia, Maryland, and New York—regulate pet bird breeding in any way. And even in those instances, the laws have more to do with containing psittacosis than protecting birds.

The American Federation of Aviculture, widely recognized as the preeminent organization representing professional breeders, came out in strong opposition to the California bill banning the sale of unweaned birds in pet shops when the measure was proposed. Though the Kansas City, Missouri–based federation has several education- and conservation-related endeavors, its primary purpose is to ensure that no regulations inhibit its industry. "AFA people consider legislation regulating birds as an assault," says one leader of the organization. AFA president Benny Gallaway said, "I have no doubt that some unweaned baby birds are killed by people inadvertently, but it is also a matter of economics at the individual level, too, and I don't know [that] it's a huge problem, given the amount of the investment."

The bird breeders and the pet industry alike pummeled the California bill, sponsored by Assemblywoman Ellen Corbett (D–San Leandro), as it made its way through the legislature. A major disinformation campaign was waged to stop the legislation. "I've never seen lies like this, never like this," said Corbett. The bill's primary supporter, the Sacramento-based Animal Protection Institute, an animal advocacy group, came under attack for being an animal rights group. Gallaway called the bill "a knee-jerk reaction from a group with suspect motivations."

An example of the misinformation disseminated by breeders aired in the San Francisco Bay Area as a local news story on KRON-TV. In the report, called "Squawking over State Bird Ban," the news reporter interviewed local pet shop owners and bird breeders lamenting the possible passage of the bill. One store owner was interviewed with some baby cockatiels in her lap. "This bill will put me out of business," she said, looking sadly at her birds. The report led viewers to believe the baby birds would starve to death without her. The interviewer never asked why the store owner hadn't obtained the birds after they had been weaned for a few weeks, or why they were taken from their parents that young in the first place. Though breeders agreed that most chain stores don't do a good job hand-feeding birds, they argued that the law would penalize the stores that do. "All of this is a smokescreen," says Linden, who had never sold her birds into pet shops.

Originally written to preclude pet stores from having unweaned birds on the premises, the bill—which had many supporters, including the California Veterinary Medical Association, the Humane Society of the United States, the Avian Welfare Coalition, and hundreds of bird lovers and humane law enforcement officials in the state—was heavily amended to allow shops to have them but not sell them until they are weaned. Baby birds could still be pulled from their parents and shipped very young from the breeding facilities. Yet now that the precedent-setting baby bird law has passed, it paves the way for other states to pass similar laws to protect parrots in the pet trade. Monica Engebretsen, senior program coordinator at the Animal Protection Institute (API), says seven other states have contacted her for help introducing baby bird legislation. (She declined to state which ones, to keep them off the AFA's radar until the legislative process is further along.)

The Animal Welfare Act, which Congress passed in 1966, is the only federal law regulating the treatment of warm-blooded animals kept as pets and used in research, exhibition, transport, or by dealers. Jerry D. Depoyster, veterinary medical officer with the U.S. Department of Agriculture's Animal and Plant Health Inspection Service, is writing amendments to the act to include birds, originally excluded from the regulations by the discrepancy authority of the secretary of agriculture. "The agency simply did not have enough funding to do what we already were supposed to do, and to add birds would result in less time spent in other areas of inspection such as dog breeders," says Depoyster. "We would not be able to hire new inspectors for the increased workload of regulating birds." As a result, scores of millions of parrots and other birds have gone unprotected for four decades.

In 2002, Congress approved the Helms Amendment to the Animal Welfare Act after the Alternatives Research and Development Foundation, a nonprofit organization that funds research using alternatives to laboratory animals, sued the Agriculture Department to stop excluding from the act birds, rats, and mice in the pet trade. (The group tried to get all birds, rats, and mice protected, but were not successful with animals bred for research purposes.) Avian welfare organizations are hoping to see the federal law amended further with requirements that include minimum cage sizes for birds, restrictions on the transport of unweaned parrots, and environmental and behavioral enrichments. No one knows how extensive the regulations will be or whether they will make little or considerable difference. But any changes might not take effect for a decade or more, according to Depoyster. "I have no best guess," he says. "It took nearly three years for a one-word change for one docket [*or* instead of *and*], and I have three [regulations] that are over seven years in the works." Plus, says Depoyster, a new president almost always shuts down the rulemaking process for months or years, especially if a new party is elected into the White House.

Meanwhile, the pet bird industry continues to fight against any comprehensive regulation, although the need for it is undeniable. (Gallaway of the American Federation of Aviculture has admitted the need for it: "I may get fired for saying this, but we need to be regulated.") In the meantime, unless animal cruelty—the intent of abuse—can be proven, birds cannot be rescued when they are discovered in bad situations. Some bird breeders are reconsidering their vocation and leaving the business. The Lindens at the Santa Barbara Bird Farm have stopped breeding altogether, in part because of the many calls they received from customers wanting to return birds after they realized how noisy or time-intensive they were to care for. Despite the good care the couple gave in raising highly socialized young parrots, the birds were still more than most people wanted to contend with.

Garry Wallen is a former breeder based in Anchorage, Alaska. After he heard Bonnie Kenk, founder of the Parrot Education and Adoption Center (PEAC), a San Diego–based organization, speak at his local bird club, his consciousness was awakened to the plight of parrots, and he helped form the local PEAC chapter there. He now says:

> I think back over my time with parrots, how little I knew at the start, and how hard-won some of the knowledge was. Many parrots lost their lives due to my ignorance or the ignorance of the people (to whom) we sold the birds. In a stated opinion that will surely raise hackles in the breeder community, I have to say that some breeding, especially for endangered species, is very necessary, but most is heartless commodity production for the sole purpose of producing income. I was one of those people and it embarrasses me now. I'm happy to have found an organization such as

PEAC where I can focus my efforts to educate people about the behaviors of these undomesticated animals, and to find new homes for parrots, to make amends for the problem I helped to grow.

Avian veterinarian Brian Speer has been a breeder of large parrots since 1984, as well as a staunch supporter of the American Federation of Aviculture for many years. He recently reduced his flock, in part because the practice was wearing on his conscience, "I'm getting older and softer in my mind and heart. I don't like seeing birds in breeding cages. I like large cages and less of a production-oriented mentality. What changed? I've learned to be more sensitive to their feelings, emotions, and intelligence and the wonder, the magic of birds. I've gained appreciation for the souls of these animals."

If ever an industry needed regulation, the captive bird trade is it. Parrots need protection, and the facilities that house and breed them should be under severe scrutiny—if not for their benefit, then for ours. The threat of an avian flu pandemic raises the question: Is public health at risk from the millions of exotic birds being kept in unlicensed, unregulated, and unmonitored circumstances?

Tracy Bennett, the avian veterinarian, points out why it's imperative that the bird-breeding community be regularly monitored. "They say, 'We have the right to do whatever we want, and you can't tell us what to do.' And I say, 'Why can't we?' My argument would be: Birds carry zoonotic, potentially human contagious diseases, so for that reason, if for no other, they should be inspected. Nobody loses but the bad breeders."

With the danger of avian flu looming stateside, parrots and chickens could be a deadly combination. Both poultry farms and large backyard parrot breeders are found in the same rural agricultural zones, which makes the threat of avian flu transmission between them high.

In 2002, three million birds, mostly chickens, were "depopulated" in Southern California to stop the spread of exotic Newcastle disease. While large poultry farms are licensed and thereby listed with the U.S. Department of Agriculture, other bird farms are not. As the disease spread, infecting birds in Los Angeles, San Diego, and Riverside counties, Agriculture Department inspectors went door to door, trying to suss out backyard breeders and those with a few birds. It took almost eight months for the inspectors to finally stem the outbreak.

To date, more than 150 million birds in thirty-three countries, either culled or infected with the avian influenza virus, and half of the humans who have contracted the highly pathogenic H5N1 strain of avian flu, are dead. The disease has worked its way to fifteen countries in Asia and Europe. U.S. government officials and flu experts say it is not a matter of "if" but "when" the flu will arrive stateside.

Seven billion dollars in emergency funding has been allocated to ramp up protection against avian flu outbreaks, and with good reason: the 1918 avian flu pandemic, considered the worst natural disaster the United States has ever known, killed an estimated forty to fifty million people in a single year. Some say those numbers, mainly based on North American statistics, are conservative. The death toll could have been double that, because accurate figures were not available in places such as Latin America, Africa, and Asia.

"The H5N1 virus is not transmittable from human to human or animal to human easily," says Jamie Gilardi of the World Parrot Trust, "but all that can change in an instant with the next recombinant strain or if a single mutation develops. Then it could be gifted at either of those things."

The 1997 outbreak of avian flu in Hong Kong dispelled the common belief that a pig or other intermediary mammal host was needed for humans to be infected. The eighteen people who caught the virus, six of whom died, did so by direct transmission from poultry with the disease. Though since then H5N1 has infected only 218 people and killed 122, the more humans contract the virus through close contact with chickens and other birds, the more likely humans will become a "mixing vessel" for a new subtype that would be contagious from human to human. That event, according to the World Health Organization, would mark the start of a pandemic.

A paper published in the May 2006 issue of *Science* magazine established conclusively that the cause of the global AIDS pandemic started in the jungles of Cameroon with the hunting (and likely, eating) of members of an isolated subspecies of chimpanzees, *Pan troglodytes troglodytes*. All chimpanzees carry strains of simian immunodeficiency virus (SIV), though they do not succumb to it and are not contagious to humans. It was only through unrelenting hunting that a jackpot group with a strain contagious to humans was finally struck, and transmission began. Subsequent transmission from human to human spread the virus worldwide. "The chimp viruses made the jump three times, one of which has caused what we know as AIDS," says Beatrice Hahn, a human retrovirus expert whose work is part of the *Science* paper. "That is responsible for over ninety percent of all AIDS cases on the globe."

If the H5N1 avian flu virus mutates, it will spread swiftly: in eight months, the time it took to stem the outbreak of exotic Newcastle disease in 2002, human mortality would be astronomical. A single cell of H5N1 releases a swarm of virus, unlike HIV, for example, which is much more contained. Predictions of three hundred million fatalities are considered plausible, given that six billion people live on the planet and the myriad of advancements since 1918 that allow disease to travel across the globe.

Larry Hawkins has been working on emergency programs throughout the United States for fifteen years as part of his job as a regional public affairs officer for the Agriculture Department's Animal and Plant Health Inspection Service. His region includes all the states west of the Mississippi, including Hawaii and Alaska, and the U.S. territory of Guam. "It would be helpful to have the names and addresses of all bird-breeding facilities in the U.S. as a resource for surveillance in case of an outbreak of avian influenza," he says. "Early detection usually improves our chance of successful disease response."

But that information is unavailable because thousands of hobby (i.e., pigeon) and pet bird breeders, producing an estimated two million birds for the pet trade each year, have fought local and national legislation to regulate them at every turn. They also have intentionally stayed off the radar of governmental organizations that would inspect them. In many states a license is required for catteries and kennels, which might have fewer than ten cats or dogs. Yet bird breeders can keep hundreds or thousands of birds, and ship them across the country and around the world, without oversight.

Estimates are that half of all pet bird-breeding facilities keep birds in dirty, substandard conditions. If operators of those facilities knew they had a serious problem, they might not be quick to report it, because the authorities would euthanize their birds. "A virus could get under way without anybody knowing about it," says Gillian Air, a professor at the University of Oklahoma's Health Sciences Center.

Experts say most bird breeders would not recognize the symptoms of an avian flu death without testing for it, because its symptoms are similar to any avian respiratory disease. "The only way of knowing which virus is responsible is to isolate and identify the virus," says Air.

Unlike most poultry farms, which have regular, thorough veterinary inspections and testing, backyard bird breeders don't. "They aren't going to use a vet unless they absolutely have to, because they don't want to pay for it," says Bennett, the avian veterinarian. "When they don't spend money on their flock, they get sick, and then they lose production and they don't have as much money. It's a vicious circle."

Birds that are weak or sickly are more likely to contract a virus like avian flu. "It's just like people," says Air. "If they're not in the best of health, they're more susceptible to disease." Plus, he says, if they came in contact with any wild birds, they could further transmit it. There's no knowing how long a virus could maintain itself in a colony without the birds showing symptoms, and birds that survive infection excrete virus for at least ten days, and can become asymptomatic carriers.

Many backyard breeding operations house birds outdoors in open-air barns that are covered only for a few months during winter. Sick birds shed diseases in their saliva, nasal secretions, and feces. If susceptible, caged birds can contract the illnesses if they come in contact with the droppings of wild birds, which dry and become airborne. Highly pathogenic viruses can survive for long periods in the environment, especially when temperatures are low.

But air is not the primary method of transmission. Avian influenza viruses are easily transmitted from farm to farm by mechanical means, such as contaminated equipment, vehicles, feed, cages, or clothing. During the outbreak of exotic Newcastle disease, feed stores in Southern California unwittingly helped transmit the virus when it attached itself to the tires of delivery trucks or the shoes of delivery workers as they dropped off seed at one bird farm after another.

Most parrot breeders are not using proper biosecurity, says Hawkins of the Animal and Plant Health Inspection Service. "We endorse security precautions that are not generally in effect in parrot-breeding facilities, and we'd be thrilled if they would adopt them," he says.

After several imported birds, including a parrot, died in a United Kingdom quarantine facility and test results were positive for H5N1, the European Union banned all imports of wild and pet birds, closed live poultry markets, and increased border enforcement to control the threat of birds coming illegally. Even so, says Gilardi of the World Parrot Trust, there are plenty of ways for Europeans to contract the virus in their own backyard. "Hunters can still kill boatloads of ducks and geese, handle them, get blood on them, and store them in their cars [where the virus would shed]. They're on the front lines for direct contact of contagion transfer. Yet no European country, even though they say migratory ducks are a prime vector, has banned hunting, because of the strong hunting lobby."

Given the negative stance of the industry regarding regulation, companion bird breeders are unlikely to voluntarily invite inspectors onto their properties if it could result in quarantine or destruction of their flocks, even if they could be a carrier for disease.

In the event of an avian flu outbreak in the United States, the Agriculture Department can locate poultry farms, which are licensed and regularly inspected. But for first responders, finding backyard bird breeders could be a repeat of the exotic Newcastle disease crisis: like looking for a needle in a haystack.

Chapter Six

Death Row and a Death Row Reprieve: The Notorious Scudder's Parrot Depot and the Stellar Cockatoo Rescue

A red cockatoo.
Coloured like the peach-tree blossom,
Speaking with the speech of men,
And they did to it what is always done
To the learned and eloquent
They took a cage with stout bars
And shut it up inside.

—Po Chu-I, ninth century

At Martha Scudder's Parrot Depot near Roy, Washington, hundreds of parrots, including many endangered species, have lived in cold, wet, filthy conditions for years, according to eyewitness and expert accounts, court testimony, and scores of postmortem reports. Witnesses and documents indicate that Scudder's, located in Pierce County about fifty miles south of Seattle, has neglected hundreds, and possibly thousands, of parrots over its twenty-five-year history. A veterinarian working with the Humane Society for Tacoma and Pierce County called the five-acre farm a "concentration camp" for birds.

Since 1999, several complaints about Scudder's have been made to the Humane Society and the U.S. Fish and Wildlife Service. Local animal control inspectors have checked the property and warned Martha Scudder that they believe the facility violates the state's animal cruelty law. Still, not a single bird has been removed or a fine issued.

The story of Scudder's, which houses eight hundred parrots and is considered the largest parrot-breeding operation in Washington State, reveals how little protection there is for birds in the pet trade, and how little oversight there is for bird-breeding businesses, locally and nationally.

According to two Washington State experts, avian veterinarian Tracy Bennett and former parrot broker Lori Rutledge, a large percentage of the state's twenty major breeding facilities for large parrots keep their charges in bad conditions—a situation other experts say occurs nationwide. Bennett says Scudder's is only the tip of the iceberg of bad aviaries. "I know of a dozen very bad aviaries that are basically no better than this," she says. "Most aviaries I've been involved with and most I know of are not doing a good job." Animal neglect is more common than abuse, and can be just as painful, given that the suffering is prolonged. Animal welfare experts estimate that for every severe case of abuse there are one hundred cases of neglect, not just in bird-breeding facilities but also in the increasing number of avian rescues opening up to take in unwanted parrots. These rescues suffer from overcrowding and are unable to keep hundreds of birds and cages clean and cared for each day.

Before even visiting Scudder's, Bennett saw evidence in her own veterinary office of the troubling situation there when the new owners of several young birds from Scudder's brought them in for veterinary care. The birds were uniformly in poor condition, tested positive for disease, showed signs of stress, and were underweight. On January 23, 2003, local Humane Society investigators went to Scudder's and asked Bennett to join them. She later described the facility as "horrifying—a scummy, filthy, horrible" place.

The main house was filled with cages and filthy with feces. "We went downstairs, and there were feces all down the wall," says Bennett. "It was all green with it." In the basement was the nursery, where Scudder incubated and fed baby birds. "Across from the babies were some incubators the size for chicks, but one had an adult bird, and he barely fit," says Bennett.

The next room downstairs was filled with birds in stacked wire cages.

"Some of the birds were brought in from the aviaries because Martha said she thought they were sick," says Bennett. "Some had clubbed feet from walking on bare wire, which was very bad. Others she was boarding and had no idea of their health status, but they were mixed in with the rest. All of these were next to her nursery, close enough to contaminate the baby birds with any diseases they might have."

Bennett saw only a fraction of the flock because Scudder would allow her into only two of the eight bird barns that house African grays, Amazons, macaws, and different kinds of cockatoos, and some rare species, such as vasa parrots. She described the aviaries as "rotten old ramshackle wooden shacks with hanging wire cages."

"They had what I call 'fecal stalagmites' at least six inches high, maybe higher," she says. "You would think seeing giant accumulation of feces would be a bad thing, but Martha Scudder didn't comprehend that. I got the impression that she saw no problem."

An automatic watering system was leaking badly and poorly maintained. Where there were water bottles for the birds, algae was growing in them. "Water was coming into the barns because the buildings were open to the elements," she says. "It was bad, but at the time I was happy about it, because all the drinking water those birds would get is what they could lick off the bars."

The birds that especially haunted Bennett were the ones left on their own. "I remember this one double yellow-headed Amazon just sitting on the bottom of the wire cage—no perch, no mate—in this cold, rainy place in winter, sitting there alone with just filth underneath it," says Bennett. "And I thought, 'This is torture for this bird.'"

Reports made public after a series of necropsies on several of Scudder's birds revealed diagnoses of aspergillis, a long-term, chronic infection in which the bird dies gasping for breath; proventricular dilatation disease or PDD, a highly contagious virus commonly called "avian AIDS"; polyoma, which causes birds to bleed to death; and mycobacterium avium, an avian tuberculosis contagious to humans.

Bennett sent a report of her findings from the inspection, dated March 7, 2003, to the Humane Society and outlined a long list of recommendations, suggesting that Scudder get rid of most of her birds, reducing their numbers to fewer than one hundred; replace the watering system; and improve the birds' diet.

Scudder received Bennett's report, which had a deadline of May 31, 2003, to implement the changes. But she didn't take the recommendations seriously. Later, in deposed testimony in a related lawsuit, Scudder said she thought Bennett's recommendations "were not conducive to flock management," and that she didn't feel required to reduce her flock just because the Humane Society sent her a letter saying so. "She [Bennett] has no right telling me how to run my business," Scudder said.

To crack down on bad breeders, Larry Gallawa, a Seattle resident and parrot lover, lobbied the Pierce County Council in mid-2003 to have its Kennel, Cattery, Grooming Parlor and Pet Store Ordinance expanded to include aviaries. The revised ordinance would have allowed inspection of any aviary wanting a license and would permit follow-up checks without advance notice. All that was required was adding the word *aviaries* to the ordinance, along with the number of birds defining an aviary. (In the case of cats and dogs, the county requires a license to house six or more.)

The county council held a hearing on the ordinance on February 24, 2004. Breeders argued against the amendment and the inspections it would bring. The Humane Society representatives countered that the revised ordinance would help them do their jobs. Bennett testified to rebut the breeders' concerns.

In the end, the breeders prevailed: without further consideration, examination, or investigation, the council tabled the proposal. Two more hearings were held in the year following, and both times the council voted down an ordinance to require bird breeders to be licensed.

Washington State can boast the best and the worst when it comes to captive parrots. A little more than one hundred miles north of the misery of Scudder's is its polar opposite: a stellar parrot refuge, Rutledge's Cockatoo Rescue.

The drive along Interstate 5 unfolds under a carpet of clouds that rolls to a stop at the snow-drenched Cascade Mountains in western Washington. Even in August, majestic Mount Rainier hovers like an apparition over the ring of clouds at its base. It's easy to understand why hippies made it a spiritual mecca decades ago, and why New Agers still consider it a prime cosmic energy vortex. Spitting rain starts to give way to sun, but only briefly, and the day becomes like many here in the Pacific Northwest, a little warmth with wet on either side.

Rutledge's parrot sanctuary is about an hour north of Seattle in Stanwood, Washington, a rural area zoned mostly for agriculture. Flatbed trucks heading south on the freeway with stacks of massive, fresh-cut logs are a common, if troubling, sight here; the Weyerhaeuser Company is clear-cutting a "shitload" of land in the foothills of the Cascades just thirty minutes east of Stanwood, Rutledge says.

Rutledge's exit is just past the Tulalip Indian Reservation, which boasts a population of 3,611 and its own casino. A few miles farther along is the exit onto Pioneer Highway, a two-lane road that leads into Sylvana, the tiny town before Stanwood, winding through miles of farmland and forest. The mist lies low on the surrounding fields, and clusters of woolly sheep graze near an old rusty truck lying on the lush, rain-fed grass.

The sheep are in odd contrast to the silvery sheen of the raised railroad tracks just above them and the looming brown mill silo that brags "Sylvana." This tableau sits outside time: fifty years ago it would have looked the same. Photos adorning the wall of the local diner show that it did.

The town is a block long and sits on a raised wooden street out of the old West. Next to the diner is the notions store, which connects through to the toy store, and lastly a crafts consortium posing as an antiques store.

"People still look out for each other here," says the diner waitress. She was born and raised in the area, but neither she nor any of her patrons (she calls out to ask), all longtime locals, knew hundreds of parrots had been living in an exotic bird sanctuary just up the road for the last several years. Rutledge intentionally keeps her place incognito.

Past Happy Valley Road, down Happy Hollow Road, and across the Thomas slough sits the sanctuary.

Rutledge quiets her three Great Danes as she comes out onto the wooden deck of her old-fashioned mobile home. Here, the parrots live better than the human inhabitant. Rutledge, forty-nine, is an attractive redhead. She wears a black T-shirt even in this chilly weather. She's vivacious and, like her birds, fiercely independent, which brushes some people the wrong way.

Many, including other avian rescuers, have criticized the way she operates. The criticism has kept her from trusting people she doesn't know, even though she could use the support of those doing similar work. But no one is doing quite what she has done. Rutledge, out in this isolated pocket of rural Washington, is doing something quite extraordinary. There are hundreds of avian rescues nationwide, but hers might be the only one of its kind providing a retirement community for breeder birds, like those at Scudder's, which number in the millions. These mostly wild, untamed parrots are locked away in barren cages in windowless warehouses for decades. They are the forgotten ones—unseen, unheard, and unknown to the public, while their babies fill pet stores across the country.

"All bird breeders take good care of the baby birds and not good care of their parents," says Rutledge. "These breeder birds have been to hell and back. Most were wild-caught in the jungle, so they knew what it was like to live in the trees with a flock. A lot of them haven't seen daylight since they were captured thirty-five years ago. It's been the worst for them. They are kept in rows of cages, completely forgotten, while everyone is enjoying their babies."

Once the breeder birds have outlived their usefulness after decades of producing young, aviculturalists often kill them to make room for younger pairs. Or they are sold as productive breeding stock and are killed as soon as their new owners realize they have been duped. Rutledge solicits the breeders for these old birds before they are disposed of. Many turn them over to her, but they laugh at her for taking what they consider useless birds.

"I know a couple of diehard, crack-their-neck, old-school breeders," she says. "They think I'm crazy because I'm sitting here feeding them and not making a profit. But don't these birds deserve it, with everything they have been through?" Rutledge calls them "death row birds," and opened her sanctuary to provide them a permanent stay of execution. At Rutledge's they are once again allowed to flock, fly, and live a freer, fuller life.

Rutledge wanted to rescue cockatoos on a large scale and had to go into agricultural zoning, and poverty, to do so. Now she lives so far from a mall, she says she could scream, and it's two exits on a freeway miles away to a grocery store. Even so, she says, "I am now living my perfect life."

There is always some apprehension among the flock when a new human comes to visit. "They fear they'll be taken somewhere else," says Rutledge. Many of the birds were moved over the years from cage to cage and breeding facility to facility, which caused long-established, deeply bonded breeding pairs to be split to be paired with other birds breeders thought would be more effective for reproduction. The birds that come here are safe for life.

The sanctuary area sits at the end of Rutledge's driveway. It is a haven of trees, lush flowers, tall grass, a running pond. Walking paths—lighted at night, lined with halved logs, and strewn with ample wood shavings— surround the parrots' enclosures.

All told Rutledge has forty acres of land, evenly divided between woods and pasture, with a salmon-spawning creek running through the property. The sanctuary sits in a large oval clearing surrounded by dense fifty-foot-tall spruce, cedars, birch, cottonwood, and alderwood trees that provide a protected enclave. On one side, a path goes through the forested area to a pristine pasture Rutledge is considering renting to horse owners for extra income.

Residents of the first and largest aviary greet us. Forty by twenty by twenty feet, it houses eighty Moluccan cockatoos, which have enough room to fly around. They move forward as a unit. Then, like mountain climbers, they scale the aviary's metal mesh to get an eye-to-eye vantage point and beg for gifts. The mesh becomes a wall of white-feathered wings and black beaks as far as the eye can see.

The birds require proper homage from all visitors and prefer it in the form of treats such as Cheetos. They are not disappointed. Clawed feet reach out eagerly for the orange crescents. There's a little competition— some try for two at a time—but there's no fighting; they are a flock. They hold their Cheetos in their scaly toes and daintily crunch them a bite at a time.

Much of Rutledge's oasislike refuge was donated by supporters. The colonies are all Costco carports a friend helped her erect. They added riveted chain link to the sides and roofing material to shade a third of the top so the birds can bask in the sun or take rain baths, a favorite pastime. The flights are lined with cedar chips that deter bugs and worms and naturally kill bacteria.

Bright red Chinese golden pheasants calmly wander around the cage bottoms, doing housekeeping chores. They pick up all the parrot food scraps, keeping the aviaries clean so rodents stay away. At night they sleep next to the parrots. Rutledge says the pheasants and parrots don't speak the same language, but neither is bothered by that.

The first two aviaries she built held Moluccan cockatoos and scarlet macaws. Once she acquired 4 to 6 of a species, they got their own colony. Now there are a dozen colonies housing 250 birds of different species: 6 house cockatoos (200 of them), while the rest hold 9 species of macaws, 6 species of Amazons, and 2 species of African gray parrots.

One special aviary houses just two birds. One is Jackson, a Moluccan cockatoo whose beak was torn off by an aggressive bird in a breeding facility. Rutledge thinks he's embarrassed by how he looks, so he hides in his nest box if anyone's around. After he arrived, a female was donated that had been attacked in the same way. Rutledge put her in with Jackson. It was love at first sight. Now the two sit side by side, hiding in their nest box when people come near.

Once a week Rutledge peeks in the box to make sure they are okay, but she says the intrusion traumatizes the pair. They have toys and food and are fine left on their own. Once an obnoxious visitor knocked on the box to chase them out. Alarmed, Rutledge ran over. "I just want to see them," the woman said indignantly. Incidents like this convinced Rutledge to stave off visitors, which has given her the reputation of being a recluse.

The other special aviary is the "killer colony." All the members are male cockatoos that have killed their mates. Mate aggression happens with this species in captivity, though it is not known to happen in the wild. Some experts consider it the collateral damage of confinement. These "killer 'toos" are liabilities that get put down fast in breeding facilities. But Rutledge says it's a mistake to give them a death sentence. "I'd like to get word out that they'd do well in a colony," she says.

At her place they live together without incident but retain their tough-guy personas. "You see how they are with each other," says Rutledge. "It's like they're saying, 'Hey, what are you in for?' 'Me? I killed my bitch.' 'Yeah, I pulled the beak off mine.'"

When new birds arrive, they have an immediate reaction to their new living arrangements with a flock. "The wild-caught birds are so excited to see their own kind!" says Rutledge. "The thing these birds are missing in captivity is choices. In the colonies they can choose their friends, where they want to hang out, if they want to sun themselves, and food—I offer a huge variety. They love it. It is wonderful to watch a female flirt with a bunch of different males. The joy in their eyes is unforgettable."

Domestically raised Moluccans—even pets whose owners relinquished them—intermingle with the wild birds seamlessly and are completely fulfilled living together, Rutledge says. "I have a few of those needy 'toos that have been passed around to seven homes in one year, the ones that scream nonstop for human attention, and then lash out and bite unpredictably. Within days they have melted into the flock and no longer want one-on-one attention from me. I offer it; they pull away."

Rutledge keeps an eye on pairs she sees doing mating dances. She doesn't encourage breeding and hopes the birds don't, but she accepts it, and sometimes helps the birds if she sees the male digging a nest hole below the logs. He will chase other birds away to protect the area. In a confined space, that can cause problems. "They're down digging in the ground at midnight, and they get so upset they can't keep other birds away from their nest hole. When they look miserable, I'll put them in their own flight cage. I keep my fingers crossed the eggs don't hatch, but I let nature take its course. I don't interfere. They think I'll be like all the other humans and take their eggs away from them, but I don't. I figure whatever makes them happy."

At times Rutledge is forced to intervene if there are problems during the incubation period. She sees the sorrow the birds experience when she removes even a bad egg, and can only imagine the grief they go through at the loss of their young.

> They'll stop nesting if an egg is rotten. They know it's bad. They will be sitting outside the nest box, not keeping it warm. And yet they'll scream and cry like I'm taking their babies when I remove it. So nobody can tell me they don't grieve. They're miserable. And that's for a rotten egg. It's awful if they [breeders] take their babies after two weeks. They're so loving towards each other; they're such a family unit. I can only imagine what goes through their heads.

Rutledge is grateful that breeding hasn't been a big problem. Just a handful of offspring have been produced since she started taking in parrots.

The macaws in her care came from a local rescue that went under. Almost all were emaciated and had to be nursed back to health. When Rutledge said she'd take them, word got out, and macaws started coming in from all over. One was a once wild green-winged male, thirty years old, who had lived in a collector's home with one hundred other big parrots. "An awful place," says Rutledge. It was so bad their owner, an older woman, moved across the alley to get away from the stench and noise. Her daughter-in-law fed them. The green-winged was kept in a dark, dank basement with rat holes in the wall. The owner had bought her birds, all caught in the wild, right out of quarantine. "There were birds everywhere," says Rutledge. "She had blacked out the windows so the birds couldn't see out and had no daylight."

There's one odd couple among them that Rutledge calls the Christmas Couple. The female is a mostly khaki-green-colored military macaw named Olive. She fell in love with a male scarlet macaw named Pimento. "He comes into the colony and falls head over heels with this domesticated female," says Rutledge. "She's a social butterfly and he's very reserved, but he follows her everywhere. He found someone that really touched his heart and he's not going to let her go."

Pimento was emaciated when he arrived, but Olive nursed him back to health by feeding him from her beak. "They're so in love; everyone notices it," says Rutledge. "She's social and comes right up to meet everyone, and he forces himself to come up with her. Then he spreads his wings in a menacing way to let everyone know she's his girl."

Rutledge says each species has a distinct personality. "The sulphur-crested cockatoos are the cranky colony, and the Goffin'ses are juvenile delinquents," she says. "They are so naughty, they should come with a warning label. Amazons are cantankerous and nasty, and macaws are low-maintenance. They're not as needy as cockatoos. The (African) grays stand apart from each other; they need a lot of personal space. But nobody is as loving as the Moluccans."

The latter are still her favorites, and the birds she spends the most time watching. Many of the stories she has to tell about them are remarkable tales of love. "Moluccans are so accepting of new birds," says Rutledge. "Everyone that comes in is welcomed like an old family member. There is the 'welcome wagon' for new birds. It is always the same females. They lead the new bird to the food station and water. They also seem to be introducing them around to the other birds, and they act like old friends. I would have expected the new ones to have a few squabbles, but they react like they know each other."

"Even in ninety-five-degree heat they do group snuggles," says Rutledge. "In a windstorm, they squat low on their perches and fan out their wings and go, 'Whooo, whooo,' mimicking the howling wind." There is "hair-pulling," just like in the playground, but sometimes things get a little more serious, like when a bare-eyed cockatoo was introduced into the Ducorps cockatoo colony, and they dive-bombed the new bird. The bare-eyes now have their own colony.

Rutledge's farmland zoning allows her to let the incredibly noisy birds scream as long and as loud as they wish. Even so, she gets complaints about it from neighbors eighty acres away. The birds have their own reaction to the squawking. Rutledge has heard them say, "Shut up," "Knock it off," "Quiet, quiet," "Stop that bad bird," "Shh, somebody will hear you," and "Night, night" to a noisy peer.

Some of the parrots can't squawk anymore because their syrinx (the equivalent of vocal cords) were cut to quiet them. "There are still a few vets that do it back east," says Rutledge of the controversial and dangerous surgical procedure.

Even with all the horrors these birds have endured, like living in the avian equivalent of concentration camps (and not for three or four years, but for decades), they have not become permanently hateful, violent, and psychologically dysfunctional, as happens to some humans exposed to similar long-term abuse. Instead, the birds have shown a remarkable emotional resilience. Their effervescent spirit and social, nurturing nature begin to return as they are allowed to heal. Rutledge has witnessed behavior in her birds that goes against the common beliefs, which further shows that parrots may be the most misunderstood animals to interact with humans, and that the people who purport to know them best, understand them least. A case in point: Rutledge feared, when she flocked breeder birds that had had no contact with birds other than their mates, that they would be aggressive toward one another, and that weak or compromised birds would be picked on by larger ones, as many bird breeders said would happen. She found the opposite to be true. "Members of the flock seem to give a wide berth to the handicapped birds, allowing them to pass by with ease," she says. "There is a female orange-wing in the Amazon colony that is blind in one eye and partially blind in the other.

Dr. Irene Pepperberg with Alex, the African gray parrot who was her study subject for thirty years. Together they pioneered groundbreaking cognition and communication research that showed that parrots had innate intelligence equal to that of three- to five-year-old children. Taught by Pepperberg, Alex learned to identify, request, refuse, and categorize more than one hundred different items. He could also read phonetically and count.

Parrots and other birds evolved from dinosaurs like this *Sinornithosaurus millenii*, a carnivorous theropod dromaeosaur that lived 125 million years ago, had a sickle-shaped claw similar in design to parrot toes, and was covered from head to tail with downy fluff and primitive feathers—precursors to the feathers found on modern birds. It was a cousin of the vicious *Velociraptor*, made famous by the film *Jurassic Park*, and recently discovered to have been covered in feathers, too.

Parrot people are a breed unto themselves. Their avian passion rivals that of cat and dog lovers. Parront Shauna Beckendorf entered this pet bird look-alike contest with her Moluccan cockatoo, Cuddles. As decked out as she was, the pair didn't win. Another contestant, who had dyed her hair red and wore body paint to match her scarlet macaw, took the big prize.

In a matter of weeks parrot lover Hugh Choi had trained his red-fronted macaws, Otis, Gizmo, and Annie, to fly to him on command. Now they travel with him uncaged everywhere, even on subways and at the beach.

Choi's macaws free-fly in New York's Central Park for hours at a time. Choi says he could never deprive them of flight again because he now knows it plays a large part in their psychological well-being.

Most parrots live their decades-long lives in cages so restrictive that if dogs or cats were kept the same way it would be called animal abuse. The cages are chosen for their unobtrusiveness in owners' living rooms, not for the needs of the birds they hold. Until he was brought to a parrot rescue, this Amazon, which would fly fifty or more miles a day in the wild, lived for years in this cage, unable to do more than stand on the perch.

Large parrots are difficult pets. Because few people are willing to put up with them for their many-decades-long life spans, a crisis of unwanted parrots has developed. It is now estimated that the average parrot has seven homes in the first ten years of its life. Ziyal had several, including a breeding facility where she was battered by a male cockatoo who had killed his previous mate. By age eight she was sold by a pet store to a man who kept her in a closet to quiet her, lit her toes with a lighter to loosen them from a perch, and threw her against a wall when she bit him. She is now living cage-free with other special-needs birds. Though parrots are usually neglected more than abused, stories like Ziyal's are not rare.

Sofia, Beeba, and Simba are feather pluckers. An estimated one in ten captive parrots engages in this painful and aberrational by-product of captivity that is never seen in wild parrots.

The only parrot indigenous to the United States, the Carolina parakeet once filled the southeastern skies and those as far north as Connecticut. The birds were described as beautiful to behold, but after their habitat was converted to agriculture, they were systematically shot out of the sky as crop pests.

Numbers of monk parakeets (aka quaker parrots), originally brought to the United States from South America for the pet trade, have gotten free over the years and formed colonies in several states. Many people feel that they fill the niche of the lost Carolina parakeet, as they do not usurp the needs of native birds. Unlike other parrots, which nest in tree holes, monks build stick nests. Each twig is honed until it is just the right length for the spot where it's used.

Architectural feats, monk parakeet nests can withstand rain and high winds and keep the birds warm in the cold. They are often built on the poles of electrical and telephone lines or other tall infrastructure as pictured here, on the baseball fields of Pelham Bay Park in the Bronx, New York. Their nests are shared by multiple families for warmth and are designed like condos with separate apartments for each. They can weigh more than a hundred pounds—at least one was reported to be as large as a Volkswagen Beetle.

Across the United States, local residents and media have championed the monk parakeet flocks in their neighborhoods. Local electric companies, however, have been in a battle with the birds. While no damage has ever been directly connected to the birds, electric companies routinely dismantle the nests, as Connecticut's United Illuminating is doing in this photo.

These boxes contain pairs of breeder parrots, the hidden minions whose eggs or unweaned young are taken for the pet trade year after year. At Beech's Bird Nest Ranch, five hundred parrots were kept in barren cages with a wooden nest box, food, water, and a mate, and little space inside for them to move. Breeders often keep their birds deprived and in the dark so they will be left with nothing to do but procreate. But large parrots are not like chickens. Many produce only one or two eggs once a year in breeding season. This facility was an independent field research farm for Kaytee Products, the large bird food company, and boasted that company's logo on its sign.

Beak bifurcation (splitting) was a practice done by an avian veterinarian and approved by bird breeders as a way to prevent aggressive males from harming the females they were paired with to produce young. Aggression is not uncommon, especially in cockatoos, when a pair of parrots are kept perpetually confined in a cage too small for them to fly and lacking enrichments to occupy their days. This Ducorps cockatoo, named Alex, had never harmed a female or shown any aggression toward one, but the procedure was done to him anyway as a preventive measure. The damage to his beak is permanent.

Breeder parrots are treated like work horses. They spend their entire lives warehoused with only the bare necessities. They are like prisoners with life sentences that are never allowed out of their cells. This male eclectus would be flying free in Australia or Indonesia, but here he lives in the shadows, pulling out his feathers.

Scudder's Parrot Depot in Pierce County, Washington, was described as a concentration camp by one witness. Its eight hundred parrots, including many endangered species, were kept in squalor. Even after the situation was exposed in the Tacoma *News Tribune*, the Pierce County Council members did nothing to rescue the birds or protect others like them in the dozen large breeding facilities in the area. Scudder's is still open for business.

Lori Rutledge's Cockatoo Rescue in Stanwood, Washington, is a haven for hundreds of retired breeder parrots, including African grays, Amazons, macaws, and eight kinds of cockatoos. If Rutledge hadn't provided a home for these parrots, they might well have been killed. Even if they had produced young for decades, they are considered a liability when they can no longer do so.

Some of these aged wild-caught breeder birds brought into the United States before the 1992 Wild Bird Conservation Act may once have lived in a flock. Any that were bred in captivity would never have been allowed to. Even so, parrots are so social that they take to their brethren as soon as they are permitted to mingle. A few female cockatoos that Rutledge calls the "welcome wagon" even work together to welcome new arrivals and introduce them to the flock.

All methods for trapping parrots are violent. About 75 percent of the birds caught are injured or die in the process. One common method uses tethered lure birds, or "caller" parrots, to encourage others of that species to land and get trapped on a baited glue stick. Some captured birds chew their toes off trying to get away. This makes them less valuable, so they are used as lure birds themselves. In Argentina, where this photo was taken, it is legal to trap parrots, but only 20 percent of adult parrots can be caught by this method. Even so, in some years nearly 100 percent of the trapped birds documented were adults.

Invisible mist nets are also used world-wide to trap parrots. Mexican trappers get their nets from Indonesia, where parrot trapping is rampant. Broken wings and legs are common, and birds can strangle trying to free themselves. Here, a bird that may have been trapped for hours in pain hangs in the net until nightfall, when trappers arrive to pull the tangled bird out.

Parrot-trapping mortality rates are enormous. Three or four are lost for every one that gets sold as a pet. Parrots that don't die when they're trapped will often perish in transit to the marketplace. They can be packed in cages like this for days, traveling in an open pickup on rough roads in the hot sun without food or water until they arrive at their final destination.

This pet and feed store is about twenty minutes south of the U.S. border in Rosarito Beach, Mexico. It is owned and run by a veterinarian, yet sick birds lie on the bottoms of their cages and scores of birds are kept crammed together in small ones next to chickens, rabbits, and other animals. The birds hanging in these tiny cages were not let out until they were sold or had died. As a result of stacking like this, the feces from the upper cages fell into the water and food of the ones below.

A marker of wild-caught birds is their tendency to huddle together for safety, as these two young yellow-headed Amazons are doing. Yellow heads are coveted as pets because they are good talkers; the demand for them has driven the birds almost to extinction in the wild. Now they are banned from trade in Mexico and internationally. Despite the ban, these were openly displayed on the curb of a major thoroughfare and the owner of the store offered to tranquilize them so they could be easily smuggled into the United States.

An American tourist is shown how to smuggle a parrot by a street bird vendor in Tijuana. The vendor grabbed a lilac-crowned Amazon (a protected species, banned from sale in Mexico) from its cage, put it in the paper bag, and rolled the bag up. The seller said the bird would stay immobile and quiet in the dark of the tourist's purse, in the trunk, or under the car seat, for the hours it would take to cross the border into the United States. He sells birds to Americans this way all the time and has done so for years.

Birds are smuggled over borders in myriad ways. The backseat cover in this SUV, coming over the border from Mexico into Texas, looked suspicious to U.S. Customs and Border Patrol (CBP) officers, so they pulled the vehicle over and tore it apart.

Hidden underneath were scores of baby Amazon parrots that were being smuggled for sale in the United States.

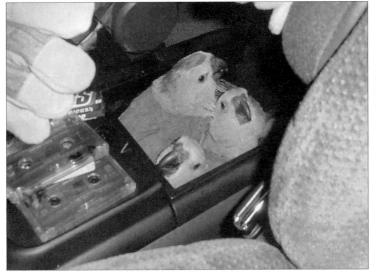

Amazons were also packed into the arm rest.

A bird was smuggled in this deodorant container.

This bird smuggler was caught with forty finches strapped to his legs. They were each rolled up in sections of toilet paper cardboard.

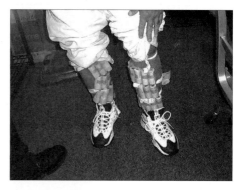

The USDA quarantine station in Otay Mesa, California, is located a few feet from the Mexican border. Confiscated parrots coming over the border in Texas, Arizona, and California are sent there for disease quarantine. This Amazon named Pirata (Pirate) by the staff was confiscated in 2003 and remained there for almost four years, though he cleared the mandatory health quarantine in forty-six days. He was allowed out only while the Isolette was cleaned once a week.

Hyacinth Valley, in Piaui, Brazil, is a protected area for hyacinth macaws, the largest of all parrots. It is supported by ecotourism and is jointly run by conservationist Charles Munn and former hyacinth trapper Lourival Machado Lima. Munn has made protected areas like this for parrots, jaguars, and other animals in a number of countries. Like the others, Hyacinth Valley is a success. The macaws' numbers have risen significantly and the local people benefit from the tourism revenue, which enables them to stop trapping animals for income.

Wild hyacinths alight on *piqui* nuts placed there to attract them. Visitors get to watch them from a blind built for that purpose. The birds would never come this close to humans otherwise. Observing them up close in the wild, we can see how important it is for parrots to be able to fly at will and live free with a flock or mate.

Carlinho, a former parrot trapper, acts as a guide to the
habitat of the rare and endangered Lear's macaws. Like most
parrot trappers, he is one of the few people who know the
circuitous route to their cliff range in the remote area of
northeastern Brazil.

The beautiful range of cliffs in Barreiras, Brazil, hours
inland from the popular coastal city of Salvador de Bahia,
is one of the few places where endangered Lear's macaws
can still be found.

Not far from
Munn's Hyacinth
Valley, deforesta-
tion to plant soy
for cow feed has
razed some of the
hyacinth macaws'
limited habitat and
piqui nut trees they
depend on to live.

The birds actually step aside to let her pass, and they make room for her at the feeding station."

One Moluccan was a self-mutilater. He suffered a serious injury his first year in the colony and could no longer fly. Rutledge hung his small hospital cage on the inside of the colony so he wouldn't be separated from the flock. Many avian veterinarians and bird behaviorists might caution against doing so because of the dangers to the sick bird. Flocking behavior has been thought to dictate banishment, or worse, for a weak parrot to protect the majority from illness and predators. But Rutledge's instincts were right: members of the flock opened the door to the hospital cage and sat inside with the handicapped bird. "They gently preened him, and it was obvious that they understood he was injured," says Rutledge. "The sick bird's visitors, both male and female, rotated all day."

After a year of rehab, including acupuncture treatments, the injured Moluccan now moves slowly and deliberately but gets around. He also stopped mutilating himself, which is a huge change. Rutledge has found that, over time, all of the mutilators have stopped feather-plucking when they live unhampered with a flock.

And all the birds have bonded as a flock even though they have never experienced this level of socialization before. Rutledge says whenever there's a loss of a bird the entire aviary is quiet. "They're such a family unit," says Rutledge. "You can tell if they're happy or not. When one dies, the others grieve. It's horrific."

Rutledge seems as connected to her birds as they are to one another. She says she doesn't care if she lives shabbily compared to her charges. She has given up most creature comforts—including her former upscale lifestyle in an affluent community where there were more people than parrots—for one where there are regular worries about keeping everything afloat.

Because she has streamlined the caretaking process with low-maintenance aviaries and emotionally self-sufficient flocks, she spends most of her time outside, enjoying the birds. She placed patio furniture settings in front of each aviary, with umbrellas so she can stay in the rain. After five years here, watching the birds is still her most treasured activity. It is like a meditation, and she sometimes stays here for hours, moving from one patio set to another. In the summer, she pulls out a hammock and naps with the birds. She'll tune the radio to soft jazz for them during the day, but still isn't sure they like it. In June and July, she will be out until 10:00 p.m., when it's still light and you can hear the frogs croaking.

Rutledge does live like a recluse: she rarely answers her phone, closes the place to visitors for the winter, and doesn't invite many up at other times. Often she won't read e-mails because so many come in with queries like, "What can you tell me about parrots?"

If inclined to answer a question like that, she could write a book. Rutledge always loved parrots. She got her first, Bosco (later renamed Sophie, since he was a she), a once wild and later rescued Goffin's cockatoo, eighteen years ago. Sophie had been kept in a small cockatiel cage, and had plucked out all her feathers. "She was stark naked, and so terrified she wouldn't let anyone touch her," says Rutledge, who worked with her patiently until even her husband could pet the bird.

After working as a buyer in the jewelry business and as an insurance broker, Rutledge started brokering parrots between breeders. She got a 10 percent commission and a referral fee on every bird she hooked up with a new owner. Over time she befriended many of the breeders, and she was one of the few people allowed inside their aviaries. "Most rescuers never get to set foot inside a breeding facility," says Rutledge. "No one but no one goes in those places but brokers or someone dropping off a bird. If it was an awful facility, I never had birds to sell them; if it was a good one, I always had them."

She found that pet birds were often given to breeding facilities by their owners, but they could never acclimate to these institutional confines, and remained terrified of the limited space and barren cage. Rutledge hated the idea of a pet locked up in a facility and started asking breeders who were offering birds for sale whether they were tame. If the answer was yes, she bought the bird herself. Soon she was her own best customer. For every bird with a sad history, she took the bird in lieu of commission. "I'd sell an Amazon and take a cockatoo in trade," she says. At the time, she was married and living in a six-bedroom home in a posh gated community in Edmonds, Washington, just north of Seattle. The birds started filling her home.

Bird breeders confided to her what they did to the birds when they were too old to produce. "They talk about Petco employees putting birds in the store freezers [to euthanize them]; where do you think they got that?" asks Rutledge. "It's the bird breeders who taught them to do that. It's disgusting, but it's real common." She felt so bad for the birds that she stopped brokering them and kept them all herself.

She says a Moluccan named Cinder is the cause of her divorce. "She would bite Dad in the butt when he went into the fridge," says Rutledge. "She broke out of her cage and let everyone else out of theirs. Then she chewed smiley faces in all the mahogany cabinets." That, and the fact that more and more birds kept coming into their home, finally generated an ultimatum from her husband: him or the birds. Rutledge says that when she got through laughing, she said, "Well, of course, it's the birds," and started looking for property.

In 1998, she parted with her husband and friends, found her land, and opened the sanctuary. As a city girl not fond of country life, it was a crossroads for her to go rural, full-time, without any financial security. One breeder Rutledge knew was ready to retire wanted her to have all her birds. So when the land was secured, the two got to work clearing it for the aviaries. "It was a rough and scary first year," she says. She operates now as a licensed nonprofit organization, primarily dependent on donations and on money she earns from making and selling bird toys.

Rutledge has broken ground in several ways with her sanctuary. Mainly, she kept her birds in flocks in large aviaries from the start, something many parrot breeders say cannot be done. As a result of the colony setup, she can easily maintain hundreds of birds without additional help. Instead of having one hundred and fifty cages and hundreds of food and water bowls to clean daily, she has twenty-two big buffet pans for the food and the same number of water bottles. The average fruit pan is filled with grapes, cantaloupe, apples, and nectarines. "They love strawberries," she says. "When I get a case of corn on the cob, the birds have corn all over their beaks." The menu varies, depending on the produce donated by local supermarkets.

Rutledge says five local rescues have closed in the last two months alone, which she blames on burnout. "There was one back East," she says. "They had two hundred birds and had to clean and service one hundred and seventy cages every day. It took several hours. I have almost two hundred birds, and it takes me just two hours to do everything." Rutledge says the fact she doesn't adopt birds out or take in pet birds as a rule (though one woman brings her bird to Rutledge's for "summer camp" every year) is a key component to her not feeling overwhelmed.

She brings out an Eleanora cockatoo that came from a breeder. "She was a big producer, but was always terrified, so the breeder gave her to me," Rutledge says. "Once she got here, she was a bottom dweller in the colony, and she plucked all her feathers out." Rutledge was concerned and went in to talk to her. "I said, 'No one will bother you in here.' She looked at me and said, 'Hi.'" The bird stepped onto Rutledge's finger and lifted her wing to get petted. She gave Rutledge a kiss. "Someone sold her to the breeder after she was a pet," says Rutledge. "She was tried with different males. She produced but she wasn't a breeder; she was being raped." The Eleanora holds on to Rutledge's finger with a death grip. She looks good now. Her feathers have all grown back "I just wish we knew her name," says Rutledge.

Rutledge believes what she has done at her sanctuary should be the standard retirement for all old breeder birds. "After their birds have given all that they can give, the breeders owe it to these parents of our pets to retire them with dignity with their own kind," she says. "They deserve to spend their final days in a place where they can fly and live in peace without the requirement of earning their keep by producing babies.

"Wouldn't it be ideal if people with land and a mild climate put up one colony dedicated to rescue birds, filled it with one species, and just let them enjoy the rest of their lives?"

The temperature dips as the sun sets behind the trees. The cockatoos don't seem to care. They are all perched, cozily huddled together, ready for sleep. The macaws swing on a hanging perch to entertain themselves as the last sunlight recedes. Some start vocalizing.

"It's the evening call from the orchestra," says Rutledge. The parrot symphony harmonizes, echoing through the trees, until dark.

Chapter Seven

A Bird in a Cage Is Worth Two in the Bush: The Illegal Trapping and Wild Harvesting of Parrots Around the Globe

Large flocks of African gray parrots live as their ancestors did in the ancient forests of the Congo. Each morning they watch the sunrise and forage greens and seeds in the open savannah. In the afternoons they play in the trees or high in the air over the jungle canopy. Their noisy banter can be heard echoing through the forest. The setting sun bathes their silvery gray bodies in golden light as thousands take to the skies for their evening roost. Bunched up along the tree branches, generations of families sleep at night, and each year they come to the same tree holes to raise their young. Throughout their lives they are always within earshot or sight of mate or flock.

But their loud calls to one another also alert humans to their location. Trappers trick flocks into nets by using a trapped comrade as a decoy. The bird is tethered to a stake driven into the ground by a string painfully sewn onto his chest or attached to his leg so he can't move. When the other birds fly over, he calls to them for aid, and many rush to him. In a single moment, these parrots, with long lives ahead of them, life-long mates, and generations of young to raise, are caught and imprisoned forever.

As their fragile bodies are grabbed and crammed a hundred at a time into a narrow crate, many suffer broken wings and bones. They might be left that way for days and even weeks until they are sold. In the unrelenting heat and crowded confinement, many will die of suffocation, hunger, or dehydration. They pine for their flock, which is now mourning their loss.

Those that survive the violence of capture will be loaded into trucks. A well-stacked pickup can hold a thousand birds. The African grays will be transported to Europe or Asia by plane or cargo ship. The birds' pleading, incessant screams can be heard through the hull, but many will be quieted en route by death or illness.

Every year thousands of grays are legally trapped in Africa to be sold abroad. More are trapped illegally, because many affluent countries around the world, whose citizens can afford to buy exotic birds and have created a demand for them, still allow wild parrots to be imported and sold as pets. More than one million wild African grays are believed to live in cages around the world, and another million are lost in the wild harvesting process that dominates legal and illegal trapping.

The term "wild harvesting" belies the violence of the endeavor, which is practiced from the Congo to Indonesia, Brazil to Mexico. Parrots are not sitting on branches, waiting to be taken, and they do not walk willingly into cages. One scientist called wild harvesting a misnomer because nothing has been planted, and we aren't harvesting a crop—it's predatory hunting.

Guyana is home to 794 species of birds and 30 kinds of parrots, small and large. Among them are 6 types of macaws—blue and yellow, scarlet, red and green, chestnut-fronted, red-bellied, and red-shouldered. Only one tenth of one percent of the country's eighty-three thousand square miles (about the size of Minnesota or Kansas) is protected wilderness. Locals typically trap parrots as a hobby for extra money, but are so thorough in their work that they have made Guyana one of the top parrot exporters, relative to its size, with 30,000 parrots shipped abroad annually.

Guyanese trappers get $8 for every Amazon parrot they capture (they retail for about $1,000 in the United States), and $25 for a scarlet or green-winged macaw ($1,500 or more retail)—small sums to some, but not in a country where $25 is considered good remuneration and the annual income averages less than $1,000. Trappers keep birds from escaping by pulling out their feathers or chopping their wings with a machete, which can cripple the birds for life. But the trapping of long-lived animals injures more than the individual trapped bird.

Gay Bradshaw, a scientist and researcher, has been studying the effects of trapping on parrot and elephant populations, two species heavily hunted by humans. She and her colleagues have found both have long memories, suffer emotionally from posttraumatic stress disorder, and might not recover from violent trauma. Says Bradshaw, " 'Wild harvesting' is not a scientific term; it's a betrayal of science. It's a political euphemism like 'ethnic cleansing.' Harvesting is the commercial killing and enslavement of parrots. We need to use the terms we use for humans for animals. Then we can see what we're really doing." In a coauthored paper presented at the 2005 conference of the American Association of Avian Veterinarians, Bradshaw wrote of parrot harvesting, "Actions that create traumatic disruptions will severely perturb the population not only from the perspective of reducing numbers but by breaking down stable structures and processes that define a social species such a psittacines. Such effects have been observed in other species such as dolphins; even when anthropogenic disturbance (i.e., boats and nets) cease, behaviours remain abnormal, reproduction rates and population increases remain depressed." Trauma and attachment theories also emphasize that the effects from systematic killing—harvesting—can transmit through the extant flock and across generations.

Bradshaw notes that an elephant's size forces us to take notice when one acts out emotionally by wreaking violence on villages and other animals. But we neither look for nor acknowledge the emotional scars parrots can carry from the trauma of having their flocks ravaged or their young taken. The damaging psychological and biobehavioral repercussions of harvesting are never factored into determinations of parrot quotas or the viability of trapping them.

The violence of harvesting methods varies. In Africa, one practice is to chase the parents from the tree hole nest and then lower fish hooks on a string to snare the chicks and pull them out. If a wing gets punctured, the bird might lose the use of it. If the hook goes into its neck or heart, it dies. Because parrot babies are free for the taking, if poachers inadvertently kill them, they just try to catch another.

Sometimes a sling is used to lasso an adult bird that won't abandon its young. Other times a wide net or metal wire is strung between trees to nab adult birds flying from their roosts in the dark or early morning. Another method is to use a sticky substance, a combination of breadfruit tree gum and coconut oil, spread on a branch next to a decoy bird. When another parrot hears the decoy's call and lands, it gets stuck. The glue is so strong, sometimes the trapped bird's feet cannot be unglued and must be cut off. In all methods the mortality rates are high. For every bird that makes it, five, ten, or even more might die in capture or transport.

While many birds (and humans) would flee in the face of danger, parrots are unusually brave and will come to the rescue of a flockmate in danger. In 1618, a European explorer traveling by boat around Brazil wrote, "The most amazing thing is that when we catch a parrot or other bird and pinch it a bit so that it shrieks, all the others that were in the neighborhood come by as if they wanted to free it, and were therefore taken. We went back to the ship with a load of feathered food."

It is still the same today, though now affluent buyers in far-off countries have local and indigenous people to catch their parrots for them. Many parrot parents will remain with their young when trespassers encroach. They cover their young with their bodies and try to fend off the intruders, but invariably they end up trapped or dead. Others will remain nearby, watching, powerless, as their young are taken and their nests are destroyed.

Parrot populations are diminishing at an alarming rate where trapping is ongoing. In Mexico, some species are down to five thousand individuals, some to one thousand. Heavy trapping there is now localized to two or three species, like the small orange-fronted parakeet, which are smuggled into the United States more and more and are diminishing rapidly. Some species are extinct in the wild in areas where they were plentiful just years before. Of twenty-two parrot species, twenty are being adversely impacted by relentless, year-round trapping. Because the birds are free for the taking, trappers go back for more to assure the income they expect.

Even those that survive, if they don't make the arduous trip across the U.S. border, have mostly terrible fates. Sold as pets in Mexico, they live chained by the foot to a wooden perch for the rest of their lives, with nothing to do all day and little to eat or drink until someone remembers to feed them. Because they are messy, and the weather permits it, the birds are often left outdoors in the hot sun all day, and are lucky if they are given any shade. A common practice of sellers is to blind the birds with a hot poker. The then docile bird is forever fearful of human touch, but needs no leg chain, cage, or wing clipping; it can't fly if it can't see. Such a bird endures chronic pain for its lifetime; the cornea of the eye is the only structure of the organ that perceives pain, and even the slightest break in a cornea results in intense pain. In Africa, a common practice performed on older wild birds, which are naturally hard to handle, is to repeatedly dunk them under water to make them submit.

But perhaps the most alarming aspect of the wild harvesting of parrots worldwide is that it is still legally sanctioned, and even encouraged. The Convention on International Trade in Endangered Species of Wild Fauna and Flora (CITES), an international agreement among 167 member countries that meet regularly to determine the fates of species around the globe, is responsible for legitimizing the violence. The convention's stated aim is "to ensure that international trade in specimens of wild animals and plants does not threaten their survival." Yet yearly the organization designates quotas on the number of parrots that can be exported from the birds' range states (the countries encompassing parrots' native habitat), knowing full well that the methods used to procure parrots for the commercial trade are producing mortality rates of three to one.

Worldwide, annual CITES quotas for wild parrots are more than 215,000. But when you factor in the number of birds killed as collateral damage, it is not unlikely that more than one million parrots a year are lost unnecessarily in the hunt. CITES's own estimates say an average of

30 to 40 percent of the African grays captured die before being exported. (The rate has been as high as 65 percent.)

In 2004, Argentina alone had a quota of more than fifty thousand parrots, the highest number of any country. Next highest is the forty thousand quota of small Senegal parrots. Beyond quotas, an unknown amount of unrecorded trade in parrots is not listed by CITES.

Cameroon accounts for 50 percent of all African gray parrot exports. In 1996, CITES suspended the country's export quota on African grays because it had shipped out twenty-three thousand birds, double its legal allowance. Poachers continue to trap and export the birds in Cameroon, using fraudulent documents to ship them. Some take advance orders from middlemen and then say to a bribed official, "I need five hundred more" of a particular species and get that number approved. Or they ship the birds using CITES permits from other countries without hindrance.

CITES reinstated Cameroon's parrot export quota in 1998, even though experts say, and CITES is aware, that each year the country is likely still exporting thousands more birds than its allowance, both legally and illegally.

As long as legal trade continues, quota issues will be problematic. Many countries fight yearly to have their quotas increased, and often the numbers are what trappers determine them to be, not what the local parrot population can withstand.

Tom De Meulenaer, the senior scientific officer for the CITES Secretariat and someone who helps establish quota numbers, said in an interview:

> Countries like Cameroon, Congo, DRC Congo (the Democratic Republic of the Congo), and other central African countries are competing against each other to export more parrots. "You send out five thousand; I send out six thousand. You send out six thousand; I send out seven thousand." So there's been this escalation of exports. There are concerns that these countries allow too many animals to be harvested annually. So what we have to do is take a look at the situation, take a look at the populations in the wild,

and then make recommendations or impose certain management regimes to these countries. That is what our convention is all about. It tries to regulate trade so that it is no longer a threat to the species in the wild. If we note levels of export that are problematic, then we can take action.

But many critics complain that CITES is more interested in enabling trade than protecting animals in the wild. "CITES is not protecting animals from the trade; it is trying to ranch wild animals so that trade can continue," says Ron Orenstein, a zoologist, lawyer, conservationist, and advocate with the International Wildlife Coalition.

CITES was formed in 1973, with twenty-one governments as signatories. At the time leopard populations were being decimated to produce fashion items such as handbags and coats. The legal trade was intermixed with the illegal, and no one could tell the difference between the two once animals had been killed and the skins made ready for export. Public outcry, especially strong in the United States, ensued because the big cats were heading toward extinction.

In response, CITES instituted three levels of export permit requirements, called appendices. Leopards went on the strictest list, Appendix I, which allows no trade in the species at all. That effectively stopped the massacre. Once all trade was forbidden, it was easy for customs to tell who was breaking the law—anyone with leopard skins or parts in their possession.

Appendices II and III allowed trade in degrees. The former is for species that might not be threatened now with extinction, but could be if trade isn't monitored; the latter is a voluntary watch list for countries to protect species where trade might endanger them over time.

"Some people think the CITES appendices are a list of what's endangered and what's not: If it's on Appendix I it is endangered and on Appendix II it's not," says Orenstein. "But an animal can be in large supply and still be on Appendix I." That, he contends, is because the listings are not about the absolute number of a species, but about the impact of trade on its population.

Now, more than three decades after CITES was formed, with more than thirty thousand species listed, some critics argue that the convention has done more damage than good by striving to keep parrots in the commercial trade rather than protecting their populations from its hazards. Some question whether the real reason CITES is concerned about the extinction of a species is the fear there won't be any left to trade.

One reason for the skepticism is that CITES considers it a failure of its system when there is commercial demand for a species, but its numbers are too low for them to be sold commercially. This reveals an underlying ideology that every species that someone wants to make money on should be available for a price, even though the repercussions of dismantling ecosystems are now well apparent.

Only reluctantly, when the situation is dire and even then often only after extensive lobbying, does CITES take a species out of circulation by putting it on Appendix I. Conservationists say that even when range states want protections for their parrot species, CITES is reluctant to grant it.

This was the case with the yellow-crested cockatoo (also called the citron-crested cockatoo). Indigenous to Indonesia, this large white parrot has a bright yellow head comb that stands plumelike when the bird is animated, and has the misfortune to resemble its cousin, the Australian triton cockatoo. In the late 1970s, the title character of the hit television series *Baretta* had a triton named Fred. The bird became a famous character on the show and public demand for Triton cockatoos skyrocketed, diminishing their numbers in the wild. But parrot dealers didn't want to lose the big money in U.S. sales so they targeted Indonesia to fill the demand with the similar-looking yellow-crested cockatoo. It is estimated that between 1981 and 1992, when research on the numbers trapped was conducted, more than ninety-six thousand yellow-crested cockatoos were exported.

Indonesia urged CITES to upgrade the birds from Appendix II to Appendix I, but the request was consistently denied, as CITES claimed that deforestation, not trade, was the primary cause of the birds' problems. Deforestation is an issue in the forest and scrub areas of the central archipelago of Indonesia, but in East Timor, where the yellow-crested cockatoos are found, overwhelming evidence shows that trade was the driving cause of the species' demise. To get the parrots out of the country, some traders "launder" them by chopping off their crests and exporting them as white cockatoos. There's no knowing how many yellow-crested cockatoos left the country that way, but the numbers overall were dramatic enough for one scientist who studied the situation to say they were "effectively eliminated" by the trade.

To stem the birds' demise, Indonesia internally legislated against trade, capture, or possession of the birds. But many make the case that, as long as CITES does not ban trade in a parrot species, any domestic legislation is crippled. Without international oversight, smugglers can channel the birds through neighboring countries and then openly sell them on the world market. In fact, as soon as Indonesia's legislation was enacted, neighboring Singapore suddenly began exporting large numbers of the cockatoos, even though they are not naturally found there.

By 2000, the World Conservation Union considered the yellow-crested cockatoo critically endangered. The organization, with ten thousand member scientists, produces the "Red List," an internationally accepted global monitor of threatened and endangered species. Recent studies show that cockatoos have disappeared from more than 80 percent of their natural range, and it is thought only twenty-five hundred to ten thousand are left in the wild. CITES finally upgraded the yellow-crested cockatoo to Appendix I at its convention in Thailand in October 2004, but many conservation organizations blame the dramatic diminishment of the birds' numbers in the wild on the long delay. Jamie Gilardi, director of the World Parrot Trust, has this to say:

Here's this country, the sole range state for this parrot species, saying to the international community, "Please help us," and CITES responded, "We don't think it will do any good, so we're not going to help." CITES consistently avoids helping species threatened by trade until the situation is very grim and the proof of the problem is absolutely overwhelming. The cockatoo proposal is a classic example. Previous proposals to protect this species have been turned down even though the species has clearly been decimated by decades of unsustainable trade. If you look at the CITES positions on these same kinds of proposals over the last several years, they consistently take a position in favor of making the lives of traders easier at the expense of the threatened species. They don't oppose this appalling trade that continues. Their track record is remarkably clear.

Parrots are not the only animals that have gone unprotected. It took CITES ten years to ban the export of ivory, even though two hundred African elephants a day were being killed for their tusks, an unsustainable number that was quickly endangering the whole population. Estimates indicate that before trade in ivory was outlawed, the illegal trade was responsible for the death of one hundred thousand or more African elephants each year. Between 1979 and 1987 alone, Africa lost half of its elephant population.

Today there is still ongoing discussion at CITES conventions about lifting the ban, under pressure from South Africa and other African countries that don't mind seeing their elephant populations killed for their tusks, and from countries such as Japan that want the ivory and will pay for it.

Though the CITES Web site states, "Not one species protected by CITES has become extinct as a result of trade since the Convention entered into force," it isn't so. The Spix's macaw went extinct in the wild because of trapping for the trade on CITES watch. And now only 100 to 125 confirmed blue-throated macaws are left in the wild of Bolivia, and many other parrot populations hover in the low double digits as a direct result of the lack of adequate protections.

Compared to r-selected species like rats, insects, and weeds that tend to be small, short-lived, reproduce often and in large numbers, and have offspring that mature quickly, parrots are k-selected species, like humans, elk, and oak trees. These species generally live in stable populations in species-historic locales, and are not well equipped to colonize new habitat areas. They operate at carrying capacity in their environments, meaning that impacts like deforestation and related food losses take a toll on population numbers because they have limited and specific dietary needs. They live long lives, are slow to mature and mate, and when they do, produce few young that require long-term care. Their young are intended to have high survival rates, and their populations are dependent on that. Given these parameters, *any* trade in parrots is detrimental to their populations because they cannot recover their numbers under continued pillaging for the pet trade.

Proof that the CITES system—allowing trade until it is incontrovertibly proven that the species is failing—isn't working for parrots is evidenced by how many have become endangered, and been placed on Appendix I. Of the known 9,700 species of birds, 340 are parrots. This means that 3.5 percent of all bird species are parrots. Of the 165 bird species listed on Appendix I, 51 are parrots. So 30 percent of all Appendix I birds are parrots, even though they make up less than 5 percent of all species of birds. Now, of the 340 species of parrots, almost a third are endangered, making parrots the most endangered group of birds on the planet.

Even from a purely statistical point of view, many parrot conservationists agree that commercial trade is devastating wild parrot numbers, and the experts at CITES know this, too. When De Meulenaer was asked about the inordinate number of parrot species listed on Appendix I, he responded, "Actually, yes, this shows clearly the failure of the convention to manage parrots properly. Otherwise we would not have to move species from Appendix II to Appendix I. And I believe it is true that many parrots are long-lived and have particular biologies which make them not really suitable for exploitation." Says Orenstein, "Small populations of parrots run right into inbreeding depression: the smaller the population, the higher its level of inbreeding, the more frequently close relatives such as siblings and first cousins meet and mate. The more inbreeding, the larger the percentage of offspring with double doses of defective genes that cause sterility and early death. If that doesn't do them in, small populations are near instant demise from flood, storm, wildlife, drought, or other natural disaster."

Aside from the biological risks it heightens, constant culling of commercial trade leaves parrot populations weak and vulnerable to natural disasters they could rebound from otherwise. Treating wildlife like widgets doesn't work; as Orenstein succinctly puts it, "Wildlife is not capable of upping its production to make up for a bad year."

The World Parrot Trust says the harvesting revenue stream gives the trappers less than 10 percent of the revenue—only a few dollars per bird—about a third to the middlemen, and the rest to the exporters at the top of the trading hierarchy. Because trappers make so little, they trap more than parrot populations can stand. This unrelenting invasion—stealing babies out of nests in breeding season and abducting the adults the rest of the year—leads to shrinking numbers, and there are fewer parrots to harvest overall. Not only is this scenario a holocaust for wild parrots, but when they are gone, the trappers will still have little money, and they will have wiped out a flagship species of their native land and an important natural resource that will never return.

Some environmental groups argue that trappers should be allowed to continue this activity because it feeds their families and keeps them from engaging in deforestation activities to make money. In fact, they say, locals will go out of their way to protect trees in order to foster parrot population growth if they are allowed to trap parrots. Gilardi of the World Parrot Trust points to the speciousness of this argument:

None of these people leave forest standing to save birds that they'll harvest in the future. That's just not done. In most cases, the birds disappear long before the forests do. Logically, if you don't own the land, why not capture the birds *and* cut down the trees? There are always more trees behind those and your neighbor will cut them down if you don't. The fact is, locals can't depend on catching parrots, because babies are limited by season, and, there are other things in the forest to catch for food. It's a fallacious argument by NGOs [non-governmental organizations] like TRAFFIC and the World Wildlife Fund that hordes of local people are living off the parrot trade. It's hogwash. I've never seen one example of that to be true. The only people making money off the trade are wealthy and driving big cars.

And there is also evidence in Mexico that trappers routinely chop down trees if they can't reach the parrots' nests. Both fronts suffer as a result of the parrot trade, and at the end of the day there is no long-term security for parrot habitat with the commercial trading of birds, and no parrot populations are increasing as a result of the trade. Almost everywhere you find trading in wild parrots, you find populations diminishing. With no good evidence that locals benefit from the trade, the issue returns to CITES not living up to its mandate. With the big money involved in the trade, it is not surprising that protecting the animals becomes secondary.

The legal commercial trade of live animals or animal parts is estimated to be fifteen billion dollars a year (including live ornamental plants and not including global fisheries or timber products). Under CITES, a species' country of origin, the people with the greatest to gain from trade, is responsible for determining the populations and proposing quotas. Many countries say they are practicing "sustainable use" but without any data to support the claim. Overall, CITES appears to be supporting a flourishing business environment over a flourishing wildlife environment.

David Morgan, CITES' chief of scientific support unit, has been quoted as saying, "We believe that wildlife trade can be beneficial to the conservation of wildlife. We have an international regime in place—CITES—which regulates this trade and it's perfectly effective in doing its job. And we don't think there's any need for more rigorous controls than those already in place other than for disease-control purposes."

Wildlife Conservation Society scientist Alan Rabinowitz, who has worked for years on tiger conservation, replied,

I know CITES well and it has failed a huge number of animals. It has probably failed all wildlife, not just the parrots. They'll say to you privately that they have failed the parrots, but have they publicized it? Have they acknowledged their mistake? Why not? Why do they still have a captive breeding and sustainability group? There are still groups there talking about exploitive hunting as sustainable hunting. They are still pushing that agenda. To me, they're worse than the hunter, because they know what they are doing is wrong and they continue doing it.

One might assume that the representatives from the various range states responsible for the welfare of the world's species would be conservationists or biologists with years of field experience and an understanding of the needs of the species whose fates they are determining. Instead, the very people with a stake in the commercial value of their commodities are the ones making the decisions. It is the proverbial fox guarding the hen house (or in this case, the parrot house).

Orenstein has attended CITES conventions for almost two decades. He describes them thus: "If you think CITES means a room full of animal-loving conservationists, you are sadly mistaken. The traders are there, and also the political flunkies who were dropped into it at the last minute. You can get laughed off the floor if you start talking about humane treatment. Some countries don't like other countries and will vote against them just because of that. There is a lot of horse trading going on."

It takes a two-thirds majority vote of members to upgrade a species to Appendix I. That determination can save a species from extinction, but it can be a crapshoot to get the votes. "There are two hundred issues covered over two weeks," says Orenstein. "The majority of delegates don't read the documentation. Some don't even know what the species under discussion are. At one CITES conference where vicuñas were being voted on, two delegates independently approached the proposing country. One asked if a vicuña was a plant, the other if it were a bird." (In case you are wondering, it's a member of the camelid family and looks similar to a llama. But you are not required to know; you are not determining its survival.)

In addition to this, some nongovernmental organizations that the public assumes are at CITES conventions on behalf of animals are actually supporting the trade. The World Wildlife Fund, one of the world's largest and most respected conservation organizations, condones wild harvesting of parrots. Deputy director of TRAFFIC (the international wildlife trade monitoring organization that is a partnership of the WWF and the IUCN, the International Union for Conservation of Nature) North America Craig Hoover said in an interview for this book, "We've highlighted the fact that there are parts of wildlife trade that are problematic. If you have to take ten birds out of the wild to get one into a pet store, that's not sustainable. But that's not saying that all wildlife trade is bad, or we're [WWF]opposed to all wildlife trade. We're concerned with conservation of the wildlife, and we do leave it to the other groups to deal with the animal welfare issues."

Since only an estimated five birds are trapped to get one into a pet store, apparently the numbers of lost parrots aren't high enough to warrant the fund's protection. This is a great loss to the birds, since the fund is arguably the most powerful international conservation organization—but by its own admission, it is doing little to stem the tide of trade where parrots are concerned. The fund's executive director for species, Sue Lieberman, elaborated on their current stand regarding parrots:

> It's true governments listen to WWF, because we're science-based. Our position in general on wild harvesting, whether it's parrots or crocodiles, is we are not in any sense opposed across the board. We're not out there promoting trade, but there are times we may support it. The question is if it can be brought to sustainable levels. I agree, probably most parrots cannot be used sustainably with market pressures. If I saw the science come across my desk that showed that no parrot trade was sustainable, clearly if a case could be made, I'd talk to TRAFFIC about reprioritizing.

But the data on parrots are pretty clear already. Gay Bradshaw, who spent ten years as a research mathematician with the U.S. Forest Service and was a fellow at the National Science Foundation's National Center for Ecological Analysis and Synthesis, concurs. "We have an automatic response," she says, "in our western-scientific paradigm: when in doubt, gather more data. Well, we don't need more data. We've already got plenty. We don't need more data to tell us that everything is going extinct. What we need is to make the difficult decisions that we avoid."

In addition to the dubious idea that locals will leave trees standing to keep parrot populations growing so they can trap them, the other major rationale for the parrot trade is based on the term Hoover and Lieberman used: sustainability. If the idea, as used in an ecological/environmental sense, is unfamiliar now, it soon will be. As natural resources dwindle, the term has risen in the lexicon of environmentalists, conservationists, ecological economists, biologists, and others, from the World Bank to the World Wildlife Fund. Sustainability is the earth's ability to replenish what we remove, in a timely fashion, so there is no cost to nature.

The idea is based on an economic model that assumes there is a surplus in nature (or one can be created) akin to interest on a bank account balance: as long as the capital remains intact, the interest can be culled without damage. With current rates of human exploitation, inevitably more of the earth's resources are being drained or damaged than nature can replace to maintain equilibrium. As a noted scientist at the World Bank said, "We are raping the earth."

Many experts believe sustainability is a myth. In a paper on the subject published in *Science* magazine, Charles Hall, an ecological economist, wrote, "It is clear that natural ecosystems seem to have some significant degree of built-in ability to adjust to natural perturbations while frequently returning to some kind of self-sustaining state, a property that is often lost when humans interfere with these systems in a significant way. We may increase the yield of products desirable to humans from that system, but we are unlikely to increase the total biotic functioning or its sustainability."

A "non-detriment finding" is a requirement for CITES to issue a trade export permit to any country wanting to export parrots or other animals. But rarely do countries perform the due diligence needed to prove their "take" will not harm the birds. The requirement is rarely enforced, and quotas are often rubber-stamped. "You always hear the argument that, 'We must make our decisions based on science,'" says Orenstein. "But it's a buzzword. In a political context that usually means favoring industry and trade. You can always find a scientist to rebuff negative findings, and governments use that against wildlife."

To see what a dramatic difference is made when a non-detriment rule is enforced, one has only to look at America's Wild Bird Conservation Act, imposed in 1992. The federal law limits the number of exotic birds listed on CITES coming into the United States, regardless of whether the country of origin allows their capture or not. The statute basically says: first prove that these captures don't damage exotic bird populations, that they can sustain this continued invasion, or don't bring us your birds.

Enactment of the law was significant: until 1992 the United States accounted for half of all imports of exotic birds, almost one million parrots a year, for more than twenty years. Now it's down to a trickle because the majority of exporting countries have not been able to meet the burden of proof. It was groundbreaking legislation. (Interestingly, when the law passed, Lieberman, of the World Wildlife Fund, was chief scientific authority with the U.S. Fish and Wildlife Service and one of the legislation's authors. She admits that in her new capacity as director of global species programs for World Wildlife Fund International, she is responsible for overseeing so many species that parrots are off her radar.)

"It was unique," says the World Parrot Trust's Gilardi of the act. "It sends a message to the rest of the world that we are no longer participating in the capture of wild caught birds."

The United States was also taking a proactive, ethical stand on the practices of the wild bird trade by putting the burden of proof on exporting countries. But the United States and Australia (which in 1960 enacted even stricter prohibitions against importing or exporting parrots) stand alone with this kind of proactive regulation. Once the act was instituted, data from the World Conservation Monitoring Centre in Cambridge, England, which tracks animal trade numbers for the United Nations and CITES, showed that birds formerly coming to the U.S. market were not diverted to other markets. Since 1992 millions of wild "harvested" birds have been spared as a result of the WBCA legislation.

Marine researchers have long tried to predict trapping numbers in ocean fisheries. There the illusion of sustainable harvesting is most evident.

As recently as fifty years ago the world's vast oceans seemed to hold an infinite supply of fish. Today an estimated 90 percent of the biggest predatory fish have been depleted. "First it was in the developed world, now it's the whole word," says ocean fisheries expert Daniel Pauly. If present trends continue, fish such as marlin and swordfish might become extinct in the near future. Once plentiful cod, a fish so common it was used worldwide for fish and chips, is threatened with extinction, as are sockeye and coho salmon and white sturgeon.

As we fish down the global food webs, fisheries of smaller and smaller fish are depleted. "Your children better like plankton, because that's all that will be left for them to eat," says Pauly. We are the number-one predator of ocean life, and we don't even live in the water.

If you're thinking this sounds impossible, given the availability of fish at your local market, that's because we are at the top of the economic food chain.

Years ago, fishing fleets set their sails by sustainability models, but the predictions had fatal flaws. "The models were mathematically correct," says fisheries scientist Cristi Cave, "but fishermen do not fish randomly, as fisheries scientists do in conducting population surveys. So the input to the equation is usually wrong. Garbage in, garbage out." Fish, like parrots, are always on the move and can travel long distances in a short time. As Cave points out, they aren't necessarily hanging around to be counted in predictable locations. And the ones that are already counted can move and be recounted in a new location. Says Cave,

> The model assumed that fish populations are easily determined and that fishing pressure will be even. Most fishes, however, are clumped together in communities. Using random sampling, their populations will often be determined too high or too low. We've learned that our best scientific techniques will not allow us to accurately project populations, or even to accurately determine a current population. Without the ability to determine

current populations, it has become impossible to draw the line between sustainable fishing and over-fishing.

Ocean experts have found that even when the line between over-fishing and sustainable fishing is accurately drawn, the concept falls apart in the face of catastrophic events such as droughts, unseasonable weather, failure of a food source, disease, or chemical spills. In those instances, fish need extra numbers to buffer the dramatic losses; without them populations sink below critical levels.

The same problems complicate sustainable harvesting models for parrots. No one really knows the actual number of parrots alive in the wild. If that fundamental piece of information is unreliable, the entire enterprise is suspect.

Marine biologists have found other unexpected repercussions of removing large predatory fish from the oceans. One might assume that with the big fish gone, the medium-sized fish would replace them in the food chain. But they don't. Instead, because no large fish are present to cull their populations, the medium fish proceed unchecked to eat all the small fish. The big fish were protecting small fish populations by keeping the medium fish at bay.

Fisheries experts say that to avoid depletion of all global fish populations, commercial fishing takes must be halved. That seems unlikely to happen, given the strong opposition from fishing interests.

There is no knowing what repercussions will result from removing parrots from their millennia-old ecosystem. "Birds are regulators of the landscape," says parrot expert Carlos Yamashita. They help maintain the equilibrium of the forest, including tree composition and distribution over generations. Losing parrots from the wild can mean the long-term loss of many plant species, altering both the structure and function of the forest.

Many parrots are pollinators, depended on by a myriad of flower species and flower-bearing trees for reproduction. Parrots also help control insects, and their nutrient-rich droppings aid other biological functions of the forests. As seed eaters, parrots help determine which seed crops dominate in a forest and how the resultant flora is distributed. Parrots take great advantage of the availability of seeds before they ripen and naturally disburse. If a tree normally would release one hundred thousand seeds, by the time parrots are done feasting, only five hundred might make it to the ground, severely limiting the reproductive chances of that species. Many trees have worked hard over millennia in what has been described by scientists as "an evolutionary arms race to keep parrots at bay. They have to develop new chemical compounds to keep birds from harvesting seeds prematurely.

Some of these flora warfare agents are drugs we have co-opted, such as nicotine, caffeine, morphine, cocaine, strychnine, and quinine. (In many cases what's poison and what's medicine depends on the dose.) But parrots are very clever, and they succeed in circumventing these defenses to obtain the seeds they want. In a published study, Gilardi found that one way parrots do this is by eating certain kinds of clay to neutralize toxins.

Aside from seeds, fruit is the other major component of the parrot diet. Parrots have a knack for knowing just where fruit is ripening and move from one ripened tree to the other, even over great distances. They ravage their fruit and litter the ground with their discards. (One avian researcher suggested having an umbrella while standing under a tree where parrots are feeding.) These delicacies would be otherwise unreachable for the ground-dwelling mammals that trail the parrot flocks, coveting their leftovers. In turn, the mammals help the germination process by dropping dung over seeds discarded by the parrots.

Though it is hard to estimate what microbes, insects, and animals suffer as a result of diminishing parrot flocks and the critical goods and services they provide in their habits, surely there is a loss to the ecosystem when parrots are taken from the wild wholesale for the pet trade. One thing is certain: nothing in nature is cosmetic. Or as Wildlife Conservation Society scientist Alan Rabinowitz says, "Each individual species has its particular ecological role in the entire web in the forest. Taking out one piece of the puzzle makes an incomplete puzzle, and that incomplete picture ensures an imbalance."

This points up a bigger problem: nature has an inestimable number of interdependencies that we have still not considered or even discovered.

Many are unlikely, unpredictable, and remarkable in ways not apparent to the naked eye. Take salmon forests, for example.

Each year, anadromous fish such as salmon return to riverheads in countries all over the world to spawn and die. Off the shores of British Columbia, hundreds of thousands of salmon trek upriver from late summer through early winter. Their most obvious beneficiaries, the bears, become well nourished and insulated for winter hibernation as they indulge in the large bounty arriving daily. The salmon are also welcomed by wolves, birds, and a host of insects and other forest and river life.

Bears, which prefer to eat only the fish's nutrient-rich brain matter, are great disbursers, and many thousands of salmon carcasses are randomly littered over the forest floor for miles in every direction. A person looking at the vast mess of headless bodies might come to the conclusion that bears have much more salmon at their disposal than they need.

Surely this would be a good example of a surplus in nature for man to legitimately exploit. In fact, if we wanted to be generous, the bears could have all the fish heads, the least appealing part of the salmon to humans, and surely we could take the rest without hurting them or anything else. But if we did, it would be another classic example of human error, born of ignorance about the role of seemingly unnecessary or random aspects of ecological systems that are not in existence for our benefit.

The seemingly useless and expendable salmon carcasses feed the entire forest, including trees, bushes, flowers, and thousands of birds that do not even eat fish. The bodies of the salmon decompose into the earth, providing nourishment to the soil in the form of nutrients critical to the forests' health. Things such as calcium, phosphorus, potassium, and nitrogen are absorbed by the roots of the trees, bushes, and other flora as well as by insects.

So pervasive is the nutrients' reach, the "salmon signature" of nitrogen can be found in a single needle at the top of a Sitka spruce tree 250 feet up in the tree canopy, in the wings of a songbird on its branch, or in the thousands of migratory birds that stop in the forest to rest and eat.

After more than a thousand years of this ecocycle in British Columbia, as evidenced in fifteen-hundred-year-old spruce, red cedar, western hemlock, and Douglas fir trees, only about 70 percent of the salmon-derived nitrogen and phosphorus is reaching the forests because of a 90 percent decline of large salmon returning to spawn. This is due to overfishing, dams, and the problems brought on by salmon farming.

Those who think they are out of this killing loop because they eat only farm-raised salmon, enabling the wild populations to thrive, should guess again. It's another manifestation of the problems of once wild animals raised in captivity: salmon hatcheries are producing fish with signs of domestication that are maladaptive in the wild. Escapees, of which there are more than a million a year, are bred to be larger than wild fish and outpredate them. They are often diseased or ridden with parasites, such as beards of sea lice, which have created problems in Europe and the United States. The parasites spread to wild fish populations in the same waters, even when the farmed fish don't escape their pens.

Furthermore, because salmon are carnivores, it takes about three pounds of wild fish to feed every pound of farmed salmon. Much of the wild fish comes from Third World oceans, such as those off the coast of Chile, where stocks are now dwindling. Affluent countries are literally taking food out of the mouths of the poor, who depend on their local fish stocks for sustenance. Studies have shown that overfishing, in this instance to feed large stocks of farm-raised salmon, also drives the poaching of more than forty species of animals for food or money to buy it. The fewer the fish, the harder the impact on land animals such as parrots.

Another good example of a scenario that could be analogous to parrot losses can be seen in the lost wolves of Yosemite. Recently it was discovered that simply returning the wolves to Yosemite (hunting had wiped them out at the turn of the twentieth century) could be positively and dramatically affecting everything from trees and grasses to beavers. It was a boldly unscientific move. Researchers guessed that the absence of wolves might have had an ongoing negative effect over all these decades, but had no way to know specifically what it was.

~ ~ ~

Countless examples of ecological interdependence between plants and animals abound, and there are infinitely more that we do not know about. No one can say with any certainty how many species of life there are on earth. Fewer than two million have been recorded (and most of those taxa haven't been tallied yet either). Conservative estimates put the actual number near three million, but some guess it could be as high as one hundred million. Why the great disparity? Only a fraction have been found and classified. One scientist interviewed for this book expressed alarm that few researchers now go into the once-booming field of taxonomy, and that those courses were no longer even offered at his university. Tragically, of the new species found, many need to be listed as endangered as soon as they are discovered, and many more will be destroyed before we will even find out about them.

To focus conservation efforts in the richest areas of biodiversity, scientists have looked to the best documented of all species: birds. In the 1980s, avian researchers with Birdlife International speculated that in remote habitat areas where unique bird populations had evolved over millions of years, they would also find an oasis of undiscovered life forms that had evolved with them. The researchers sifted through all available historical records of birds known to live in ranges of thirty thousand square miles (the size of South Carolina) or less. They produced a global bird map of limited ranges in tropical forests and mountain areas, islands, and inaccessible valleys.

They found that one-quarter of all the world's bird species, including one-third of all parrot species, one hundred and fifteen or so, were naturally found in these areas. And their hunch proved right: where they found parrots, they also found a wealth of other elusive and exotic species of insects, plants, and mammals.

But this is also likely to mean that when birds disappear because of trapping, habitat loss, and introduced predatory species (such as rats and cats), a treasure trove of unique biodiversity disappears with them. As with salmon, the decline of birds has a ripple effect down the food chain.

Where key wildlife has been depleted, a phenomenon known as "empty forests" is occurring. The trees are left standing, but all the birds and mammals are gone. Where once songbirds sang and parrots squawked, it is now silent. These forests aren't thriving; they're dying. Some scientists call them the "living dead."

When we are not taking parrots out of their trees, we are taking their trees out from under them. For the 70 percent of all bird species that live in the world's forested areas, one of the most devastating aspects of the wild harvesting of our natural world is the "desertification" of the planet as forests are unsustainably harvested across the globe, leaving parrots and other species homeless. Simply put, about a football-field-sized area of rain forest is being cut every second, equaling an area of lost forest the size of Utah or the United Kingdom every year. Recently the World Wildlife Fund sent out an appeal letter stating, "In the time it takes to read this sentence another eight acres of rainforest will have been bulldozed and burned off the face of the earth." Parrots are having an increasingly hard time finding suitable nesting sites because they are "site loyal" to their nesting trees, and many will not reproduce if their trees are gone.

Each old-growth tree provides food and shelter to a wide range of diverse birds, mammals, insects, and microbes, which affect and enhance the ecosystem of the tree and its habitat. Many of these millions of species are unknown and will never be discovered because they are lost before they are found when their trees are destroyed. Parrots are severely affected in every area of the world where they are found. At least fifty parrot species aren't hunted for the pet trade because they are unattractive and even louder than most parrots (which is hard to imagine if you've ever heard a cockatoo scream). These birds are equally imperiled because, when deforestation tears down their trees, they may die with them. "There is a common misconception that birds who lose their trees to bulldozing or fires can just move to other ones," says ornithologist Kimball Garrett. "Most share territories of the same species, and there are no vacancies. It's like saying if your house burns down, you'll just move to the one next door."

As rain forest is fragmented, it suffers from the collateral damage of "edge effect," where more light and wind enters, drying out the formerly protected inner forest and allowing opportunistic species to take hold, creating an imbalance in a cohesive ecosystem. A study done in 1994 estimated that more forest in the Amazon had been changed as the result of edge effect than the amount of land cleared.

Because of the edge effect, parrots that live in the forest interior are faced with invasive species that thrive in open spaces moving into their neighborhood, making the remaining habitat less ideal for their needs. Food shortages also abound when trees are lost en masse. Some migratory species, including some parrots, depend on forest they don't occupy full-time to be there when they need it, which can be some distance away and under different governmental rule each time they arrive. Almost half of all bird species have deteriorated in just the last five years, and 1,211 bird species (12 percent of the total) are globally threatened. Human-related factors now threaten almost all of the most imperiled bird species, and bird extinctions already far exceed the natural rate of loss.

Strides have been made to protect forests, but some are more form than content as countries designate land allotments that look good on paper but contain low biodiversity and, coincidentally, are the least desirable economically. Greenland National Park, the world's largest national park, is one example. Though it encompasses about 375,000 square miles (about 972,000 square kilometers), it contains only a small number of animal species.

Tropical birds also depend on pristine, or near-pristine, primary forest, and show low tolerance even when logging is selectively done. When a forest is clear-cut, only stumps remain. It can take more than fifty years to return to its former biological vibrancy, if it is allowed to do so, which is rare. In addition, an ancient forest can't be replaced with new growth. Habitat is not just trees; it includes all the life systems supporting them, like anadromous salmon, that have been destroyed as well.

The Forest Stewardship Council, the gold standard on sustainable wood-harvesting certification around the world, says only 5 percent of all the wood products sold in the United States are harvested sustainably. It's not a surprising statistic, since it is more work and less profitable to produce sustainably harvested wood, and the demand for exotic woods for homes in developed countries, with the United States in the lead of imports, is rampant. Americans relish the idea of having parrots' trees as their floors and kitchen cabinets. Our nomenclature distances us further from the reality of their loss, and the loss to the environment when it is coveted: first, it's timber; then lumber; then wood; and it becomes a house frame or a floor, furniture or siding. Soon we forget it was and always will be from a tree.

Few Americans realize that every time they discard a tissue or flush the toilet, they are likely disposing of pristine ancient forest. And this may be the most egregious use of virgin trees. While much of global deforestation occurs in faraway tropical climes, out of sight of the end user in affluent countries in Europe or North America, widespread deforestation is happening in our own backyard, and North Americans are directly responsible for it. "It takes ninety years to grow a box of Kleenex, but only a few seconds to throw away a tissue," said Richard Brooks, Greenpeace Canada's forests campaigner. "It's wasteful and irresponsible for Kimberly-Clark to use virgin wood fiber from ancient forests to make disposable tissue products like Kleenex when it could easily use recycled paper."

Kimberly-Clark is the world's largest manufacturer of tissue products such as Kleenex, Viva paper towels, and Scott and Cottonelle toilet paper. The company produced nearly 1.3 million tons of tissue and toilet paper products in 2003. Thirty percent came from virgin pulp from Canada's ancient boreal trees, and they continue to use more of the boreal each year. Much of it goes to the United States, which is the largest consumer of boreal-produced products. Canada's boreal forest is larger than the Brazilian Amazon and plays a more crucial role in regulating global climate, clean air, and water systems.

"Canada treats its land like a Third World country when it comes to selling off its natural resources," says Richard Thomas, a bird expert, environmentalist, and author of a study for the Special Places Provincial Planning Committee in Alberta, Canada.

Scientist Philip Fearnside is considered one of the foremost authorities on the Amazonian rain forest. For thirty-five years, since he left his position at Princeton University, he has lived in the heart of it, in the city of Manaus, which is surrounded by the rain forest on three sides and the Amazon River on the fourth. "There's money on the table for oil and coal, but there's nothing on the table to keep a forest standing," says Fearnside. "It is looked at as worthless, so there is only money for tearing it down."

Fearnside believes the only way to save the world's forests, thus staving off problems such as global warming, is for the leading developed countries of the world to put money on the table to allow forests, and the creatures in them, their natural, and self-evident, rights to exist without exploitation.

Chapter Eight

Smuggling

You never know what is going to climb or fly out of a person's luggage.
—Mike Osborn, law enforcement supervisor and wildlife inspector,
U.S. Fish and Wildlife, San Diego, California

Next to habitat destruction, illegal trade in wildlife is the greatest threat to endangered species worldwide. Smuggling abounds wherever there are coveted exotic birds and restrictions against their export. In the United States, illegal animal smuggling is second only to drug trafficking in revenue and proliferation. Worldwide, it is third after drugs and illegal arms, with revenues estimated at $10 billion a year or more. The two go hand in hand; traffickers in narcotics and humans will also smuggle animals. Clandestine routes used to smuggle slaves over a century ago are still being used today for illegal animal transport.

When you lift the curtain on black-market birds, you find barbaric practices. Parrots are routinely drugged, their tails clipped, and their beaks wrapped with packing tape before they are stuffed into PVC tubes and smuggled into the United States, Europe, Australia, or the Middle East. Some are taped into spare tires and locked in car trunks, hidden in luggage, forced into empty deodorant canisters and handbags. Small birds are put in toilet paper rolls and wrapped with tape onto people's limbs. Large birds are wrapped, taped, and lined up in the side panels of trucks or in the door panels of cars. Others are covered in blankets or stuffed into women's nylons.

Many parrots smuggled into the United States across the Mexican border are given tequila to quiet them. The combination of alcohol, heat, and lack of air in the confined spaces where they are stashed away often kills them.

Sam Jojola, a U.S. Fish and Wildlife Service special agent, has seen birds come over the Mexican border with their wings hacked off nearly to the bone. "It's incredibly painful and cripples the birds," he says. "There isn't a punishment suitable for people who do that. The Mexican mafia is ruthless, and they have no conscience."

For every crate of a hundred smuggled birds pried open at their destination, fully half are lying dead on the bottom. The rest—filthy, starving, dehydrated, and terrified—are standing on the bodies. During the terrible journey, they are forced to cannibalize one another or die from lack of food. "For every bird smuggled into the U.S. that we intercept, ten are lost during the capture and transport," says Mike Osborn, a Fish and Wildlife Service enforcement officer.

In Mexico, parrots are free for the taking from their nests in areas such as Chiapas and Vera Cruz, making them highly profitable regardless of the number of birds lost. One U.S. official said that, pound for pound, parrots are worth more than cocaine on the open market.

More than sixty million people a year travel through Los Angeles International Airport, the number-one gateway into the United States from Asia and the Pacific and the fifth busiest airport in the world. It is also the largest designated U.S. port for live animal imports, which account for 80 percent of the more than two million tons of goods imported a year. The Port of Los Angeles in San Pedro Bay is the busiest container port in the United States, and the eighth busiest in the world. Faced with the sheer volume of air traffic and cargo, it is virtually impossible for the limited number of U.S. customs officials to catch a significant number of smuggled animals. This is especially true given that their primary missions are to stop terrorists and find illicit drugs. Lately, smugglers have made finding animals even harder for them.

Fertilized parrot eggs are being smuggled out of their native countries and incubated on arrival at their destinations. They are easy to transport and hard to detect, which makes them nearly impossible to find. With eggs, smugglers avoid all the problems of transporting live animals on transcontinental flights. It is now believed egg smuggling accounts for much of the traffic in endangered species. "There are changing trends with these smuggling networks," says Jojola. "It's like a jigsaw puzzle, putting all the pieces together. Interpol doesn't even understand how it works. It can be a year before you even figure out who all the players are, before you develop an informant and get someone inside. In Australia, they're finding birds only found in captivity in the U.S., so they know there is a courier smuggling eggs from here and vice versa. Collectors are obsessive about getting birds they can't have."

Lisa Nichols, a Fish and Wildlife special agent, is on the front lines fighting the illegal animal trade. She says a big percentage of her time is spent fighting the international smuggling of parrots into California. In the last five years, just working the San Diego–Mexico border, she has been involved in dozens of arrests of commercial quantities of birds. "Wildlife trade is a fairly big business," says Nichols. "In some cases there is no difference between wildlife smugglers and drug smugglers."

From San Diego to Brownsville, Texas, lies eighteen hundred miles of unsecured border with Mexico. It was long thought a fence was not necessary, that the rocky, desolate land itself would be a natural deterrent to encroachers because it is hot, lacks shade and water, and has no roads. Pecos, Texas, alone has 420 miles of border with Mexico. With a population of 11,661 and an average income that isn't much higher, 30 percent of its residents, 75 percent of whom are Hispanic, live below the poverty level. Pecos is a town rife with illegal trafficking in parrots, people, and drugs because of its location, wide open space, and easy access from Mexico.

A similar situation exists in Redford, Texas, with a population of 142 (up 10 from the last census in 2000). Redford sits across from Mulato, Mexico, and is a town with a reputation. "Everyone smuggles, knows someone who has smuggled, or will smuggle," says Jojola, who spent time in that area busting parrot smugglers.

Redford is made up of unnamed streets, unpainted adobe homes, and a church. A gas station and a small market were its only stores until they closed. The town lies along the Rio Grande and looks out onto the desert bordered by the Chihuahua Mountains. Jojola says that when the river is low, people can almost walk across it. "It's like a puddle in a parking lot," he says. "There's plenty of room to get anything through." And when it isn't, there's a boatman who charges a fee to take people across. Sometimes he will trade a ride for contraband.

When the river is high, traffic is slow, but when it is low, some will come across from Mexico in SUVs and take ranch roads, often driving straight across ranchers' property to avoid detection. The U.S. Border Patrol has planted special sensors along the border to detect trespassers. The patrol also can launch a sensor-laden balloon that can cover large areas. But savvy smugglers will send out an alert saying, "The balloon is up," and travelers lie low until it goes down.

Jay Miller is an assistant U.S. attorney and chief of the Alpine, Texas, district office. It covers Brewster and Presidio counties, which include, among others, the border towns of Redwood and Pecos and the border city of El Paso. Alpine is eighty-three miles from the Mexican border and the county seat of Brewster, which is about the size of Connecticut. It is the largest county in Texas but has a population of just 9,226. Miller says that for the entire area, which also encompasses hundreds of miles of border, there are only forty border patrol officers, including administrative staff, with a dozen, at most, on patrol at any one time. There are two main checkpoints, and trespassers do their best to stay off their radar.

Miller goes from Alpine to Pecos to try trafficking cases, which are mostly drug-related, but he has seen his share of parrot cases as well. He now averages 350 cases a year in Alpine and Pecos, and in one year got 467 indictments. "We catch the same people two or three times, but everyone says it's their first time," says Miller.

San Ysidro in San Diego County is the busiest land border crossing in the world, and the hub of illegal wildlife (as well as narcotics and migrant smuggling) moving into the United States across the San Diego/Mexico border. I watched the port of entry from the control tower as a sea of cars and trucks moved bumper to bumper, nonstop, in twenty-four north-bound lanes from Tijuana. They stream into the United States all day long, every day of the year, fifty thousand to sixty thousand vehicles and twenty-five thousand to thirty-five thousand pedestrians a day, more on weekends and holidays.

To be allowed inside this high-security area, I needed clearance from three governmental agencies, the Department of Homeland Security, the Department of Immigration and Customs Enforcement (ICE), and the Fish and Wildlife Service. Kevin Talbert, agricultural assistant, port director for Customs and Border Protection (CBP); David Johnson, chief inspector, Anti-Terrorism Contraband Enforcement Team; and Vincent Bond, CBP press officer, are giving me a day-in-the-life look at the challenges border security officers face in trying to maintain U.S. security and catch contraband.

Inside the control tower it feels like a *Star Wars* spaceship, dark and cool, compared to the sun-baked and slow-moving parking lot outside. It is only early February, and temperatures are hitting 100 degrees Fahrenheit. I can only imagine how unbearable it will be in the middle of August. The checkpoint officers are stationed in open booths in the stew of hot sun, radiating automobile heat, and engine fumes.

Before me in the tower is an extensive control panel and monitoring system with fifteen video screens and picture windows overlooking the incoming traffic. A large staff quietly watches for suspicious vehicles, monitors the checkpoint officers, and listens for reports.

While officers are on the lookout for smugglers, smugglers are on the lookout for them. "The smugglers will watch and notice there's beefed-up security Wednesday through Sunday, so they come through on Monday evenings," says Johnson. "It's easy for them to change and hard for us to adapt."

They say it's more an art than a science for the checkpoint officers to know which vehicles to pull over. They need the ability to recognize what's normal in an occupant's response and listen for stories that trail outside the norm. Some of the signs are nervous behavior in the driver or passengers, unusual body language, or visibly elevated stress levels. But the amount of traffic makes it impossible to physically examine each person or car. If that happened, Talbert says, the border would shut down.

Talbert says some bird smugglers are so blatant they will have an empty birdcage on the backseat, always a sure tip-off. In one instance, a passenger was wearing an overcoat in summertime. Officers found nineteen parrots underneath it.

One ploy to bring birds in involved recruiting members of the Mennonite community in Mexico. They were successful for a while because they didn't fit the criminal profile. "Who would think to check Mennonites?" says Jojola.

Through the windows of the control tower, two officers can be seen walking a black Labrador retriever through the stream of cars. The dog gets a hit on a white Bronco, and the SUV is directed into the secondary inspection lane for suspect vehicles. By the time Talbert and I get there, the Lab is tugging on his leash and barking at the car's trunk. "It probably has a false bottom," says Talbert.

Recently, a "graduate" course in secret compartments was taught here for local police officers, California Highway Patrol troopers, and law enforcement officers from other states. Talbert and Johnson say among the worst tricks they find are coffin compartments built under a van. The stowaways are laid out coffin-style, stacked on top of one another like sardines, head to foot, and locked in a rectangular box. They can't move and can barely breathe. If there's a problem with the van, they can't save themselves because their arms are pinned against their sides in the narrow space. "On those cases the U.S. attorney will usually prosecute," Talbert says. "They consider those the most egregious cases."

With smuggled birds, secret compartments in cars include taillights, dashes, and quarter panels. "They'll put 'em just about anyplace," says Talbert. They have found more than twenty birds, some dead, some alive, in one taillight alone. Terrified, the birds had pecked one another bloody. "It was very sad," says Johnson. "The dead ones are the cost of doing business; the live ones are the profit," adds Vincent. Another time a car was rigged to use a small alternate fuel source and had red-crowned Amazons laid out in the gas tank.

Once the Bronco is open, the dog lunges inside, sniffing frantically along the rim. The two occupants watch from the side as they are questioned. An officer brings out an electric saw and slices open the trunk floor. Ten minutes later marijuana bricks are exposed. The Bronco is impounded. It now belongs to the U.S. government.

"Sometimes," Jojola tells me when I talk with him afterward, "smugglers get emboldened and gun it, trying to run the border. They have everything to lose by getting caught and nothing to lose by trying to get away." They don't make it through, even though it looks like a clear run. Easily accessed red-light-alarm buttons can close control arms at three points in the lane. If those don't work, the tire shredder a little farther down stops every car cold.

Our next stop is the pedestrian checkpoint inside the main terminal. A long line of resident aliens and visitors walk single file toward the X-ray machine and place all manner of packages, purses, and other carried items on the conveyer. Some have government-issued border crossing cards or permanent tourist visas. The former allows a visitor seventy-two hours in the United States, but he has to stay within twenty-five miles of the border. This is one reason a lot of the illegal transactions by short-term visitors take place in border cities.

I stand behind the X-ray machine with a direct view of the screen as officers watch the people and their contents move past. They explain the intricacies of distinguishing neutral items from contraband. "Here, you see this," the inspecting officer says. "It's dark orange; that means it's organic," which in this situation equals illegal. The inspectors are well trained to pick out the subtleties in the X-ray. "A hair-spray can should look dense," he tells me. "When it doesn't, we know it's been tampered with." Sometimes they see bird skulls or false bottoms in bags. Once a surfboard lined with marijuana came through. They caught it on the X-ray because there were bar lines where it should have been solid. Plus, the man carrying it was suspicious; he looked like a field-worker, not a surfer. One woman caught smuggling had a parrot stuffed in her nylons. The bird was jumping up and down between her legs. When her skirt started moving, they figured something was up.

Talbert says that in another instance a bird dropped out of a woman's skirt. "It was almost full grown and drugged on tequila," he says. "It was flopping around on the floor. We thought 'Okay, one bird.' Then we checked her and there were three other birds in two pockets on each leg. That's the extent some people go to." When he finishes, an officer nearby leans over and whispers in my ear, "Everybody smuggles."

In 2005 alone, CBP officers performed fifty million inspections. On a typical day they can catch illegal birds and people, and between thirty and seventy-five kilos of drugs. In one two-week period there were a thousand arrests. Only the drivers were charged, because there are more cases than the prosecutors can handle; the passengers were processed and sent back to Mexico. Just upstairs from us now, thirty people are being processed for crimes.

Based on the number of seizures, at least twenty thousand birds (including eggs) are believed to be smuggled into the United States each year. Some officials say it could be ten times that amount because no one knows what percentage of the total they are intercepting. One apprehended smuggler admitted he had moved birds into the United States between sixty and seventy times before he was caught. Based on information he provided, it is estimated he alone might have smuggled fourteen hundred parrots and other species, with a total street value of more than $280,000.

Even the number of illegal animal seizures isn't clear because each of the three main law enforcement agencies at the border—Immigration and Customs, Fish and Wildlife, and the U.S. Department of Agriculture— has a different way of classifying that information. Plus, each port is operated separately, and there is not a lot of cross-reporting of confiscated animals. It takes about two weeks to get information from Fish and Wildlife, and about two years to get the same information from the Agriculture

Department. Immigration and Customs and the Agriculture Department are now under the Homeland Security umbrella, which might enable information from both agencies to be available on a central database at some point in the future.

In 2004, at the twelfth CITES conference in Bangkok, John Webb, chief prosecutor of environmental crimes at the U.S. Department of Justice, said of international smuggling, "This is a real problem and we are not giving it sufficient attention. It is a business that reaps tremendous profits for those who want to take the risks and there is a great deal of wildlife that is being illegally traded. We are just barely putting a dent into it."

John L. Brooks, a veteran Fish and Wildlife special agent, says this is because of insufficient manpower assigned to the task. His San Diego office, which has only five officers, is responsible for catching animal traffickers for the entire border crossing there.

The least monitored of all access points are border waterways, which provide an easy way to move contraband. "Though boats are supposed to clear customs in San Diego, a lot of people blow this off because the office is not open twenty-four hours, and it takes time to pull into harbor. Most people just want to get where they're going," says one longtime Southern California sailing enthusiast. "We usually stop, it is the law, but sometimes we blow it off. It would be somewhat easy to smuggle something back like drugs or animals. We have never been boarded in twenty years of sailing, and we have cleared customs maybe seventy percent of the time." Regular U.S. Coast Guard and other law enforcement water patrols, he says, are focused on speedboats, which are more likely transportation for smugglers because they can make faster trips, not sailboats.

Pedestrian smugglers are not uncommon. Parrots are being walked into the United States from Mexico on "ratpackers," the name border agents give to the teenagers who sport knapsacks filled to capacity with illegally trapped parrots. With no education and few prospects, the youths are easily recruited by organized smuggling rings offering easy money. For just a few U.S. dollars they cross the border, betting that overburdened border officers are not likely to prosecute them. Osborn, whose area covers the San Diego border, says the people who hire these mules have it down to a science. "Smugglers tend to profile inspectors' habits," he says. "For the most part, big smugglers are not going to drive the car across themselves. Often what they'll do is have one ratpacker come in. Then five minutes later another will come. If one gets caught, they don't care, because the inspectors are paged, there's a bottleneck of enforcement personnel, and four others will get through."

Border officers from all agencies say catching animal smugglers is an insurmountable job with the minimal resources available. One solution, put forth by border enforcement personnel I interviewed from every agency, is bird-sniffing dogs. Programs with dogs trained to detect wildlife are already in existence in several countries, and others are being formed because of avian flu concerns. Brooks says a good example of a missed opportunity involved two crested hawk-eagles infected with H5N1 avian flu virus that were smuggled from Bangkok to Belgium in 2004. The birds were bound and taped in wicker tubes and stowed, with their heads exposed, in an overhead compartment on a commercial airline flight. "Everyone on board was exposed," says Brooks. The birds were to be sold for $7,500 apiece, enough financial incentive for smugglers to risk getting caught, especially when bird crime is low on the list of jail-time offenses. Had dogs sniffed that carry-on baggage at check-in, the infected birds would never have made it on the plane.

According to Brooks, who helped institute a brief canine animal detection program here, dogs can find many more times the wildlife than can an officer doing the same job: the officer can inspect between thirty and sixty packages in an hour; the dog can do thirty times that. "With spotters timing is everything," he says. "One dog equals thirty inspectors in efficiency of catching contraband animals, and when you add up salaries, uniforms, etc., it is completely cost-effective. Live animals are one hundred percent better than an inspector at catching smuggled wildlife, and still there is no program."

~~~

Mason, a yellow Labrador retriever with a sweet disposition, was a loved dog. Many who worked with him were saddened when he passed away in December 2004, and still sing his praises. Mason was the first and last dog trained in the USFWS wildlife smuggling program.

In 1995 Erin Dean, a Fish and Wildlife agent based about two hours from the border in Torrance, California, was assigned to train Mason to detect wildlife. She taught him to sniff out parrots by smelling loose feathers. Working only part time because Dean was a full-time wildlife inspector working on other cases, Mason spent his down time sitting in a cage. When Dean had time away from her primary duties, she would drive Mason to the border, where he did his job well. Management scrapped him and the program when they looked at his record and didn't think he found much, given how long he'd been at it. They hadn't taken into account that he was working intermittently, and that dogs on patrol need thirty minutes off for every ten to fifteen minutes on because they get "nose burnout." And at a location like the border, dogs are bombarded by engine fumes and a thousand other scents that overwhelm their sensitive olfactory sense.

The federal government has had plenty of precedent for dogs in this role. The Agriculture Department uses the "beagle brigade" to smell out illegal fruits and vegetables at airports. "There are plenty of dog programs all over the country," says Jojola. "Local sheriffs have dogs that sniff out dead bodies; ATF [the Bureau of Alcohol, Tobacco and Firearms] has a hundred bomb-detecting dogs; and we don't have one at the border to detect wildlife."

Field tests to see whether search and rescue dogs could be cross-trained to sniff out animal parts, Asian medicinals, and reptiles were successful. They could even sniff out parrot eggs. Mason was trained on parrots, ivory, bear gallbladder, and live reptiles.

After the pilot program ended in 2001, the agents involved tried to get an allocation for a full-time handler and team of dogs that could alternate shifts and cover the border effectively. But their petition fell on deaf ears, and the program was shut down. "They didn't run the program the way it should have been run," says Brooks.

Before the federal ban on imports of birds in 1992, illegal birds were coming through the normal channels with fake documentation. "We would see a large amount of 'laundered birds,'" says Marks, "birds that had legal paperwork from one African country but had been poached illegally from another." Marks and his colleagues would trace the paper trail to prove the birds' origin was fraudulent and then prosecute the offenders.

As long as legal trade is allowed, many conservationists argue, there will be illegal trade. When the United States shut its borders to imported birds and the quarantine stations were closed, they say the U.S.-bound traffic in laundered animals stopped by default. Before the 1992 ban, an estimated $40 million in illegal parrot trade was done yearly in Texas alone. Jamie Gilardi of the World Parrot Trust argues there is much less now. "The numbers go the opposite direction," he says. "The two segments are correlated, so reducing or ending legal causes a drop in illegal. It still continues, of course. It just becomes much harder, and prices go up."

But some experts say that when you close doors to legal trade, you do the black market a favor. Ordinary citizens will break the law to get birds illegally if they can't get them otherwise, making illegal birds more valuable in the marketplace. Nichols of the Fish and Wildlife Service agrees with them. She says the federal ban hasn't stopped the flow of illegal birds over the San Diego–Mexico border. "It's obvious that it hasn't," she says. "We used to go a month without a big load. Now it's every other day. Are we just skimming the surface? Yes."

I wanted to see how easy it was to buy an illegal parrot on the Mexican side of the border. I wondered whether they are an underground commodity or readily available on the streets to anyone who wants one. I decided to find out by heading south to the border towns that tourists frequent.

I travel with my building manager, Jacqueline, and her boyfriend, Tony, who is Mexican and has agreed to translate for me. Both are in their midthirties. Tony is from an upper-class family in Guadalajara. He has the maintenance and landscaping contract for my building complex. He and Jacqueline come down to the border towns of Tijuana, Rosarito Beach, or Ensenada about once a month. We meet at my Motel 6 in San Ysidro, and take their car. Mine will stay in the parking lot at the motel until we return.

I've arranged with the front desk to have two rooms when I come back. In one, I will shower and bag my travel clothes. The other I'll sleep in. I've left a clean set of clothes in my Jeep and Clorox spray to disinfect my shoes. I have to take huge precautions not to bring back contagious diseases to my parrot. Many avian diseases can be transmitted through the air from a bird's dander or dried feces. The particles can cling to body parts or clothes or be inhaled. Even small amounts can start an epidemic.

While waiting for Jacqueline and Tony, I have breakfast in the Denny's next to the motel. The freeway is just overhead with a sign stating, "Last Exit in the U.S." I call Jojola to get last-minute tips, since this is his neck of the woods. I tell him I'm in San Ysidro. "There's a Denny's there," he tells me. "It's where a lot of the smuggled bird deals go down." I tell him I'm in a booth there. He says he's done a lot of undercover deals here, probably in the same booth I'm sitting in now. "Smugglers like it because it's convenient, just five minutes from the border crossing," he says.

Tony and Jacqueline arrive, and we cruise over the border, passing the lines of cars in the other direction. Traffic going south is minimal, and there's no border checkpoint to enter Mexico. It seems the Mexican government is not concerned about anything illegal coming from the United States.

We take the coast route heading to Ensenada and bypass Tijuana, which we decide to hit on the return. We stop for lunch in Rosarito Beach. The wide main avenue hosts small one- and two-story businesses and residences, and an inordinate amount of bars that cater to weekend vacationers. As we drive out of town we pass what looks like a feed store with birds in cages outside. I make Tony turn around so we can see what they're selling. As we get closer, it's a horrible sight: parrots of all kinds in filthy, rusted cages with feces-filled drinking bowls and no food or a little seed scattered along the bottom, resting in feces. The birds, all without shade, sit in the blazing sun. The temperature is in the nineties.

There are cockatiels and parakeets, large parrots like scarlet macaws, and an eclectus. Some sit on the cage bottoms or hang on the bars because there are no perches. Others lie on the cage bottom because they are sick. One is flat on its stomach, trying to eat while a stream of diarrhea emanates from it. All the birds are being given black oil sunflower seeds and water. It's a poor diet, and, mixed with feces, a dangerous one.

Two lilac-crowned Amazons sit in a low, rusty cage near the curb, engulfed by the exhaust from cars and trucks on the busy thoroughfare. Lilac-crowned parrots are found in Los Mochis, Culiacán, and Mazatlán in the state of Sinaloa along the coastal area of the Gulf of California. They have low reproductive rates, are highly endangered, and are illegal to trap or sell.

Hanging off the storefront are pigeons and songbirds of all kinds. Many are illegal to trade in Mexico. They are stacked in rectangular cages, each maybe five by ten by eight inches. The birds live full-time in these tiny confined spaces. All of them, even the large parrots, are too quiet. None makes a sound, and they barely move. I've never seen so many birds so lethargic. It's not just the heat, which is intense. It's probably illness and depression.

Just inside the doorway are hundreds of birds, some rabbits, and chickens. Fighting cocks infected with exotic Newcastle disease and smuggled into the United States from Mexico are believed to have caused the outbreak in Southern California in 2002. Since then, the Agriculture Department has cautioned that chickens should be kept away from other birds. Here they are mixed in with sick parrots and songbirds.

I take photos and make notes. One of the men who works here comes out. He looks tough. Tony tells him Jacqueline and I are tourists. I ask why the birds have such dirty water. He doesn't speak English, so Tony translates. He says they get clean water in the morning. I tell Tony to tell him that if the water is in a cup on the bottom of the cage, it'll be filthy with feces in no time. Tony tells him but he just shrugs and looks me over, trying to figure out why a tourist would care and why I'm writing everything down. Another guy comes out, similar to the first. Neither strikes me as an animal lover. They seem annoyed to be out in the hot sun. That the birds are without shade and baking in the heat doesn't concern them. When I have him ask, they tell Tony the birds don't care.

Now I'm incensed. I tell Tony to tell them I want to give the birds fresh water. They don't have to help; they can just show me a spigot. Tony doesn't want to say that. He tells me they won't think I'm a tourist anymore if I press it, and I won't get information for my book, or worse. I tell him I don't care; we have to help the birds. He thinks for a moment, then smiles and tells them I'm a bird lover, that I have a parrot at home and want to give their birds some water. They tell him it's up to the owner, who is inside.

It's dark and cool in the large store. The owner is about forty-five. He's behind the counter, helping two customers fill bags of feed from some barrels. I wait for him. The place is packed with all manner of animal foods, boxes, and empty cages stacked almost to the ceiling. The two guys from outside come in and whisper something to the owner. He looks at me and then comes over. He speaks English.

"What's going on with the birds?" I ask him.

"What's wrong with them?" he responds.

I tell him. He says they're fine, that he should know; he's a veterinarian. I'm flabbergasted.

"How can you keep birds in the hot sun with filthy water and dirty cages?" I ask.

"They dirty their cages, not me," he says.

Tony touches my shoulder. I turn to look at him. He is shaking his head no; it's not safe to pursue this. I take a breath and go for information instead.

"And if I wanted to buy one? How would I get it back to the U.S.?" I ask.

"It's easy," he says. "We give the bird a shot. It'll be out for three hours. It won't make a sound, and it'll be fine when you get home."

"A shot of what?" I ask.

"A tranquilizer, ketamine," he says.

"But we could sit for more than three hours, trying to get across," I say.

"Well, then we'll give you the needle and you can inject the bird yourself," he says.

I tell him I can't give a bird an injection.

"It's easy," he says. "We'll show you."

"What about customs?" I ask.

"They won't search you, you're a tourist," he says. "And if the bird is quiet, they won't know you have it. Just keep it in your bag."

We are not twenty minutes from San Diego, and I'm already being told how to smuggle birds over the border.

"What if I get caught?" I ask.

"You won't," he assures me. "We do this all the time. Americans come back and buy more birds from us because it's so easy."

I'm not surprised. The prices are unbeatable. I can have the rare lilac-crowns for $300 the pair, the scarlet for $250, the eclectus for $125. I seriously consider buying them all and fantasize smuggling them over the border, driving them straight to a real veterinarian, and then finding them homes. I can't imagine leaving them in this squalor. Then I imagine the looks on the faces of the border officers when I'm pulled over. Tony beckons me out of my reverie. He says I've caused enough suspicion. The owner and his workers are not thrilled with the questions, and he worries we've overstayed our welcome.

We depart, but I am haunted by what we have just seen.

The coastal ride to Ensenada is spectacular. We are on a two-lane winding road with the ocean just on our right and lush, volcano-formed mountains to our left. The sky is blue, the clouds and vista are beautiful, and I am sitting in the back of the car, morose. I can't get the image of the birds out of my mind. It could be worse, I think to myself as we head south. They could have been blinded.

A man I know witnessed such a thing. Like many Southern California residents, he has spent time vacationing in Mexico because it is close, cheap, and exotic. A few days before I left for the border, he told me about the birds he saw blinded. "You know what they do to them? They put a pin in a fire and when it's red hot they put it right in the bird's eye, then they do the other one. They say this way you don't have to clip their wings and they stay tame." They stay tame, and live in perpetual darkness. A blind bird is a dead bird in the wild, so they resign themselves to being dead.

I have arranged for us to have dinner with a PROFEPA agent, Oswaldo Santillán—the Mexican counterpart to Nichols, Brooks, and Jojola—once in Ensenada. PROFEPA stands for Procuraduría Federal de Protección al Ambiente, the Federal Ministry for Environmental Protection, which is the equivalent of the U.S. Fish and Wildlife Service, Fish and Game, and the Environmental Protection Agency combined.

We reach Ensenada about 7:00 p.m. We meet Santillán and his wife, Alejandra Lazo de la Vega, a local veterinarian, at a fashionable restaurant downtown about an hour later. Everyone enjoys dinner, but Santillán and I eat very little because all we can do is talk about parrots. Tony bears with the constant interruptions to translate things my incompetent Spanish and Santillán's reasonable English don't compute.

Santillán is a biologist and an expert on birds. He and his wife are nursing six confiscated baby parrots at their home now. The closest government rehab center that would take them is a dozen hours away by car, too far to move them. The zoos don't have the personnel to hand-feed them, and there's no other alternative. "The law is blind to them," Santillán says. "Legally they are not my problem. I'm allowed to kill them if they're not protected species. It's hard for me because I respond to the birds."

It is not unusual for him confiscate fifty-five babies at a time from individual trappers during breeding season, he says. His wife wants to start a wildlife rehab in Ensenada. It would be the only one in several counties. She wants a location near the water where seabirds can stay close to home while they recover and the parrots can have a view. But money is hard to come by for projects like that here, and she hasn't had much success raising funds for it.

Santillán has worked in field law enforcement for PROFEPA for thirteen years. He worries with every regime change that the new person assigned to run the organization will curtail his budget and the scope of his work. Once the birds are laundered, he says, it becomes very hard to follow their trail. In one case, the smugglers deposited a large number of illegal birds in a zoo and then got permits to move zoo birds, which on paper are the most legitimate. When PROFEPA busted the people that arranged it, they found more than a thousand parrots in their possession. "Laundered birds is big business," Santillán says. "Parrots bring the highest prices. They get more birds than we know. There is money under the table, and with big money it is easier to corrupt officials, Mexican and American. It's an open secret."

Mexicans can get a permit to trap songbirds in certain zones. The government gives out an allotment of bands with the permit, but Santillán says the people trapping illegal numbers of those birds don't use the bands until an inspector comes to count their catch. And he says many people use old-fashioned, rudimentary traps that kill the birds. "They die needlessly," he says.

Smugglers are fined only if they are caught with nonendangered species. For endangered birds, they get prison terms. Santillán says the laws are getting tougher here, and now more birds are illegal to possess. If someone is caught trapping in a federal environmentally protected natural zone, there is no bail, and the prison terms are doubled. "A few years ago I caught a smuggler but couldn't put him in jail," Santillán says. "Now, if someone's caught with a protected animal, they get years. Some say, 'Why? I'm not selling drugs' when they get charged with six years in prison."

Santillán says he has made a lot of enemies among smugglers. "A lot of guys and their families hate me because I catch them," he says. "I tell them, 'It's my job. Your job is your job.'" He's received many death threats, but says he's not worried about them because they have come only "by pen, not by gun so far."

I tell him about the store we stopped at in Rosarito, which is part of his patrol. He.says he knows the place and has busted it before. The owner is often reported as a dealer. He says he'll do another inspection this week. I suggest he go undercover, but he says he's not allowed to because in Mexico undercover work is illegal. He can be reported if he doesn't announce that he is an inspector when he arrives.

When I tell him the owner offered to tranquilize a parrot for me, he's surprised that they would entice a tourist to commit a federal offense like smuggling. I told him the owner offered without hesitation, and he admits he normally wouldn't hear this side of the equation, the tourist side. Americans on vacation don't know about PROFEPA, let alone report incidents to them, especially if they're not fluent in Spanish. Santillán isn't as versed in smuggling as in the internal trade, also illegal, within Mexico, which is equally hard to stop because it is culturally embedded to have birds as pets. "All Mexicans have birds as mascots so the house isn't stagnant," he says. "Some people have changed their minds in that they don't want to see birds in jail. But the new generation, if they have the money, will buy a bird. And if a type of parrot is seen with a famous actor, then everyone wants it. It becomes fashionable."

He thinks that perhaps when Mexico develops a captive breeding program, the smuggling will stop. I tell him what is happening with captive birds in the United States, and he shakes his head in dismay. "One of the biggest problems is poverty," he says. "It's not the smuggler or the middleman that's the problem, it's the end buyer. If there were no one buying, there would be no market and no one selling. Then the birds could remain in their trees. The U.S. is a magnet for pesos and dollars. The business is to sell to the best buyer, and the best buyer is the gringo."

Santillán's findings were later confirmed in an exhaustive 120-page report on parrot smuggling by Juan Carlos Cantú Guzmán, director of programs for Defenders of Wildlife, Mexico Bureau, and María Elena Sánchez Saldaña, president of Teyeliz, A.C., in Mexico. Both are nongovernmental conservation organizations (NGO). The report, titled *The Illegal Parrot Trade in Mexico: A Comprehensive Assessment,* was published in 2007. It was the first to uncover the inner workings of the parrot trade in detail and with statistics. It revealed a staggering number of parrots trapped overall, between 65,000 and 78,500, each year by an estimated 2,500 trappers. On average these were professional trappers that had been capturing birds for almost two decades, and many for five, having been taught as children by their fathers and grandfathers, who were also career parrot trappers. With these findings, and through the continued concerted efforts by NGOs to lobby legislators, in April 2008 Mexico's senate unanimously passed a bill to ban the capture and export of wild parrots. The bill, which as of this writing awaits ratification by the country's president, would put an end to the legacy of generations of killing and capturing millions of parrots there.

Mexico has twenty-two species of parrot, of which six are endemic. Eleven are in danger of extinction; five are listed as threatened; and four are under special protection because their populations are so low. All are being impacted by consumer demand domestically and internationally. The report showed mortality rates higher than previously realized, averaging about three birds lost for every one that survived to reach the end buyer, resulting in 50,000 to 60,000 dead parrots per year. Given that statistic, the border confiscation in the summer of 2007 of 600 baby parrots would mean that those 600 baby birds were taken from 2,400 birds—1,200 pairs—a huge number, given that many birds don't breed in a given year, and that the survival of long-lived species with a few time-intensive offspring is dependent on those offspring surviving (versus the ratio of offspring survival in animals that have many). Six hundred baby birds may well have represented a generation of that species.

Baby birds were taken during breeding season; out of season, adults are captured. Trappers use mist nets, made of meshed filament like fishing line, that are impossible for the birds to see and equally difficult for them to get out of. The type of mist nets used by Mexican trappers are imported from Indonesia, where they are used for the same purpose by trappers there.

Trappers sell to a "hoarder" (*acopiador*), many of whom are women, who stockpiles birds from several trappers until there are enough for a load to a city or market where the birds are sold. According to the report, "Hoarders can be very unscrupulous and uncaring for their hoard of parrots. For them it is all about profit from volume sales, so they will accept a high percentage of mortality as long as enough survive to make a profit." One hoarder in the southern state of Chiapas, where some Amazon species and smaller white-crowned parrots come from, runs an operation with child trappers capturing nestlings for her. The hoarder then gives the birds to transporters, who give them to salesmen at their destination points. It's no wonder the mortality rates are so high, given the circuitous route to a consumer.

In Mexico, because trapping was legal, there are long-established trapping unions, which operate more like organized crime syndicates than labor unions. A handful of people control the membership. These unions, the report said, control the majority of the illegal bird trade in the country and distribution internationally, to the United States and elsewhere. They also run some of the street markets where birds are sold, such as the Sonora market in Mexico City. Their trappers give birds to hoarders, and the standard process occurs after that, but the birds' destinations are determined by the union leaders.

For smuggled birds, it's a long journey from their native habitat to the U.S. border. It's a thirty-two-hour ride from Guadalajara, with no stops, and fifty hours from Chiapas.

PROFEPA estimates that it catches just 2 percent of the birds, which reflects the level of law enforcement in place: if there were more personnel, there would be more caught, which USFWS agents agree is the same situation stateside. The report estimated the percentage of birds being smuggled into the United States to be between 4 percent and 15 percent of the total trapped, which would be between 2,600 and 11,000. This estimate is based on USFWS seizure data, however; since USFWS has no idea what percentage they're catching, other than that it's tiny compared to the number getting through, and since there isn't a unified reporting system between enforcement divisions, the total number is hard to determine. In terms of numbers of birds coming into the United States, the total may well have been exponentially higher than the report suggests.

Jojola is cautiously optimistic about the effect Mexico's pending bird-trapping ban will have on parrots smuggled into the United States. "There will still be smuggling," he says, "there will always be smuggling, because there are poor people in Mexico that still need the money and are willing to do what it takes to get it, and there are people here that still want the birds. Everyone has to remain vigilant even if there is legislation in place, because if you don't have authorities out there enforcing them, what good are the laws?"

When we get to Tijuana, it is Sunday, and the narrow streets are congested with people. It is already late afternoon, but the temperature is not cooling down; the packed cars and concrete keep it sweltering.

Tony knows the city well, but not where parrots can be found. He stops the car and asks some vendors. They direct us to the backstreets. We come to several people lined up, selling puppies. A few deal them off the backs of trucks or supermarket shopping carts. There are a few ten-year-old kids on the sidewalk holding puppies in their arms and in bicycle baskets. All the puppies are very young, too young to be away from their dams. The puppies are lethargic, like the birds in Rosarito. They are eerily silent and barely moving. Tony queries them, "¿Dónde están vendiendo loros?"—"Where can we buy parrots?" They point and say we must go to another neighborhood, one block east of Avenue Madero. We drive there, then park and walk. The streets are dirty and dug up. It's an industrial area on the periphery of downtown, with some retail stores mixed in. There are machinery shops and metal works across from a drugstore. On Second Street, across from the Mercado de Artesanas, there is a pet store. We wander inside.

I'm nervous at first, but it's nowhere near as bad as the one in Rosarito. The animals are all indoors and out of the sun. I'm starting to feel good about this place when I see items on display that rivet my attention: tiny razor-sharp scythes lined up in a velvet box. Next to them are miniature leather boxing gloves. They're not for tiny hands; they're to sheath the scythes. These, and more in the glass cases in front of me, are the accoutrements of cockfighting. The blades attach to the back of the roosters' legs so they can fatally hack at their opponents. When President Bush signed H.R. 137, the Animal Fighting Prohibition Enforcement Act of 2007, all of this paraphernalia became illegal in the United States, subject to up to three years' imprisonment for bringing it into the country or transporting it from state to state. I pick up a small, expensive-looking glossy magazine on the counter. It's a cockfighting quarterly. Inside are photos of proud owners with their winning roosters. There is a feature on their farms. The photos show the roosters restrained on short chains, spaced apart from one another in neat rows, with small chicken houses behind them. That is the extent of their life, and when they fight it is their death. All I can think looking at these things is that it's a strange hobby, to breed violence for money.

In the rest of the store are some doves and a few chickens (no roosters), but very few parrots. Whether it's puppies or parrots, Mexicans don't like to buy their pets in retail stores. They prefer to buy them on the street at a discount. The average customer doesn't care how they got there.

We emerge from the pet store to see parrots for sale diagonally across from us on Avenue Negrete. A man and his teenage son stand in front of some large piles of dugout rocks with several cages. The main street is a busy thoroughfare, and he is trying to sell the birds to passersby.

On close inspection, it is another dismal sight. There are seven rickety cages, each maybe a foot square, stacked and attached to one another as they were at the pet store in Rosarito. They are all rusty and filthy. The top one holds a lilac-crowned Amazon that can barely turn around in the cramped space. He is trying to dig some seed out of the meager offerings in the dirty food bowl.

The others hold a pair of canaries, a pair of cardinals and parakeets, and conures. They all have just a few seeds, lying in dirty dishes. The birds can't help but defecate in them with so little room to move, and their water is undrinkable. A badly clipped baby lilac-crowned Amazon stands atop the cages to attract buyers.

The seller is jovial, proud of his wares and happy to see some gringo action come his way, especially since it's late in the afternoon and he is eager to sell some birds before he goes home.

Jacqueline and I query him about the parrots and how we would manage to get one across the border. Tony translates. The seller says the lilac-crowned Amazons are $175 apiece, and very good birds. While he talks, his son retrieves a small brown paper grocery bag. The seller says, "Look, you can just put the bird in here," and grabs the Amazon on top of the cage, shoving it headfirst into the bag. He lays it flat on the bottom and rolls up the bag. It looks like a parrot cigar. Jacqueline and I are stunned but try not to show it.

"It won't move in the dark, and it will be very quiet," he says.

"But what about air?" I ask. "How will the bird breathe?"

He says it's no problem. The bird can stay in there as long as we like, or we can take it out once we're across the border. I tell him I'm not convinced. He says he can put the bird out with a tranquilizer, but it's not necessary; it's fine in the bag, and safer for the bird. We can just put it in our handbag. We won't be checked because we are American women.

He says he has many longtime American customers. They come back and buy birds from him because he is so close to the border, just twenty minutes away.

I quickly take a photo of Jacqueline holding the bird in the bag. The seller urges us to buy it and reduces the price by $25. I tell him it's a nice bird, but I am really looking for a double yellow-headed Amazon. Double yellow-heads are on CITES's Appendix I, which means no trade in them is allowed worldwide. There are stiff penalties for selling Appendix I birds. But there is also a huge market for yellow-heads, which, as their name suggests, have a taxicab-yellow crown on their otherwise green body, and are coveted because they are considered great talkers and sell for double the amount of some other Amazons. Mexican sellers will routinely dye the heads of other Amazons yellow and palm them off as yellow-headed Amazons to make more money.

The baby lilac-crowned shakes itself out when it is returned to the top of the cage. There is no food or water available for it. I ask the seller to give the bird some water, but he says it doesn't need it, and will be given food when they get home that night. The bird has been out all day with nothing to eat or drink.

The seller, whose name is José, says he might have a yellow-head for me if I'm really interested. I tell him I am. He looks around to make sure there are no police around, then walks over to the trunk of an old Chevy parked a few feet away and pulls out a cage with a double yellow-headed Amazon inside. The bird has been kept in the hot trunk all day, out of sight of law enforcement officers who could arrest José.

He wants $350 for the bird. It looks sickly, but I figure it's probably dehydrated from being in the trunk all day. The seller lets me take a photo of him with the bird, but then rushes to put it back in the trunk when I tell him I'm not comfortable taking a chance crossing the border.

He tries to convince me otherwise. When I don't budge, he hands me his business card. It's four-color, glossy, with a photo of a scarlet macaw and a cardinal, and says across the top that he is a member of a union that breeds, captures, transports, and buys birds that sing and are ornamental. It also states his full name, José Nieto Tapia; his home phone number; and a slogan boasting, "You can trust us!" He says that when I'm ready, I should call him, and he will get whatever I want and be waiting with it for me here. I ask, would he meet me on the U.S. side? He says he's happy to, but the price will be higher.

As we approach the border, Tony points out some prostitutes standing along the side. "It's a slow ride back to the U.S.," he says. "For $20 they provide entertainment to drivers while they're waiting in line." The prostitutes stand among the endless line of vendors, some housed in small open stores perched two steps up from the closest lane of traffic, selling everything from furniture to glass baubles. Our car is swarmed by them until we are twenty cars from the border. I look to see whether anyone is selling birds, but they don't dare this close to U.S. law enforcement.

For the ninety minutes we are in bumper-to-bumper traffic, Tony and I argue. He says there are long-standing traditions in Mexico, and pulling parrots out of trees is one of them. It's bad that some are endangered, but he thinks people should be allowed to sell them overall. "That guy on the street," he says, "was just trying to feed his family." I respond, "He shouldn't feed his family by keeping endangered and fragile creatures in deplorable conditions."

This segues into a heated discussion about cockfighting. "It's part of our culture," he tells me. "How can you judge it if it's part of our culture?"

I tell him that around the world there are human rights violations against women and children that are culturally embedded. Just because countries have long-standing traditions doesn't make them all good. He counters that the roosters will fight anyway. "They do it naturally, on their own," he says.

I tell him the roosters aren't the issue; the people who bring them together and then stand around to watch them kill each other and cheer them on are. "Plus," I say, "roosters don't fight with sharp knives attached to their feet." I'm surprised Tony doesn't respond. I look over and see from his expression that my point is actually sinking in. He would have ended this conversation long ago if he wasn't captive in his own car. As it is, he heard more than he intended, and now his self-delusions are giving way to the deeper, innate awareness that blood sports are inappropriate and unjustifiable pastimes. I figure I'm the only animal welfare person and the first woman to have won an argument with him in a long while. But more important, after all the terrible acts to parrots we've witnessed in Rosarito and Tijuana (which will keep me awake at night for the next week), his realization restores my spirit and confirms my belief that long-held cultural traditions can be toppled in an instant when people are educated to the suffering animals endure at human hands.

To follow the chain of succession for the smuggled birds, I get permission from the Department of Agriculture to visit its avian quarantine station in Otay Mesa, California. All birds caught illegally entering the country across the western half of the United States are brought there.

I'm going to spend the night in the area. Mark Gabele, the quarantine enforcement inspector, has told me there's not much in the way of hotels (or anything else for that matter) nearby, so I keep an eye out for a motel before I get there. I see a couple that look nice, but when I get close they turn out to be mortuaries, so I opt not to check their availability.

Though it is just about seven miles from San Ysidro, the town of Otay Mesa feels like the middle of nowhere. It is surrounded on three sides by desert as far as the eye can see, and by Mexico on the fourth. Visible from the main road is a large cluster of state and county correctional facilities that make up the Otay Mesa prison area. I didn't know then that I was heading to a prison myself. It was an irony that would occur to me later as I drove away.

About a half mile of empty road past an Exxon gas station is a three-block-long central area with some fast-food restaurants, a few housing developments, a single Best Western hotel, and several manufacturing businesses in corporate parks. Another block in any direction, and it's back out on open land. The largest structure in the area is the Richard J. Donovan State Correctional Facility, which I pass on my way into town.

The large government complex housing the quarantine facility is at the end of one of the corporate parks. The building itself is just seventy-five feet behind the triple rows of barbed-wire fencing cutting off Mexico from the United States. It is quiet on this side, bustling and congested with truck and car traffic on the other. Like San Ysidro, Otay Mesa also borders Tijuana.

Gabele and I talk in his office before he takes me on a tour of the facility. He started working for the Department of Agriculture in 1977, when millions of birds were coming into the United States each year. Back then he worked at Los Angeles International, conducting plane inspections on cargo shipments of birds and assisting the Agriculture Department's chief veterinarian with the government's imported bird program. "Then the death rates were just disgusting," Gabele says. "Fifty percent were dead on arrival."

He took this job in 1980 and since then has seen it all, from smuggled birds to spoiled ones. One pet rainbow lorikeet, quarantined on its return to the United States, wouldn't touch the lory food Gabele offered. When he called the bird's owner, she told him it was on a diet of McDonald's French fries and Coca-Cola. The bird hadn't eaten in days, so Gabele went to McDonald's and got him some food. "Some of those birds are our toughest cases to deal with," he says. "Many are used to eating at the dinner table with their owners and have some very strange diets."

Pet bird owners pay a $9.25-a-day fee, plus the $44 in lab fees for their birds thirty-day required stay upon entering the country. The Fish and Wildlife Service covers the costs of the quarantine for any smuggled birds. The quarantine's "bread and butter," as Gabele calls it, are the many small commercial shipments and pet birds that generate a steady stream of income to meet the facility's operating expenses.

Before 1980, there were a hundred government facilities like this, and many more that were privately owned with Agriculture Department permits. But none housed smuggled birds, which for many years were routinely destroyed. "It was a terrible waste of wildlife," says Gabele. Pressure from the public halted the killing, and in 1980 quarantines were established for confiscated birds to make sure they were healthy before being released.

Today, there are imports of captive-bred species from other countries, and the businesses that bring them in are required to have their own quarantines, strictly overseen by the Agriculture Department (an inspector opens them in the morning and secures them at night with a lock and official seals), but there are nowhere near as many quarantines, or birds entering the country, as there were before the 1992 ban took effect.

The Otay Mesa facility is one of only three government-operated quarantine stations left in the country; the others are in New York and Miami. Otay Mesa gets all the birds criminally seized or abandoned by their owners, pet birds entering the country, and legitimate shipments of small commercial loads of birds for zoos (and similar situations) from as far east as Chicago and as far north as Washington State.

Gabele says they average three hundred to six hundred birds a year, with a steady stream of smuggled birds coming in all the time. Often they are in very bad shape. "They are extricated from hubcaps, gas tanks, and undergarments," says Gabele. "They have had poor sanitation and poor ventilation during travel. They can be droopy from alcohol, which is toxic to them, or bound and wrapped. Some arrive dead or near dead. Sometimes you wonder, 'How many seconds do they have left?'"

Often baby birds arrive looking as if they are well fed with a full crop, but in fact they are starving. Many have been fed masa, a cornmeal mix they can't digest and that hardens in their crop so they can't eat anything else. If the birds don't die of starvation, the masa will soon grow bacteria and kill them. To remove it, Gabele and his staff add warm liquid to the crop and massage it with oil until it loosens.

Though most of his time is spent caring for birds, Gabele says his primary job is keeping contagious diseases out of the United States. There is no treatment for viruses such as exotic Newcastle disease, so the infected birds have to be euthanized. When I'm ready to start the tour, Gabele hands me a towel, coveralls, and plastic covers for my shoes. I have to "shower in and shower out" of the quarantine area, as do all employees, every day and every time they leave and return for lunch. No diseases come in or go out of this place. When birds arrive, they do so in bio-secure containers.

Gabele instructs me to wash my hair and to clean my eyes, nose, and mouth thoroughly to avoid any avian disease particles smuggling their way in on my clothes or in open orifices. It happened to Gabele in 1982. He was home sick with what he thought was a terrible case of the flu when he got a call from the hospital to say the smuggler that brought the birds in was dying of psittacosis, not pneumonia, as originally diagnosed. Gabele and the wildlife inspector that confiscated the birds were both infected with this highly contagious avian disease, which affects the respiratory system in humans as well as birds. They were all treated with antibiotics, but only Gabele and the inspector were cured, because they had been diagnosed early enough. Gabele said it lingered in his lungs for a long time afterward.

Once out of the shower and wearing protective glasses, I'm ready for the tour. There are seven large isolation rooms measuring eight by nine feet, with eight-foot ceilings, where large groups of birds are kept. Every time a room is cleaned, staff members take showers and put on new coveralls and clean protective gear (gloves and goggles) before going to the next room. Biological protocol is strict. "There's a big reason for it," says Gabele. "Viruses jump pretty easy from one thing to another."

The facility takes in everything from ostriches to hummingbirds. Gabele has had to rig string-width perches for hummingbirds and ones as wide as telephone poles for visiting African crowned eagles. When a group of woodpeckers arrived, he bought cork for them to peck at. The current residents of the seven large rooms are about sixty show pigeons, some with feathered feet. They are a proud group, and Gabele thinks their owners pampered the birds before they were seized. They all tested negative for disease, but Gabele doesn't know what their future holds.

He and Bertha Peña, the technician who has worked with him since 1984, have seen their share of parrots over the years, many of which have been dyed. "Red-lored Amazons will go for $80 to $200," he says, "but yellow-headed will sell for $400 to $700." Peña says they have had half-moon conures with dyed yellow heads that sellers pass off as baby yellow-headed Amazons. They have even seen military macaws dyed yellow and sold to unsavvy tourists as yellow-heads. "Their friends tell them to look for a yellow-headed parrot, so they buy whatever has that," says Gabele.

Beyond the seven large rooms is another isolation room containing seventy-three Plexiglas boxes measuring twenty-four inches square. They look like miniature gas chambers with a single perch in each. The birds kept here have zero contact with the outside. Air, food, and anything else is pumped in through a connecting hose. Without openings, the boxes are soundproof as well. Built in 1979, they are old and fragile. Gabele says it takes two hours to clean one. On this day about half are filled with parrots.

While pet birds stay thirty days because they are considered low-risk, smuggled birds are required to have a forty-five-day quarantine to be sure they are not manifesting signs of any disease. During that time, the birds are given blood tests and swabbed twice. When both results come back negative and their time in quarantine is over, they are eligible for release, but few actually are. Most parrots remain isolated in the Plexiglas boxes indefinitely. Gabele says six months is average.

Part of the reason is that they are held as evidence to prosecute smugglers, and it takes time to get to court. But Sam Jojola of the Fish and Wildlife Service says the agency started using video footage of confiscated animals in court, rather than live birds, a decade ago. "It's not in the government's interest to keep them there," he says, because of each bird's daily costs, which become astronomical over months-long and sometimes years-long stays. And it's not in the birds' interest to stay here either. "These are small Plexiglas units that are biologically controlled and contained," says Gabele. "They are not like a regular open birdcage where birds can communicate with each other and socialize with humans." In an isolation unit, a bird is alone in a silent box.

When the government no longer needs the birds, they are auctioned off to the highest bidder. This makes the birds thrice victimized: first by the people who stole them from their trees; then by the smugglers who drugged them, hid them, and put them through other terrible ordeals; and lastly by the U.S. government, their would-be protectors, who cleaned them up, kept them sensory-deprived in isolation for months, and then cashed in on them just as the smugglers had planned to do in the first place.

But it doesn't end there. More than one Fish and Wildlife agent told me they know smugglers, many who got only a slap on the wrist or a fine when caught, come to the Agriculture Department auctions to buy back their confiscated birds at wholesale prices. Then they pick up where they left off before they got busted. Only this time the government has done them a favor. Now the parrots are well fed, in good feather, and come with an Agriculture Department health stamp. Best of all, they are no longer contraband, so the smuggler can sell them without any worry about being arrested again.

But not all birds can be sold. Parrots that are on the CITES' Appendix I list cannot, and the facility long ago stopped selling macaws because their numbers in the wild are questionable, even though all the species aren't protected by CITES strictest regulations. If a bird fits into either of those categories, it remains in isolation.

One yellow-headed Amazon, who the quarantine team lovingly named Pirata (Pirate) because he has only one eye, has been held in isolation in the same Plexiglas box for three and a half years. Gabele says the missing eye is an old injury and that Pirata is by no means a wild bird because he is very tame with them. Pirata's quarantine number is AB-44-NG. The AB stands for abandoned; the NG, for Nogales. He was a pet abandoned by his owner after she was caught trying to cross the border with him. Gabele says it's a shame, because he would have worked with the woman to get the bird back if she'd tried, but she never did. Now Pirata has fallen through the cracks of the Fish and Wildlife Service's bureaucracy and sits languishing here. Staff members give him new toys every once in a while when they clean his cage, and he gets to see them in person, so to speak—though sometimes they are covered head to toe in protective glasses, gloves, orange suits, and plastic shoe covers.

Once, a pair of nestlings was confiscated so young they hadn't even grown down feathers yet, and the staff couldn't tell what kind of birds they were. The pair, called "the Twins," were given the names Seth and Ethan. They turned out to be double yellow-headed Amazons. Tragically, they have been in quarantine so long they've literally grown up in their box without outside contact, the feel of fresh air, or ever seeing the sun. The Twins look at me curiously as I photograph them through the Plexiglas. I'm sure to them it's one more strange occurrence in the strange reality they live in. They look healthy enough, but they exist in a dimension outside of any reality their DNA would prepare them to know.

Gabele tells me about the other smuggled birds. There are three lilac-crowned Amazons in one Isolette. Terrified, they run and huddle in a corner as we approach. "That's how you know they were wild caught," he says. From other biologically secure Isolation modules we are peered at by a military macaw, a spectacled Amazon, two lilac-crowned parrots that came in with their heads dyed yellow, and a red-lored Amazon.

After I've showered, back in civilian clothes and driving through the desert again, a huge sadness comes over me. Waking up in an isolation unit day after day seems one of the saddest things I can imagine for those birds. That feeling remains with me until I attend the auction a few weeks later.

It's 9:30 on a Saturday morning, and already ninety degrees. There is no shade, so I am standing in the hot sun across from the quarantine building with about sixty other people who are here to bid on the birds I saw during my visit. The birds, including the pigeons, some colorful Australian rosellas, parakeets, and others, are in stacked cages lined up under an awning on a truck-loading platform. I greet Gabele, but it's hard to hear through the cacophony of talking and squawking. This is the first time some of the parrots have felt fresh air in more than a year.

The Agriculture Department started holding the public auctions more than twenty years ago, and it has been doing so regularly since. Before the federal import ban they were often scheduled on the forty-sixth day of a group quarantine, or as soon as there were enough birds cleared to hold one. Generally, the birds were moved out as soon as their time was up. Now, because of CITES and the long delays in releasing birds kept as evidence, they average about two or three a year.

Gabele places ads in local newspapers around the state, including the *Los Angeles Times,* to announce the sales. They are held as public auctions, and no questions are asked of the people who attend or bid. The Agriculture Department feels no responsibility to ensure the lives of the birds it has nursed back to health remain improved after they leave here. "I don't like it," Gabele tells me as he finishes setting up, "because I know we get people that don't know anything about birds, but there's not much we can do about it. We get bird dealers, too, people who are buying these birds and they make money [reselling them]. But that's okay. I mean, they do the same thing with cars that are seized by U.S. Customs."

Gabele says they've contemplated instituting an adoption program, but even if they check people out, there are no guarantees. "They may love that bird for a few days, but that's it. They turn it over to their kids, and the kids play with it for a few days and that's it. Then these animals are forgotten about."

I want to know the demographics of this group, so I walk around interviewing people. Most are friendly, but many won't talk when they hear I'm a reporter. Of those who do, a lot are breeders who have come for specific species. They say there is a lot of inbreeding in private aviculture because wild parrots are no longer available. They are happy this auction exists, because it's the only place they can legally obtain new bloodlines, and some have come long distances, more than five hundred miles, to get them. Others say the price is what brings them. The birds can be had for a fraction of what they would cost retail, and they will be reselling them quickly. "I ranch every kind of animal," one breeder says. "I've bought twenty-five birds here over the last four years."

I've spoken to only a small number of people when the auction begins. Gabele is the cashier, and his colleague John Grise is the auctioneer. Gabele gives me a seat next to him on the loading dock. He has a checklist and notes the prices as they go. There are eighty birds to be sold.

Gabele says he's willing to let the pigeons go for fifty cents apiece just to get them homes. "They're orphans," he says with a twinge of sadness. Before the auction, I connected him with some members of local pigeon clubs. A few are here to bid on the birds and distribute any they don't keep to other members. They were motivated by the interesting variety of pigeons and the fact that Gabele would have been required to euthanize the ones he didn't sell.

Grise begins with some Amazons, and the auction gets off to a good start. The red-lored goes for $260, the rest of the Amazons between $200 and $350. They would retail in a pet store for about $900. When the Amazons are done, a few half-moon conures are sold. The birds range from $20 to $80. These birds would sell for several hundred dollars retail.

Halfway through, Gabele introduces me to the crowd and gives me the microphone to take a quick poll. I ask for a show of hands: How many are breeders bidding for breeding stock? How many are buying pets? How many are reselling? I count fifteen breeders and the same buying pets. The rest of the group, more than half, doesn't respond.

The pigeons are up last. Many go for $6 each. The ones that don't, Gabele gives to the pigeon club group, since no one else wants them. Gabele says the auction did okay. It brought in $9,492.82. "Any revenue is better than no revenue," he says.

There are few options for birds not sold at auction. A few times over the last few years Brooks and other Fish and Wildlife agents organized a program to repatriate smuggled birds to Mexico after they finished their quarantine stay. Santillan was the Mexican contact and helped expedite the arrangements for the birds to be returned to the wild. He wishes the United States would return all of Mexico's confiscated birds, and was shocked to hear they were regularly being auctioned off by the Agriculture Department. "Three to four times we did it," says Santillán, "but we can't say to the U.S., 'Where are the other birds?' The saddest part is these birds are going to live condemned in a cage."

There is talk of another repatriation, but for unexplained reasons, the Fish and Wildlife Service has not instituted this as a normal practice. Meanwhile, Pirata remains in isolation, and the Agriculture Department quarantine station is planning another auction later this year.

Chapter Nine

The Invisible Man

Once illegal parrots are in the United States, locating them and building a case against their perpetrators that will hold up in court is all the more difficult. Those investigations are the domain of U.S. Fish and Wildlife Service Special Enforcement agents like Sam Jojola.

For twenty-five years Jojola has dedicated his life to apprehending criminals in the animal trade. He is one of an elite group of law enforcement agents specially trained to infiltrate smuggling rings and organize sting operations.

Jojola is five feet nine, with hair just beginning to go gray. His jovial, unassuming disposition doesn't betray his fifty-three years or that he's in undercover law enforcement. The fact that you'd never know what he does to look at him is one reason he's been able to infiltrate parrot smuggling rings. And it's why he works, the invisible man in the midst of illegal animal traders, on long-term, undercover sting operations so successfully.

Over the years Jojola has confiscated animals and animal parts including narwal, elephant tusks, and live spitting cobras. "You have to make sure there's nothing loose on the floor," he says, citing a house search that produced forty illegal animals (hots), including highly toxic snakes such as black and green mambas, a deadly taipan, massive Gaboon vipers, highly toxic Mohave green rattlesnakes, rare jumping vipers, king cobras, and other reptiles. "Those who deal in hots always have something out. It's part of their persona." In that instance he discovered a sleeping four-foot-long caiman when he looked under a spare bed.

Most of Jojola's busts have involved reptiles, since the sheer number smuggled is astronomical, but his primary passion is parrot crimes because, he says, "It's the most heinous of all wildlife smuggling."

On one bust, six endangered black palm cockatoos, worth upward of $160,000, had been smuggled thousands of miles in a circuitous route from Australia to Indonesia and then to a safe house in Mexico City. From there they were going to be sold around the United States. Through his undercover work, Jojola intercepted the birds after they came over the Mexican border into San Diego. But it was too late. They had been overly drugged on the tranquilizer ketamine to subdue them so they would go undetected by Customs and Border Protection. Once across the border, the rare birds went into convulsions and died in front of Jojola. More than twenty years later, he still can't get the image out of his mind.

Jojola's deep appreciation for animals and his outrage at those who steal them from the wild for profit traces to his upbringing in the Pueblo Indian culture.

Jojola's father was born in 1906, before New Mexico became a state. He was beaten on the reservation for speaking his own language and ostracized when he left the reservation for a better life. But he was determined to maintain his Indian roots and pass them on to his son. "I became interested in wildlife because of the stories he would tell me about animals in his beliefs," Jojola says of his father. "I was taught that every animal has an important place in the natural world."

Hunting was a religious event that required Zuni fetishes, four days of fasting, and having your face painted anew each day of the hunt. One couldn't just take an animal's life without ceremony.

"We took a medicine man on sacred mule deer hunts," Jojola recalled. "They would greet the morning sunrise and sprinkle corn pollen to each of the six directions in the world. A prayer would be said for all of mankind and the entire world each morning of the hunt. Then there were prayers asking permission to take a mule deer that morning. It was a very special time and place of sacred ceremonies that reminded me of the beauty of nature and how humanity should learn to respect our environment."

During one sunrise in northern New Mexico, among swirling red clouds and magnificent jagged peaks covered in Ponderosa pines, Jojola's father shed tears while chanting a native prayer. Then he said to his son, "You're in the natural world. You feel a bond with nature and it'll always be with you, a part of your life." Decades later, Jojola took his own son to the same spot. "I told my son, when I die I want to be buried right here," he says.

By the time Jojola was ten, he had started studying birds in his backyard. He began keeping notes on the weather, the kinds of animals he saw, and where. He memorized their calls. He had parrots as pets, both early on and though college. His early experiences with nature and his time in the army, which included recruiting informants, helped make undercover work on parrot crime his forte when he became a Fish and Wildlife field agent in 1983.

The law enforcement arm of FWS includes everything from conducting inspections at airports and seaports to preventing contraband wildlife and animal parts from coming into the United States and enforcing U.S. wildlife laws, regulations, and treaties, such as the Lacey and Endangered Species acts. Agents are also required to guard against illegal commercial exploitation of protected species in the United States, and safeguard the animals' habitats.

Theirs is a never-ending job, and agents say they don't make a dent. Among other factors, this is due to the lack of animal-sniffing dogs and, equally important in terms of covering the volume of animals coming into the United States, the lack of inspectors at major ports. When Jojola started in 1983, there were eight undercover field agents in the Special Ops branch. By 1995, and with the advent of computers that made illegal animal smuggling easier for perpetrators and harder for the agents, there were just five agents left for the entire country. Then on February 1, 2008, when the number of Special Ops agents was down to three, the unit was disbanded, even though there's more crime than ever before, and senior agents are in other districts to fill those posts. "*National Geographic* made our agents famous in the 1980s," says Jojola; "then we lost all visibility in the 1990s, and now the public doesn't know what we do. That problem is compounded by the fact that we're a law enforcement entity under the umbrella of a non-law-enforcement organization, the Department of the Interior, that doesn't understand our needs. We should be under the Department of Justice, like the FBI. We need to be FBI Wildlife agents."

Over the decades, Jojola has become expert at living dangerously. He has infiltrated smugglers' networks by pretending he is one of them, uncovering their contacts and export channels and collecting enough evidence to arrest them.

He has turned "intel" into an art. ("You can't catch them if you don't know their inner workings," he says.) He finds out everything he can about a suspect in advance. His one-page criminal "profile sheets" (an idea he copped from the Charles Bronson movie *The Mechanic*) document the person's daily and personal habits, known associates, hobbies, likes, dislikes, even food choices. He uses the information both to befriend his targets and understand how they think. "It's surreal, knowing everything about someone before you meet them in person," he says. "It is like a live chess game, with real people as the pieces."

The chess analogy is fitting for the tactics employed by both sides in the smuggling game. Jojola has noticed more than once that there are only a few degrees of separation between him and the people he stalks. "We're alike in some ways: we're after them the way they're after the animals. They hunt the animals, and we hunt them."

To protect himself, Jojola lived like an invisible man throughout the 1990s. He used the same tactics as the 9/11 hijackers and the suspects he investigated: shady identities, assumed names, fake addresses, and false IDs. He still maintains some of those tactics because he has gone in and out of cover repeatedly since he was last on a major sting operation. For example, he hasn't received a single piece of mail at his home address in fifteen years. All his mail goes to fake addresses that read like street addresses, but actually are at a Mailboxes center. These addresses go on his income tax forms (the Internal Revenue Service doesn't get his real home address either) and his driver's license. And he changes them regularly. He doesn't vote or apply for something as seemingly innocuous as a grocery card. "As soon as you use a supermarket discount card, it goes into a database, and voter records can be traced," he says. No phone is listed in his name, and he keeps two undercover cell phones just for calling "bad guys."

Jojola might be the one person in the United States who has never gotten a telemarketing call, because his real name and contact information don't show up on any search engines, and nothing comes up for him on an identity search. He knows because he searches for himself regularly on Autotrack, one of the largest databases used by private investigators, detectives, and the government.

His thoroughness at hiding his identity has been tested more than once. One suspect, whose clique Jojola was trying to infiltrate, didn't trust him because he hadn't been able to find anything out about him. He asked Jojola for a business card, and the agent took out his wallet. The guy grabbed it and started rifling through it, looking for evidence Jojola was a cop. "Hey, you got a badge," he said to Jojola, half joking. Finding nothing but the dummy identity on all the credit and ID cards, he quizzed Jojola, who verified everything on the cards. "You become the new identity," he says. "You even know the [fake] Social Security number by heart. The only time they find out my real name is at the indictment."

Another time, Jojola was the passenger in a smuggler's car crossing the Mexican border into the United States. An inspector pulled them over, and the driver was terrified. "He says to me, 'Oh, no. We're going to get strip searched,' because he had a long record. But they didn't run him; they ran me and came up with nothing. Not even that I was an agent. They let us go. He couldn't believe it. And neither could I. I was hoping we'd get busted. He was bringing animals over in the trunk."

For four and a half years, until 2000, Jojola worked as part of a Special Ops unit in Sparks, Nevada, on two operations known as Chameleon and Botany. His alias, Nelson DeLuca, was a shady animal dealer with a wholesale parrot and reptile business called Silver State Exotics. The front enabled him to buy illegal exotic animals, while setting up their sellers. It was a full-time job, even when he wasn't working. "I didn't go into a government building for four years," he says of the extreme precautions necessary to avoid blowing his cover.

One night a primary suspect in Los Angeles called, saying he was in the neighborhood, and asked to crash at Jojola's place. Jojola still thinks it was a test to catch him off guard. Jojola was with his wife and children at their home in Reno, far from prying eyes. To avoid suspicion, he immediately said yes, but told the suspect his father suffered from Alzheimer's and might get up in middle of night and get in bed with the man. The suspect declined the invitation, but had he said yes, Jojola was prepared. The real estate agent who rented Silver State's office space knew Jojola was a government agent—he had had to tell him because neither the business nor Nelson DeLuca had any credit history. Jojola knew he could count on him for keys to an empty furnished rental on short notice.

Aside from the locals allowed into their confidence out of necessity, Jojola and his partner, another Fish and Wildlife agent, ran Silver State as they would a legitimate business. To avoid suspicion that it was anything else, they took credit cards ("When you run MasterCard and Visa, people think you're a bona fide business," says Jojola) and paid rent, utility bills, and even taxes. Their federal tax ID was a special one issued by the District of Columbia office of the Internal Revenue Service. It flagged the business as what it really was, but the county considered Jojola and his partner to be running a real business, and expected them to file with the state. For four years the agents had two full-time jobs: operating what amounted to a large pet store, with hundreds of animals to feed and cages to clean daily, and running an intensive undercover investigation.

To give the operation credibility on the street, Jojola got distributorships from manufacturers of exotic animal accessories, such as bird cages and parrot toys, and set about selling them to pet stores in places like Reno, Tahoe, and Carson City, Nevada. If smugglers called, Jojola could refer them to the other stores he had supplied, where he had good references.

Silver State was based in a small warehouse in a corporate park. A special room, always maintained in the reptile comfort zone of eighty-five degrees Fahrenheit, housed high-end exotics like black-headed pythons that retailed for four thousand to seven thousand dollars (the higher price for females). In the rest, aside from office areas and the business's catalog items, were seventy parrots, many rare or endangered species confiscated in previous busts.

The other business front of Operation Chameleon, called Pac Rim, was set up to infiltrate the international networks of wildlife smugglers trafficking in reptiles from Malaysia, Africa, and Indonesia into the United States. Jojola sold the animals Pac Rim bought through Silver State, further proving the front to be a genuine wholesaler with good contacts. He picked up hundreds of protected chameleons, Komodo dragons, snakes, and on one occasion a two-foot-long Gila monster smuggled from Madagascar in a Federal Express box.

Smugglers insured their shipments in creative ways. A crate of endangered tortoises, living treasure to collectors, was topped with a layer of water monitors, nasty lizards with sharp teeth that smugglers knew wildlife inspectors wouldn't want to mess with.

Pac Rim was run by Jojola's mentor, a veteran agent and reptile expert. The agent taught his protégé how to force-feed the emaciated but still dangerous Gila by gripping the back of its neck and pushing "fuzzies," young live mice just getting their fur, down its throat with forceps.

Because of their sheer numbers in the wild, there are more reptiles than parrots being illegally traded. But Jojola has always felt his calling was to save parrots in the pet trade. "Parrots are the very top of what is being impacted most severely," he says. "Reptiles are right behind them, and plants behind them. If you have to pick one species most prone to widespread decimation over a short period of time, it is parrots."

Because he was fluent in Spanish and had amassed expertise in the Mexican parrot trade, "Nelson DeLuca's" primary focus became CITES Appendix 1 birds coming over the border. It was an area Jojola would monitor for the rest of his career, regardless of where he was in the United States.

For Silver State Exotics, Jojola attended parrot trade shows in California and Florida, where he handed out business cards and infiltrated dealer networks with talk about the rare birds he could get or queries about black-market parrots he wanted. Sometimes Silver State took a booth to attract "dirty" sellers with their displays of hard-to-find birds that would show any collector or illegal smuggler that these guys were connected.

Unlike the other vendors, Jojola did his best *not* to make sales of anything, even a birdcage, because each required a mountain of paper-work—the standard retail business recordkeeping, plus more for the Wildlife Service's stringent internal accounting. "You couldn't be off ten cents," he says of his agency requirements. "It would be sent back if it was off a penny."

Soon his name got out, and smugglers began contacting him. "They're very cagey," Jojola says. "They want to know who you sell to, how long you've been in the business." They asked whether there was "paper"—a street term that alludes to the lack of documentation on illegal animals—on some of his wildlife. He was offered reptiles like bearded dragons (their name comes from their ability to puff out their throats) that Jojola describes as "hotter than two-dollar pistols."

Ultra-wealthy collectors fall into the category Jojola calls the "untouchables." They have extensive collections and an insatiable appetite for collecting the rarest parrots. They move with impunity, combing the global black market for parrots and offering exorbitant sums for the rarest, most endangered species. "It's a trade of greed," Jojola says. "Some are willing to buy a pair of Lear's macaws for $75,000 to $100,000 a pair, and in cash. They are the epitome of the wildlife criminal world involved in the deep underground black market. Those are the ones we all like to catch, the ones with bucks deluxe who have private jets. It takes a special kind of criminal mind to continue doing illegal work and not get caught. It doesn't mean they can never be caught, but we would have to spend an extraordinary amount of time, effort, and manpower over years to penetrate these people. That's why I say they're untouchables."

Even when Jojola tracks average smugglers, it takes months and even years of undercover work to make inroads into their networks or estab-lish a case that can be successfully prosecuted. Unlike Drug Enforcement

Administration agents, who can arrest suspects as soon as they're apprehended with illegal substances, the burden of proof with animal crimes
is on wildlife agents to show, even in the most obvious situations, that
the animals in question are illegal and the perpetrator had the intent to
sell them. "Three hundred and fifty dollars is a minimum buy for a felony charge," says Jojola. "If you can't prove it's commercial, it's a misde-
meanor. And it's entrapment if only the government buys from him. Even
if you can prove multiple buys, they say they're only a collector."

Even when there is proof the person smuggled birds, Jojola still must
prove the birds in the suspect's possession are the ones that were smuggled. To do so he subpoenas phone records, bank records, and wire trans-
fers. In a day's work he might also do a "trash run," going through the
suspect's garbage on the street or in an alley, for evidence of illegal transactions. Jojola got a call from another smuggler who said, "My luggage
came in and it's sick." That, along with the other evidence amassed, was
enough to get the man arrested.

To get the stiffest penalties, Jojola tries to apprehend perpetrators
committing more than one felony. As soon as endangered animals cross
state lines, the offense becomes a felony under the Lacey Act. Jojola will
"bootstrap" that with the Endangered Species or Interstate Commerce
acts. Informants are another key tool. They not only provide information
on deals that are about to go down, but also give insight into the personalities of the crooks involved. In the bird world, it is not unusual for informants to be colleagues of dealers who might not be criminals themselves.
"The reptile people don't dime each other out," says Jojola, "and they're
[often] dealing with collectors. The parrot people do, because it's more
competitive. Bird people want others to get nailed."

Jojola says working with informants is a dying art. A lot of it is intui-
tive, such as knowing who can be used. You have to be able to speak the
language of the bird smugglers. And there's a huge time investment in
grooming the person, to bring them to your side. "We'd use an informant to check on an informant—run an informant on another informant.
If somebody's playing you, you won't know, otherwise," says Jojola. On

one occasion he was buying eight black palm cockatoos for $27,000 in a Target parking lot. Before meeting the seller, Jojola "ran him"—pulled his phone records—to try to detect who the dealer was getting the birds from. Waiting for the dealer to arrive, Jojola watched with a four-hundred-millimeter lens from a beat-up truck. "They sent a guy I knew on another case," he recalled. "That's why intel is so crucial. You think you're going in to meet one person, and it's another who knows you."

Hunting smugglers is always dangerous, but exposure while working undercover can mean an agent's death. Federal agents used to have an upper hand because of their access to databases, criminal records, and other information that put them ahead of those they were watching. Now the Internet and nongovernmental information technology is eliminating that advantage. Well-funded criminals who suspect someone can conduct background checks that rival those of the federal agents pursuing them. "You're at risk every time you do a transaction with a bad guy," says Jojola. "When you're alone with them, anything can happen." And the longer Jojola works undercover, the harder it becomes to keep his real identity secret. "These groups are all hip to hidden mikes, tape recordings, covert operations, and undercover businesses," he says. "They watch *CSI*. They know about body wires and pinhole cameras. You have to be a lot more careful and a lot more creative than when I came on twenty-five years ago." When socializing or at a party while working undercover, Jojola says he's allergic to cocaine or marijuana to avoid doing drugs, but it's still a fine line between being believed and being found out.

One dealer sneaked up behind Jojola in a parking lot, accused him of being a Fed, and frisked him for a wire by running his hand over the agent's chest. The only reason he didn't find it was because of Jojola's intuition that something was wrong. The dealer had been particularly paranoid so, as a precaution, Jojola put extra tape on his chest and wore a thicker shirt to mask the mic. "He was a lunatic kind of guy. A felon. There's no telling what he would have done. I had no backup or anything."

Even after years of investigating and building a tight case, agents see some defendants plead out and get short sentences, house arrest, or even probation. Some cases never get to court. Jojola says agents never get the sentences they want or that the dealers deserve. "We're competing with the FBI, IRS, and DEA to even get our cases tried. It's a big-time sales pitch to convince prosecutors why these crimes are as important as alien smuggling, drugs, or even a tax case. And judges don't understand parrot smuggling and that the implications are disease and environmental issues."

Jojola says that in all instances agents prefer to make arrests rather than have the accused turn themselves in with a lawyer. "We like to make arrests on a Friday so they spend the weekend in jail," he says. "That may be the only time they spend in jail. When you put the hooks on them, you want them to remember that moment as you read them their rights. That they know they did something really bad. They may beat the rap, but they're not going to beat the ride."

When Jojola was young, his father blessed him by sweeping him from head to toe with the outermost feathers of a golden eagle, mimicking the movement of the bird in flight. "I recall my dad telling me, 'You are a part of nature and that nature will be a part of your future,'" says Jojola. His father's words were prophetic, given his career path and that, as a tribal member, he is one of the few agents who can infiltrate the Native American trade in illegal eagle feathers.

There is a resurgence of Native Americans returning to their cultural roots. Many are getting involved in powwows, where the community comes together to socialize and celebrate customs such as traditional tribal dancing. Those dancing on the "powwow circuit" need eagle feathers to make the dance regalia, which are composed primarily of feathers and intricate beadwork on the "roach," or headdress, and bustle. Many powwows have dance competitions that boast large cash prizes, $10,000 to $15,000, for first place. "The bustle needs fresh eagle feathers constantly to keep a regalia fresh," says Jojola. "If it's worn before, it can't be entered again. If you're a powwow dancer, your phone rings off the hook, everyone offers you feathers. Powwows are a good thing, but there is a dark side to them."

The Eagle Protection Act prohibits killing of eagles, but there is a long waiting list for feathers from the Wildlife Service's National Eagle Repository in Denver, Colorado, which was set up to supply them to Native Americans for religious purposes. Orders are placed for specific eagle parts. "The normal requisition is two to three tail feathers and a couple of wings," says Jojola. Most of those waitlisted seek the coveted "black-and-whites" of immature golden eagles. These are in limited supply because the government gets feathers only from eagles found dead, from electrocution or being caught in wind turbines, which kill an enormous number of birds. When called, wildlife agents pick up the carcasses and send them to Colorado.

Because of the competition for best regalia, the long wait to get feathers, and the financial incentives to obtain them, a black market permeates Native American communities in Canada and across the United States. Jojola busted one operation run by a Native American who was shooting eagles off power lines and freezing the birds. Jojola found scores of dead eagle carcasses in the man's basement. "He was popping golden eagles with a scope rifle. So much damage was done to eagle populations by one or two people, it's incalculable. Money corrupts beliefs and customs. Nothing is sacred in the wildlife trade."

Jojola says some dancers place orders in advance, paying $500 to $1,250 for a dozen golden eagle tail feathers, the most sought after of the black-and-whites because they lie flat. Dead eagles often are found minus their tail feathers, talons, or even their heads—the markings of a killing for regalia or other Native American uses, Jojola says. The Wildlife Service has reports of birds found that way all over the country.

He understands the need for feathers in Native American traditions better than anyone, but sees a pivotal difference in the rampant killing of the birds taking place now. "I don't have a problem if it's for a bona fide religious ritual," Jojola says. "The Hopi Indians have historically trapped live eagles, and they are still allowed to do so today. The problem I have is killing and selling for profit."

On June 28, 2007, after four decades of intensive conservation work, the Wildlife Service announced that the bald eagle was being dropped from the federal list of Endangered and Threatened Wildlife and Plants. "The eagle feather trade is out of control, and nobody wants to talk about it," says Jojola. "They downlisted the bald eagle because they think any trade is limited to a few people. They'd be shocked to know how active it is."

In 1963, America was watching its national symbol head toward extinction. Bald eagle populations were declining so severely that a mere four hundred nesting pairs remained in the lower forty-eight states. Forty years of conservation have increased the number to ten thousand nesting pairs today. Calling the improved populations "a true success story," the U.S. government requested that the bald eagle be moved to CITES Appendix II. This made the trafficking of eagle parts into the United States from Canada a minor offense, in comparison to the penalties for being caught under the previous Appendix 1 listing. "There are a lot more eagles in Canada than the U.S.," says Jojola. "At the Gathering of Nations, Natives come from all over the U.S. and Canada. They'll come down with a trunk load of eagle feathers to sell here. There's an incredible black market."

Ten thousand nesting pairs is not a huge number when compared to the hundreds of millions of common birds like starlings and pigeons. Even a declining native species like the bobwhite quail has a population of 5.5 million, though that's down from 31 million in 1967. "There were three to five billion passenger pigeons; now there isn't one," Jojola says. "There's no safety in numbers. The bald eagles should always be afforded the highest protection as a symbol of our country."

In the twenty-five years since Jojola joined the Wildlife Service, the number of special agents has decreased to 199 from 260, while wildlife crime has seen a global explosion in sales and revenue. He estimates black market revenues have gone from hundreds of millions in the 1980s to billions today. The staggering profits—animals are free for the catching in the wild, and trappers get pennies compared to the distributors—have attracted international organized crime syndicates, such as the Russian mafia, which is also involved in other animal-related activities like illegal caviar smuggling.

The Internet has exponentially fed the growth in the wildlife trade. Like an unrestricted virtual shopping mall for natural resources, it has enabled thousands of illegal transactions from one side of the world to the other, numbers that were not dreamed of twenty-five years ago. "The Internet has opened an entire new segment of illegal wildlife traffic larger than anybody ever imagined, but nobody even has a clue how large," says Jojola.

Global shipping services can be a smuggler's best friends. They don't screen packages, but do provide online tracking and automatic delivery confirmation. The more animals arrive safely, the more dealers use the services. As Jojola says, "The reptile arrives fine, and that's the problem."

In one DHL package arriving from Singapore, the customs form declared the contents as "toys." Inside were new packages of Power Rangers. But a Customs and Border Patrol inspector at the Brisbane, California, mail facility knew something else was inside when the box went through an X-ray scanner and he saw movement.

Inside were fifty-one threatened Indian star tortoises smuggled out of India and headed for a dealer stateside for sale across the United States. Wildlife agents marked the tortoises' carapaces with black light and repacked them. Jojola donned a DHL carrier uniform and delivered the package to thirty-one-year-old Wai Jo Gin, who went by the name Bobby Gin, at his business in Diamond Bar, California. "That's how you prove smuggling," says Jojola.

But it's rare to catch animals smuggled this way without an animal-sniffing dog, and if the smugglers are hiding parrot eggs, it's almost impossible. "We have six wildlife inspectors at the FedEx location in Memphis to check thousands of packages a day," Jojola says. "Smugglers are raping the world's wildlife resources, and we're standing by watching. We are languishing in bureaucracy." Jojola says the number of special agents in the Wildlife Service needs to be doubled to four hundred or even five hundred to win wildlife wars and successfully cover the seventeen major air- and seaports. "Without deterrents in place, like a canine program for birds, both at U.S. border checkpoints and FedEx, Airborne, and other expedited mail carrier hubs, and a change in the USDA/USFWS protocol for smuggled wildlife, we in the U.S. are enabling, and inadvertently adding, to the victimization of these birds," he says.

The lack of detection encourages the trade. That combined with a demand for inexpensive parrots in large numbers is fueling the influx of captured parrots into the United States from Mexico. Aside from American tourists trying to sneak pets over the border in their handbags or luggage, the majority of the incoming parrot traffic is generated by the demand for the birds in burgeoning Hispanic communities.

Some immigrants from Mexico and Central America are realizing a new level of affluence after being in the United States for a generation or more. Many spent their first years struggling financially while they learned English and worked to bring in family members left behind in their homeland. Now they are living the American dream—buying homes and spending disposable income like the rest of America. Latin cultures have traditionally kept parrots and songbirds as pets and many upwardly mobile Latinos can afford a large bird and want one in their homes as a sign of their success.

In their native ranges the birds are easy to find and inexpensive to buy, averaging from a few dollars to twenty for a large bird, depending on how close the buyer is to the bird's habitat. Here, a hand-raised baby bird, pretty much the only kind you can find from breeders or pet stores, costs a fortune by comparison. To many Latinos, spending $900 in a retail pet store for birds that are native to them is an absurd idea, so they look for alternative means.

In the early summer of 2007, when Amazons and other parrots fledged in the wilds of Mexico and Central America, Customs and Border Patrol agents intercepted several smugglers with scores of fledglings in numbers Wildlife Service agents hadn't seen in years. A few weeks later, Mexican authorities apprehended a shipment with 550 young parrots being trucked north to Tijuana and, ostensibly, the U.S. border. For the two young poachers, both male Mexican nationals in their twenties, to be smuggling that many live young birds, statistics show five times that number would have died in the process of procurement. The two smugglers could easily have wiped out an entire flock, a generation of parrots in their wild range.

In August 2007, undercover work by special agents exposed a parrot-smuggling ring, the first found in almost two years. That case and others revealed the new boom in illegal parrot trafficking to authorities, and Jojola says Latino communities are absorbing smuggled birds as fast as they come in and creating a demand for more.

The birds—which include lilac-crowned Amazons, recently added to CITES Appendix 1 because they are "threatened" in their native ranges—can be bought at swap meets, bird marts, and street corners in low-income areas, any place they can show up for sale without question. Latino consumers, who shun retail pet store prices for something that costs next to nothing in their homeland, go looking for a bargain. They may not know, or care, how the birds got here, and they don't connect the parrots they buy with a trade that is destroying their home country's ecology and future generations of its wildlife.

"I've been in the parrot trade since 1983," says Jojola. "I've seen it evolve over the past decade. Now it's socioeconomic-based, involving primarily the Hispanic communities. They are moving up the social ladder. They want to buy pets and, in particular, ones that remind them of home. There's an active trade going on within the community, surprisingly active. It's probably a lot more than we even know."

In the 1980s, the boom sucked millions of legal and illegally caught birds from their forests into the United States. The illegal activities were easier to uncover back then because they came from a Spanish-speaking source into visible arenas—bogus quarantine stations, pet stores, breeders, and the like—all in white, mainstream America. The language barrier alone helped in apprehension. Today, the birds are funneled into a closed culture that enforcement agents have never penetrated. They have no networks set up with informants, and lack the manpower to do so.

And because all those involved speak the same language, from trappers to end buyers, and come from similar cultures, it's much harder to penetrate their operations. Jojola is one of the few agents who speaks Spanish fluently and in enough dialects, including street and prison Spanish (he picked up the latter when he worked as a prison guard early in his career), to work undercover without detection. He was recently promoted to a desk job, supervising his fellow special agents across a third of Southern California, from San Diego to San Luis Obsipo. His higher-ups have since discouraged him from doing what he loves: investigative work in the field.

Still, on a hot day at the end of June 2007, I tell him about a neighbor seeing parrots in terrible conditions at an indoor swap meet at Vermont and Santa Monica boulevards in the middle of Los Angeles. Jojola's investigative nature prevails. He wants to see for himself what's going on at the swap meets, which he and his agents have known for years are a hotbed of illegal activity, even if they couldn't always prove it.

I go along for the ride, embedded, as it were, and undercover with Jojola. It's sweltering in the inner city, especially inside the non-air-conditioned building filled with stuff and people. It's a permanent indoor swap meet not far from downtown and ten minutes from trendy, upscale, artsy neighborhoods like Silver Lake.

Jojola wants to check out some other swap meets, but it seems implausible to me that they will produce results, especially on a slow summer weekday when the cover of crowds, and thus also the likelihood of making a sale, isn't there. Historically, swap meet animal dealers are like carpetbaggers—there one hour, gone the next. That's no longer true; now they're a staple, like the ubiquitous cowboy boot and T-shirt vendors.

The scrap-paper map my neighbor drew to the parrots was accurate. The stall was hidden in the middle of the back row, as far away from the street, and any chance of daylight or prying eyes, as one could find. The other vendors in the mart were less glitzy than the sneaker place that welcomed you off the street. It had name brands, a hundred of them, on display, and bright lights to draw in passersby. By comparison, the parrot seller's row was quiet and low-key. The stalls were the least expensive in the place, and the wares for sale on either side of the dealer were a nondescript mishmash of cheap stuff from China. Nothing to draw a crowd.

This was in direct contrast with the wares in the pet store, if it could be called such. The stall was small, filthy, and in the middle of the darkest area of the ten-thousand-square-foot place, but it held the most expensive items of the eighty or so stalls in there. Its owner was hiding his wares in plain sight. His name was John, and he was hard to pin down ethnically, possibly Filipino or some kind of Asian mix. The dozen or so birds were Amazons, cockatiels, and one macaw. All were confined in small, maybe ten-gallon, fish tanks with a single perch lengthwise. The fluorescent fish-tank light was almost touching their heads, and two were hunched, trying to avoid hitting their heads. There was no avoiding the glare. The lights were meant to highlight their plumage, but the gray-green fluorescent light cast a pall across the feathers of the mostly sick-looking birds. There were small bowls of black oil sunflower seed, the equivalent of potato chips for kids, and dirty water. Some had no water.

Jojola and I acted as if we were tourists who had stumbled on the place by fortuitous accident. My friend Sam, who was visiting from San Diego, had been looking for parrots to buy at the right price. John the seller was more than happy to answer our questions and let me take photos so we could remember which bird was which when Sam and I were deciding on one later.

I asked John about the heat and lack of water. He said the birds were fine, something he repeated often, even the one on the perch that couldn't stand straight or keep its eyes open. He said he gave them water at different times through the day, so they didn't need it in their cage; all they did was make a mess in it with their feces. That was surely so, given the little room the birds had. They were confined with their faces on display like statues for the crowds to gawk at, nothing between them and whoever wanted to come and poke or harass them.

It was the same at the four other pet stores we visited that day, not more than twenty minutes apart from one another in the center of the city.

In the later ones, the din was relentless. One was near a store that sold stereos, and rap music blasted nonstop to show off the speaker systems. All the birds bore the telltale signs of young, once-wild parrots. They cowered in a corner for safety, the instinctive action to retreat to the back of their tree hole nest when predators approached. Birds raised by humans don't categorize them as predators and don't have that reaction when people come near.

By the time I returned home I had a case of heat stroke and had seen the plight of more than forty-five parrots as surely smuggled into the United States from Mexico as I was born here. They were carbon copies of the trafficked parrots I'd seen in the isolation units at the Department of Agriculture quarantine center. Caged in circumstances rivaling those for psychological damage, they were in the hands of unfeeling human sellers who felt no emotional response to the piercing suffering in their eyes.

A few months later Jojola and his team were invited to Mexico to conduct a seminar for their law enforcement counterparts. This was a direct result of efforts over the last several years on the part of U.S. wildlife agents to connect with Mexican agents at PROFEPA. About forty officials, from PROFEPA, the judicial police, and the Mexican navy—who attended because they regularly board boats suspected of smuggling—were present.

Jojola's and his agents' expertise in areas foreign to their colleagues, such as how to conduct undercover investigations, won over the group and formed a bridge for the two countries to work together. "There's no undercover work with PROFEPA," Jojola says. "They're not allowed to do investigations or police work. And they're not an arresting authority. Now that they've realized what we can teach them, they're dying to work with us to end the illegal trade."

But Jojola can't get approval to do more seminars from his bosses. "We should have been doing this twenty years ago, not at the end of our careers," he says. "It's tragic. We have so much to give them to resolve the bird smuggling issue at their end. A lot of agents get frustrated. They say we always have to fight our own people to get the job done. It's an uphill battle. The easiest part is the work, even the undercover work; the hardest part is selling it to the people who are approving it. Imagine that! Our biggest obstacle is our own higher-ups."

As a direct result of the newly forged bond between the field agents in Mexican and American wildlife enforcement, officials in both countries provided the permits needed for repatriation of confiscated parrots, a huge undertaking two years in the making. On August 22, 2007, the residents of the Otay Mesa quarantine were released to Mexican officials to be brought back home. It was the first in many years and, with 150 parrots, the largest ever. "We want to do this as righteous as possible for the birds," said Jojola. All told, more than 200 were handed over.

Some of those birds, like Pirata, the one-eyed macaw, had been there for years, held as evidence in pending cases against their perpetrators. Most of the latter are out on bail almost immediately after being caught, and then plead guilty in exchange for no jail time and minimal fines. But the birds, unable to be returned to Mexico or released into other facilities, are like inmates without a trial date, stranded indefinitely in the quarantine station's small soundproof Plexiglas boxes, barred from seeing sunlight or hearing or feeling anything outside, air, food, and water pumped into their little isolated universes. Jojola said you could see the change in them immediately when they were brought outside. They were laughing and calling to each other, thrilled just to be out in fresh air.

Mexican officials said the birds that can be repatriated to the wild will be. Jojola is staying in touch with his counterparts to track the birds' placement.

But on the home front it's still a battle for Jojola and his colleagues to get the funds, manpower, and permissions needed to combat the ever-growing rise in parrot smuggling. "We're not keeping the public trust," says Jojola. "I'm not covering for them, my agency. I speak my mind. We're supposed to be the guardians of these animals, and we have to be accountable. We all need to do more of that with respect to wildlife, because they don't have anyone else to do it for them.

"Our whole ecosystem is being torn apart. With respect to wildlife, this is it what we've got. In twenty-five to fifty years, when parrot populations are so diminished because we didn't stop this crisis now, bird smuggling will be a serious crime. Then smugglers will go to the big house for a lot of years, but then it'll be too late."

Chapter Ten

A Brazilian Journey with
Global Parrot Conservationist
Charles Munn

*A society grows great when old men plant trees
whose shade they know they shall never sit in.*

—Greek proverb

With so many species on the verge of extinction, parrot conservation has never faced greater challenges. Parrots that have not been captured are still imperiled by the loss of their habitat. Even so, a new hope for their future and a revolutionary way to protect endangered birds has shown itself in the work of Charles Munn, a biologist and real-life Indiana Jones.

In 1994, *Time* magazine voted Munn one of the fifty young leaders for America, and one of one hundred for the world in the next millennium. He is as comfortable at a black-tie dinner with heads of state in Washington as he is hanging from a tree in the jungle, looking for macaw nests, or on the ground in a sting operation, busting international bird smugglers.

Munn is tall and fair-haired with boyish good looks (he's fifty-one but looks forty-something). Like Indiana Jones, he's a ladies' man—dapper, dashing, and charismatic. For decades, parrots have consumed his time, energy, and focus, yet he has never had a parrot as a pet or even gotten to know one personally.

What about them has driven him to devote his life to their welfare? "Imagine," he says in response, "that you have all the great Impressionist works of art in one room. They are about to be destroyed, and no one will ever see them again. These birds are like those masterpieces, and for the same reason that we protect great paintings we must protect them. That's what they mean to me."

Considered the world's foremost expert on macaws, Munn first went to the Amazon in 1976 to research small forest birds for his thesis, and has been going back ever since, spending two or more months there a year.

His nonprofit conservation organization, Tropical Nature, is funded by a for-profit ecotourism business, Tropical Nature Travel, and has secured millions of acres with habitat fortress projects for birds and other wildlife. Thus far he has created havens in the Bolivian Amazon, eastern Ecuador, Peru, and Brazil. Munn is a maverick, and some of his methods—such as hiring local parrot poachers to protect the same birds they once imperiled—are considered radical. As a result he has come under fire from his peers. Still, no one is accomplishing what he has for parrot conservation around the globe.

Once called "Terra Psittacorum," land of parrots, South America contains a third of all the bird species on earth and half of all parrot species, about 160. Brazil alone is home to one-fifth of the world's parrot family, including parakeets, macaws, green maritacas, parrots (which includes Amazon species), and jendayas. Brazil is also home to all the problems facing birds worldwide, and parrots in particular—deforestation, smuggling, and a lucrative national pet trade in wild birds. More than 100,000 are still trapped each year in South America, most in the Amazon and in areas of northeastern Brazil where Munn has established an important conservation project.

But Munn's work isn't limited to Brazil. He has projects in Ecuador and Peru, where he began his work with parrot conservation in 1983. Then he not only had to thwart local trappers; he had to educate them and the neighboring Indians not to kill their wildlife for food. Then and now, in many areas macaws were caught and eaten. "If it's bigger than a breadbox, the locals will catch it and eat it," he says.

His method was simple and effective. He would buy land to protect the birds and other animals living there, and then empower local residents to work on ecotourism instead of ecodecimation. To protect parrots where they were most vulnerable and visible, during their routine feedings at a clay lick (the clay aids their digestion), Munn created the Manu Wildlife Center, bordered by Manu National Park and the four-hundred-thousand-hectare Amarakaeri Communal Reserve. The clay lick, now one of the most popular ecotourism sites, was dubbed "the most intense wildlife experience in Amazonia" by *Condé Nast Traveler* in 2002. The need to protect the lick was apparent from the start. Before he could get guards to protect it, some Indians from communities downstream came in boats on a trip to a festival in another area. The Indians knew there were always a lot of parrots at the lick, so they stopped and shotgunned forty macaws. "There were four hundred or five hundred birds that used that clay lick," says Munn. "So they may have shot ten percent of the entire population that uses it in one morning."

Because shotgun shells are expensive, just under a dollar apiece, Munn says it's generally not cost-effective for Indians to shoot small animals like macaws, given the little amount of meat on the birds. "You have to shoot two to three to make it worth the shell," he says. "When the birds are sitting next to one another, they can shoot two. And if they have a baby, they can shoot all three with one shell and then it becomes worth it to shoot them." At the rate it takes macaws to mature, it can take a decade for nature to replace a single pair.

As a result of Munn's ecotourism excursions to the clay lick, which have financially enriched the local communities, Indians in the whole area now know that macaws are worth more alive in the trees than stewed in a pot. He has enough resources on the ground to monitor any other poaching activity on the protected land. "We know so much about what's going on in every watershed that it would be impossible for anyone to operate what's needed for smuggling birds," he says. "Cocaine you can grow in one area, fly it to somewhere else, do some processing, and then ship it off. In this case, you have to operate in large areas to get enough birds, and we would immediately hear about it."

Munn is at the São Paulo airport to meet me and four other American bird lovers: Marc Johnson of Foster Parrots avian rescue; Brian Cullity, his friend and board member; Lin, a demure young Japanese woman; and Jean, a disease expert. The five of us have embarked on a journey with Munn to see the largest parrots in the world in their native home, the Brazilian outback.

We travel from the coastal metropolis of São Paulo, which is so heavily populated it makes New York City look uninhabited by comparison, on a puddle jumper to the inland city of Barreiras, about a thousand miles northeast in the state of Piaui, a 156,000-square-mile oval that provides a transition from the semi-arid climate of northeastern Brazil to the tropical Amazon to the west. Munn says few Brazilians have heard of Barreiras, which has a population of 150,000, let alone been there, and even fewer have gone to our final destination, Munn's Hyacinth Valley Lodge, 150 miles farther inland by car. Hyacinth Lodge is home to the endangered hyacinth macaws, the largest parrots in the world.

Barreiras means "cliffs" in Portuguese, and small caves in the ancient sandstone cliffs indigenous to that area provide the birds with nesting sites when they don't find tree holes large enough to accommodate them.

Once we're off the plane, it takes us only thirty seconds to see parrots. A giant fig tree just outside the airport is alive with the high-pitched squawks of a hundred yellow-chevroned parakeets. They are a good size, about eight inches long. Their upper wing feathers are a warm shade of banana yellow. A boisterous lot, they move so fast it's hard to track them. It is feeding time, and there is heavy flock action as a hundred or so joyfully ransack the tree for its fruit.

These birds, once routinely trapped for the pet trade, and wild populations in Florida that were loosed accidentally or illegally released by unhappy owners tired of their noisy ways are now thriving. To see them this way, to feel their vibrancy as part of the fabric of their natural climate and environment, is rejuvenating, and I'm glad for the opportunity so soon after our arrival.

We are met by two men, Lourival Machado Lima and his brother-in-law Raimundo Nobres. Lourival oversees Munn's Hyacinth Valley and Cliffs lodges. He is forty-seven, about five feet eight, tanned, and stoic.

He speaks no English. As he and Raimundo load the luggage, I ask Munn about him. "Lourival is an honest man," says Munn. "He doesn't lie or drink. He's an upstanding member of his church and one of the two or three most respected members of his town." And for twenty years he was godfather of the largest illegal animal trapping ring in the northeastern area, poaching thousands and thousands of birds.

Raimundo, handsome and in his early thirties, is a "sensitive guy," says Munn. "He writes poetry." He was Lourival's number-one trapper of hyacinth macaws. Others in Lourival's family are waiting for us at Hyacinth Valley. They are now in Munn's employ, caring for the birds they formerly hunted.

Munn says this time of year is when repaving and asphalting is done on the roads inland. There's no evidence of it, and we drive the next four hours like tricked-out cars on Hollywood Boulevard, bouncing up and down as we go in and out of potholes. Lourival gives wide berth to the ones we wouldn't make it through, and we hold on, careening back and forth like an amusement park ride.

It is mid-June, and winter is getting under way. The weather will remain hot, humid, and dry without much rain until southern hemisphere summer, which runs from December to April. The view is consistent, desertlike red dirt and dry-looking shrubs in all directions as far as the eye can see. Munn calls it "typical Brazilian terrain—dry and drier." It has a name: the Cerrado. There are a few types of *cerrado: campo limpo,* or "clean fields," which are open grass fields sparsely bordered by small trees; *campo sugo,* "dirty fields," those forested by small trees and shrubs; and large dense trees called *cerradao,* "big cerrado." Munn's Hyacinth Valley, which encompasses 2,500 acres, has some of each.

The Cerrado usually contains thirty to forty species of trees in a square mile (compared with the Amazon, which hosts about six hundred species in an equal area). Cerrado trees are a tough bunch, able to withstand extremes of intense drought and rain, and the diversity in terrain accommodates a plethora of wildlife.

Studies done here estimate that sixteen hundred species of plants, fungi, and animals thrive in this area. This includes a remarkable array of birds numbering about 550 species, and five thousand species of plants. At one time 85 percent of the central Brazilian great plateau, almost 2 million square kilometers (about 1.25 million square miles), equaling about 20 percent of the surface of the whole country, was made up of *cerrado* plains. Now *cerrado* areas provide grazing for 70 percent of the country's cattle, which are usurping wildlife habitat at an alarming rate.

We pass some skinny kids on the side of the road carrying heavy pails of clean dishes from a water spigot. Fifty percent of Brazil's population, about ninety million people, are malnourished. The number is higher here than in any other South American country. Most of the poor live in the interior of the country, where we are now. This is the third poorest area, with the biggest hyacinth parrot "loads," populations of birds in a given area. The soil is nutrient-poor, but the land is animal-rich, so it is unsurprising that the selling and trapping of these high-priced and highly coveted birds became a local industry. People found a free resource they could make money on in land you can barely farm without intensive, expensive fertilizing. Munn thinks the flocks of hyacinths once would have been seen over hundreds of miles from Barreiras. He has seen some east of Hyacinth Valley, but they are otherwise all almost gone because of trapping.

Parrot expert Carlos Yamashita (it is said there is no place where there are parrots in South America that he hasn't been) estimates that macaws have lived in this area for a million years. In just the last fifty years, because of intense poaching in the 1970s and 1980s, the locals wiped out so many generations of macaws and other parrots that the birds were brought to the brink of extinction. In 1995, Munn instituted programs here to stop the decimation and turn things around. Now he would like to recolonize the area with hyacinths.

"Parrots divert people to Brazil. They're the heavy lifters of ecotourism," he says. "No animal can help maintain what's left of habitat by drawing people to it like parrots. With them, you can save one hundred million acres of forest because they make the forest come alive for people." Yamashita told me to think of parrots at the top of an ecological pyramid:

"If you save the tip, you save the pyramid." If parrots are thriving, everything below them will be, too.

By now the terrain outside the vehicle has become familiar, but Munn, who has taken this ride for years, still seems thrilled by it. "You don't see this as landscape, do you?" I ask. "No," he responds, "I see it as habitat. I want to know what's living in there."

This isn't just the response of a trained biologist. Munn's interest about the natural world has always been with him.

By the time Charles Alexander Munn III was born in 1954, his father's family had filled the society pages for decades. His relatives include foremost American families such as Drexel, Astor, Biddle, Paul. There were dukes and duchesses of European aristocracy, and members of Philadelphia Main Line society.

His aunt, Pauline Munn, was considered the "most popular international debutante" of 1937. His grandmother was Mary Astor Paul, a Philadelphia socialite and granddaughter of financier Anthony J. Drexel, a pivotal player at the family-founded banking house Drexel & Company, a philanthropist, and one of the founders of American finance. A biography about him is titled *The Man Who Made Wall Street*.

Being a risk-taker might have been passed down to Munn through his DNA. When his grandmother divorced in Paris in 1929, she remained there. Instead of fleeing the Nazis during World War II, which she had the means and connections to do at any time, she stayed and risked her life fighting for her homeland and her adopted country by becoming a spy, cracking German codes and overseeing covert agents around Europe for the French Resistance. She arranged for the shelter and return of six hundred American airmen to Allied-controlled areas. Dubbed the "Angel of Paris," she was twice honored for her bravery by the American and the French governments after the war.

Munn's great-great-grandfather and the patriarch of the Drexel fortune, Francis Martin Drexel, was an Austrian immigrant and artist who lived and traveled throughout Mexico and South America in the early nineteenth century, as Munn would more than a hundred years later. He made his living painting portraits, including one of General Simón Bolívar. But it was in South America, where, also like Munn, he found his passion, for international finance. When he returned to the United States, he settled in Philadelphia and founded Drexel & Company.

Munn has something else in common with both his relatives. Though born to a rarefied life, he is as happy to sleep on a tent floor as a nice hotel bed and is egalitarian in his dealings with people of different classes, religions, and cultural backgrounds.

His father, Charles A. Munn Jr., was the socialite son of a wealthy Washington, D.C., family. Charles Munn Sr. owned Tropical Park racetrack in Florida and the American Totalizator company, which provided tote boards for racetracks. After serving in World War II, Munn Jr. ran American Totalizator and married Loretta Philbin Strauff of Baltimore in 1950. A year later their daughter, Mary Paul Munn, was born. Tragically, Mary was killed by a milk truck in 1953. Munn was born the next year, but when he was just three years old, tragedy struck again when his father died of ALS (Lou Gehrig's disease). Fearing he would have no heir to run the company, Munn's grandfather sold American Totalizator to Remington-Rand. Munn has never been to a horse race.

He was raised a cherished child doted on by his mother, whom he describes as one of the most interesting and vibrant women he knows. The family home in Green Spring Valley, Maryland, sat on five acres, most of it forested and connected to a forty-acre park. Young Munn began bird-watching at age nine. Within two years he knew all the birds in the eastern United States and their vocalizations. Munn says he was "a weird birding prodigy." He was invited to birding forays with respected ornithologists such as Chandler Robbins of the Patuxent Wildlife Research Center. Robbins wrote one of the most popular bird guides of the 1960s and was an active conservationist.

Munn's mother kept her focus on her son's future. She nurtured his passion for birds by taking him on school vacations to places like Australia and New Guinea, where he could bird-watch. And though she could have lived lavishly on her inheritance, she saved it for him. "Now I'm squandering it," he says of the sums of money he has invested in conservation.

Though Munn describes his inheritance as just a "trickle" of the Drexel fortune, his wealth has allowed him throughout his life to reject any ties that would bind him or alter his mission. That mission became apparent very early on. When Munn was sixteen, the forest adjacent to the family home was threatened with development. The trees were to be razed to accommodate twenty homes. Munn told his trustees he wanted some of his inheritance to buy the land and protect it. They balked because he was a minor. He convinced them only after he promised not to sue them when he came of age at eighteen. (Since he was underage at the time, he could have later argued he wasn't able to make responsible decisions.) He bought the land and turned it into a conservation easement. After graduating summa cum laude fom Princeton University (he recalls that his paternal grandfather thought it was "inexcusable" that he went there instead of Harvard), he earned a master's in zoology from Oxford and returned to Princeton for his Ph.D. and then went to work for the Wildlife Conservation Society, which is based at the Bronx Zoo in New York and manages wildlife conservation programs around the globe. Munn says he liked his job but told his boss he didn't need the money, and if the society wouldn't let him do what he wanted, he would leave in a heartbeat. Munn worked there for sixteen years and was promoted to the highest level in the field division, senior conservation zoologist, tasked with researching macaws, giant otters, and monkeys. He became fluent in Portuguese by spending time in Brazil. He also speaks Spanish, German, and French.

During this time, Munn worked on ecotourism models. That work moved to the forefront when he decided more research on animals would be redundant for the purpose of protecting them. "We had done all the science we could do to learn how to create a lot of jobs at a clay lick," he says. "I wanted to apply the research to make sustainable development systems rather than pile up more and more science to be read by a few thousand colleagues that don't create any more jobs."

Munn's work has now produced the largest network of rain-forest tour lodges in the world, and he is consulting in countries, including Honduras and Costa Rica, that want to build their own. "We've cracked the code of accessing wild animals for ecotourism and making protected areas that are self-sustaining," he says.

Munn now has working lodge projects in Bolivia, Peru, Brazil, and Ecuador. All are overseen by his umbrella organization, Tropical Nature, which is based in the District of Columbia, but all are legally separate entities. In each case, local communities have a stake in the lodge and benefit financially as long as they protect the land and wildlife. "Tropical Nature is more like an ombudsman," says Munn. "As long as the enterprise is kept up properly, there's no issue. Otherwise the land can be taken away."

The project in Ecuador has shown dramatic results in just the last two years. Before then the twenty-nine Indian families that live in the protected rain-forest area and run the lodge garnered about five thousand dollars a year in income, but now it's up to one hundred thousand dollars. "The park is now self-protecting," says Munn. "Now the Indians are the park's best friend instead of its biggest threat." He says that with their newfound wealth the families are turning into "Indian yuppies."

About five and a half hours after leaving Barreiras, we turn off the main road and drive down a winding rocky path past a few scattered homes to arrive at Hyacinth Valley. The lodge is a beautiful enclave made up of seven concrete one-room dwellings and an open-air *pilapa* for dining. There is a wood-burning stove in the back house behind the *pilapa,* and a fire pit on the side for grilling.

Each red-roofed bungalow has wooden floors; two wooden tables, one at the bedside; and a bathroom with a flush toilet and cold shower. The wooden bed frame has a comfortable mattress and is covered with mosquito netting. I am glad for both. A single bare lightbulb hangs from the ceiling in the middle of the room. It is fed by a generator that goes off at 9:00 p.m. After that, it's candlelight at night. During the day, sunlight comes through two large glassless windows with large wooden shutters.

After hours on the dusty road a shower and a nap are enticing, but Munn rushes in and ushers us out of our cabins at breakneck speed. The

Hyacinths might be feeding, and we can get a glimpse. We shuffle onto the truck for a quarter-mile ride and then hike the remaining quarter mile on red powder sand.

We get to know each other as we walk to the blind. It's an interesting group. Jean, about sixty, is at a renowned San Diego research facility. She is squat, has short dark hair, and wears glasses. Her camouflage outfit reflects her trooperlike demeanor and the fact that she is ready for a serious safari. Munn calls her "the bug lady" because she loves insects.

Lin is in her twenties, lanky, and lives in Maryland. A bird lover, she found out about the problems with parrots and has been trying to persuade her countrymen to help their cause. One of her goals is to write a book on parrots in Japanese. She is married but is traveling alone and has invested in an expensive camera. (But not as expensive or as large as Jean's, we soon come to find out.)

Marc Johnson of Foster Parrots and Brian Cullity, who is on the board of Foster Parrots, are friends from Massachusetts. Cullity, an antiques dealer, lives nearby and funds their frequent excursions to tropical locales. Cullity recently lost his wife to cancer, and there's a layer of sadness in every step as he walks slowly in front of me to get our luggage. "Linda and I—," he starts to say. He still talks about his wife in the present tense. Cullity and Linda traveled the world to see wildlife, and now he takes trips with Johnson in her memory. Johnson and Cullity have also traveled to Guyana, where Johnson is working on a conservation project with some Amerindians in the village of Nappi. Parrots there were hunted relentlessly until Johnson brought them the idea of ecotourism. Plans are in place for a lodge to be built and for education programs to be incorporated in the local school curriculum. Johnson, interested to see how Munn had set up this lodge and worked with locals, was anxious to come—more so because the unending demands of three hundred parrots and being constantly faced with the suffering of new ones he saves from dismal situations have drained him. He's burned out, feeling that his work doesn't make a difference, that the problems with parrots in the United States are insurmountable.

A two-hundred-yard-long thatched tunnel tall enough to stand in leads into a bomb-shelter-like blind, providing us with cover so the birds don't see us arrive. Munn slows and steps lightly as we near the entrance so we don't spook the birds. We are to remain hidden in the cement bunker buried in the sand.

Inside, it is cool—a nice respite. Circular peepholes in the walls at eye level allow us to see out at ground level without impinging on the birds' natural behavior or encroaching on their surroundings. We must be quiet to a whisper while we are here. Now we are the ones hemmed in by a cage, watching the birds free to come and go.

Through one of the holes, twenty feet from me, is the reason we came.

True to their name, the hyacinth macaws are a deep hyacinth blue from their large heads to the tip of their fifteen-inch tail feathers. Locals call them *arara preta*, "black macaw." Their wingspan is four feet from tip to tip. Their faces have an oval of yellow surrounding marble-sized black eyes. Their black, crescent-shaped upper mandible arches widely over the lower by about three inches, and there is a yellow splash where it meets feathers on their cheek. They have a cartoonlike appearance, so big and lumbering on the ground. They are meant for flight. The yellow at the edge of their mouth gives the impression that they are perpetually smiling.

Ten birds are foraging on a pile of piaçava palm nuts, which make up 85 to 95 percent of their diet. They seek nuts with plenty of meat, which limits them to two or three species. Each bird holds a giant brown nut, the size of a chicken egg, in his foot and bites into it as if it is a chocolate egg. Later, when Raimundo tries to open a nut with a knife, it takes him two minutes to make a dent in the tough outer layer before he gives up. He says we'll get to see the inside of the nut later, when he has a machete.

After the birds eat, they play, noisily nosing their big beaks at each other. Some sit preening in a nearby jatobá tree, a hardwood otherwise known as *Hymenea courbaril*. Others feed their young. They all stop and look out over the grand vista from the tree branches before they fly off to their roosting spots.

I've known several hyacinths individually, as pets living in captivity, and all had sweet dispositions. One would hide her head under her wing when her owner was displeased, though she could have retaliated with a severe bite, given the power of her beak. In captivity, the birds always struck me as oddities, giant parrots too big for any home. Seen in the context of their natural setting, they are endlessly mesmerizing, and it is as if everything surrounding them is here precisely to nurture their existence.

After observing the birds, we return to the *pilapa*, where Lourival's wife Antonia and the family cook serve us a delicious dinner. They will stay in the main house to care for us while we're here. They all make money by helping out. This is part of ecotourism. The locals benefit directly from our presence.

That night a maned wolf comes by the lodge. He lurks in the shadow of the veranda on the main house behind the *pilapa*. Raimundo draws him closer with raw chicken pieces and chunks of bananas. He eats the latter by the dozen, which makes a funny sight. He is lanky. He looks like a tall, thin fox, with many of the same features: large, upright, pointed ears and long rust-colored fur with patches of white under the chin and at the end of the long fuzzy tail. But this wolf also has long black stockings and mane.

He is called "big fox," *aguara guaₓú*, in Guarani, the Amerindian language, and is the largest canid of South America. Maned wolves date back to the early Pleistocene era (which began in 1.81 million BCE and ended around eleven thousand years ago), and though they have few predators, agriculture and human encroachment have usurped their habitat of these many millennia. With diminished food sources, the wolves have developed the unfortunate habit of swiping chickens from humans, who retaliate by shooting them. That, plus the fact that their eyes are considered good-luck charms, has further reduced their numbers, so they are now an endangered species.

They are protected on Munn's land, though he informs us that the nearby property owners are not above shooting what might be one of just 250,000 left in all of Brazil (another 2,000 are estimated to live in

Argentina). Munn says the wolf doesn't seem to mind camera flashes, and Jean wastes no time bombarding him with hers. We all feel sorry for him by the time she's done, and he wanders off in his unusual gait, front and back feet in tandem, the only canid that walks this way.

The blanket of stars above us is so immense, there is no horizon line. The southern hemisphere has large Magellanic Clouds cradling star clusters, and there are some in the sky above us. Lin thinks she sees the Milky Way, but no one's sure. Constellations look different on the other side of the world.

The next morning Munn is up at dawn to get to São Gonçalo, the nearest town, to meet his young daughter, Paulina, and her nanny, Edilene (pronounced Edge-a-lan-ee). They arrived today from Salvador. Edilene is Lourival's sister-in-law. Though Munn has two college-aged children from his first marriage, Paulina is the heir apparent to his work. Seven years old, she speaks English, German, Spanish, and Portuguese fluently. She has traveled with her parents since she was a baby and is comfortable in diverse countries, cultures, and customs. Her favorite dish is skewered cow heart, Peruvian style; she's undaunted going off-road, and, like her father, expects to get her way.

Her language acquisition was helped in large measure by the fact that her mother, Mariana, also a biologist, is Peruvian, and that she and her younger brother spend a good deal of time there with their maternal grandparents. It's not unusual for the kids to live in Peru when their parents are off working, and Paulina has had stays long enough to warrant attending a local German school. Within minutes she makes her presence known, impulsively talking nonstop to each of us in turn. Munn doesn't mind. He encourages her, much as his mother must have done with him.

Jean was also up early this morning. At breakfast she produces a giant black bullet ant (Latin name *Paraponera clavata*) locked in an amber prescription bottle that is not too big for it. About an inch long, bullet ants are the largest of all ants, and highly venomous. Munn tells us one sting can send you to the hospital (though there's no hospital close enough to prevent us from dying first).

Jean is excited by this information. "It's quite the ant," she says. "Quite the ant" is struggling to find a way out. "Don't hurt it," says Paulina, who instantly wins my heart. "It'll suffocate in there," I chime in. "I know," says Jean without compunction. She plans to sneak the dead bug back to show her friends in San Diego.

I figure Paulina and I are alone in our concern about the suffering of a single (and lethal) ant, and that Munn, a respected and published research biologist, would side with Jean in this instance. But he sees it the way we do, and has made his opinions known on the issue of killing live specimens even to his professional detriment.

In 1985, on a research trip to Peru, Munn discovered a new parrot species, a huge accomplishment. He took photos of the small birds at a small stream and sent them to all the top experts on Amazonian and Peruvian birds to confirm his determination. They all agreed it looked like a new, undescribed species. But he refused to kill one of the birds as a specimen to prove it, a standard requirement to get credit for a scientific find.

"I had wanted to put a few birds in luxurious captivity in a huge flight cage in the wild until they expired from old age and claim them as living specimens on which to justify the species description," says Munn. "But I was told that a living specimen in luxurious captivity would not fulfill the rules, as the specimen had to be dead." He protested to no avail, and made the unusual decision not to get credit for the find rather than kill a parrot.

Because of the photo documentation, the ornithological community called the birds "Charlie's parrotlets," though the birds were officially unrecognized. A year after Munn's discovery, some researchers found and shot some of the birds. On examination of the skins, they determined that they were just the second known species in the world in the small parrot genus *Nannopsittaca*. It was a remarkable discovery.

Though Munn found them originally, he had no formal claim to their credit, but those who did gave him second billing on the published paper. Munn further persuaded them to name the bird after a dear friend of his, Barbara d'Achille, a martyred Peruvian housewife—turned—environmental journalist who was killed by Shining Path guerrillas in 1989. The official Latin name of the bird commonly called the amazonian parrotlet is *Nannopsittaca d'achilleae*, the d'Achille's parrotlet.

It was not known at the time of Munn's discovery how large a d'Achille's parrotlet population existed. Given the accelerated depletion of wildlife, it seems an outmoded and dangerous standard to require a killed sample when the population could be small, or the species is known to be endangered.

When scientists found the recently discovered Calayan rail, a beautiful large black bird with a long orange beak and orange feet, they estimated that just two hundred were left on the island where it was found in the remote northernmost Philippines archipelago. The birds were so isolated from humans that they were unafraid of strangers, who had only to reach down and pick one off the ground.

I saw photos of one of these birds sitting guileless in its captor's hands, looking calmly and curiously at the camera, moments before it was killed. When so few exist, one would think that biologists, whose primary concern is conserving species, would do their utmost to find a way to verify their discovery through video, X-rays, blood and feather samples for DNA, or other noninvasive tests. Munn agrees that this standard should be changed for endangered species.

He urges Jean to release the ant and tells her he could be held liable, shut down even, if any wildlife taken under his auspices is found in her luggage. But she tells me as an aside she will sneak it back home anyway.

We are in the blind this afternoon for some hours, and it's hot, maybe ninety-five degrees Fahrenheit, and muggy without a breeze. About a dozen hyacinths sit in the jatobá tree. On one branch a baby begs for food from its mother, while the father watches. The mother regurgitates for him, grabs his beak in hers, and pumps the food in, pushing it into his crop. The baby looks as if it will fall off the branch from the shaking, but it holds firm. As soon as she's done, he begs for more. He's a big baby, but they're still feeding him. Another hyacinth lands on the branch near them, and the mother lunges for the interloper, chasing him away.

Few adult hyacinths reproduce. As the largest parrots, they take the longest to mature, and that may be the reason. Like humans, they take years to come to reproductive age, which ranges from six to ten, and the population here is still on the rebound from decades of trapping. Their numbers are also low because of the lack of suitable nesting holes in the cliffs, which are prime real estate among parrots. In the Pantanal, a wetlands area to the west where Munn has a macaw project, there is an apartment shortage, and if a pair of birds loses a tree nesting hole, they might never reproduce again. The hyacinths here watch over their cliff crevices even outside breeding season to stave off usurpers.

After a pair lays eggs, they incubate them for twenty-eight days. The young hatch and stay in the nest for four months, until their feathers have grown in sufficiently for them to fly. Most pairs have two young, but only one out of ten second babies fledge; the parents usually have only enough food for one to succeed. The young can remain with their parents for another eighteen months or more after that. From three to ten, they, like human kids, have fun socializing. Then they start getting serious about settling down. They mate for life.

We soon figure out it's no secret to the birds that we're here. They can hear our camera shutters, and all look in our direction when Jean's machine-gun-sized camera goes off. Silly primates, they must think to themselves. We shuffle around in the blind a little too much, and the foraging birds get spooked and flee to the high branches of the nearby trees. Their cackle is deafening as they go. Unlike the Calayan rail that was not afraid of humans, these macaws know better. They know the treachery of primates, our kind and the monkeys, which will tear the wings off the birds and eat them if they catch them.

Lourival tells Munn that they are angry. Having stalked the birds for years, he and the other former trappers know their every call and what it means. For days at a time they watched them and their behaviors. They noted where and what they ate, where they roosted, nested, and played. When they learned their routines, they set traps for them and their babies. Munn knows Lourival isn't trapping, because of the stable adult population and the increasing number of babies each year. But he says he has no illusions about Lourival; he believes Lourival could go back to poaching if Munn weren't supplementing his income.

But Munn doesn't seem to notice how Lourival lights up when the birds arrive, the joy in his eyes as the birds forage and feed their young, and the love of openly sharing his knowledge about them as Munn translates Lourival's comments.

After the birds fly off, we walk out front to examine the piaçava nuts. The birds have eaten through almost all of what looks to be a couple of hundred. Lourival's team brought three sacks of the nuts each day to this site every day for months to lure and acclimate the birds, so they would be here when we arrived to see them. They even lay seeds under a barren piaçava palm so the birds think it's seeding. "It's a tree that perpetually fruits," Lourival tells Munn with a smile. Hyacinths have highly specialized diets; they eat only a few species of palm nuts, the yellow pulp of the mauritia palm, and the seeds of a few other plants. This diet requires them to remain in the limited area where the environment supplies the food.

Munn tells us the piaçava nuts evolved over time to be dispersed by animals that weighed upward of a ton. All these large mammals, such as the eight-ton ground sloths and giant mastodons, were hunted to extinction by humans between six and ten thousand years ago. The giant sloths would have swallowed the whole nut and digested off the mesocarp in their forestomach before regurgitating the clean hard seed the hyacinths seek. Or they could have processed it through their intestines and expelled it, surrounded by fertilizer. The hyacinths would have foraged for those clean nuts either in the dung or the regurgitation. The birds, the nuts, and the large mammals evolved to be interdependent, and the birds were happy to follow their food sources around. "They don't actually want to waste their time cutting off the exocarp and the mesocarp," says Munn. "They'd much rather have that service provided by large animals that are now extinct."

Munn says that in areas like the Pantanal, horses and cows now provide this service to hyacinths. There you see flocks of twenty to thirty hyacinths wandering around in cow pastures and horse corrals, looking for clean seeds. They drink water out of the cattle troughs and sit on the cattle fences, waiting for the cows to come and regurgitate more.

I had commented to Munn that one thousand acres seemed like a lot of land for just fifty or so hyacinths. "It's not enough," he responded. "We could use another thousand acres, and it still wouldn't be." That makes perfect sense, given that it takes a year for the nuts of the piaçava palm to ripen, but less than one week for a flock of forty birds to eat all the nuts in up to one hundred palm stands. Yamashita said at least twenty-five square miles of palm stands are needed to support one small flock of hyacinths.

As we walk back, we see the footprints of a large cat. Raimundo measures one at just about three inches. He and Lourival figure it is either a small jaguar or a large puma. Munn jokes that wildlife tours without good animals make artificial paw prints in the sand and tell tourists that they just missed a jaguar.

Back at the lodge, the men put overripe bananas and other soft fruit on a platform built on a nearby tree stump, a makeshift bird feeder that fills with tanagers and myriad bird species I've never seen in a matter of moments. Lin has been waiting for this opportunity and runs to get her bird book. She turns the pages frantically, barely keeping up with the parade of birds.

That evening the maned wolf invites his girlfriend to join him for the chicken and banana dinner at the lodge. She hangs back until she sees that the food really is a free buffet. They come so close they're eating chicken right out of the bucket, about five feet from where we sit on the veranda.

After dinner I finally get Munn and Lourival to sit down in the *pilapa* for an interview, with Munn as translator. The interview lasts over an hour. Lourival answers all my questions easily, without hesitation or pretense. Throughout, Munn remarks that he is hearing much of what Lourival says for the first time, even though he has known him and they have spent considerable time together for a decade.

Lourival's grandfather ran a mule mail service around the interior of the state of Ceará, which borders Piauí and the Atlantic Ocean to the northeast. His father liked animals and figured out the only way to be around them and make a living was to trap and sell them. His grandfather didn't want his son doing what he considered a low occupation, and would spank him when he caught him at it through his teenage years. Still, it wasn't long before Lourival's father became a specialized distributor, supplying local traveling circuses with sought-after animals such as pumas, ocelots, giant anteaters, jaguars, monkeys, marmosets, and "everything else imaginable," according to Lourival. He made good money but drank it all up, leaving his wife and eight children to go hungry.

Lourival Machado Lima was born in 1957 and raised in the town of Campo Sales. Like his father, he had a natural love for animals. He says he always wanted to go to school. But his father said, "What do you need to read and write for? Just trap animals," so he never did. At thirteen, Lourival started working with his father full time. He carried fifty to sixty kilos of merchandise on his back, things like watches, guns, and clothes, to swap for animals. They would come back with cages full of songbirds to be sold in São Paulo, where they would command a high price. When Lourival worked alone he walked or hitched rides on passing trucks to make his rounds.

By the time he was fourteen he had graduated to larger birds, mostly blue-fronted Amazons, which were illegal to trap. Three years later he was trading even bigger moneymakers like blue and gold, green-winged, red-bellied, and some hyacinth macaws. He spent the next three years on the road, traveling and trading animals. He estimates he supplied distributors with a thousand birds a year, which were then smuggled out of the country. I ask if he had any guilt. He says he was raised to believe that animals were meant to be eaten or trapped and sold. "It was normal to me," he says. "I didn't have the slightest feeling of guilt."

At twenty, Lourival moved south to Piauí because he'd heard the area was rich in parrots. By now he had bought a truck, which was turned into a well-stocked traveling dry goods store. He would leave home with cane alcohol, matches, coffee, sugar, men's and women's clothes, shoes, a variety of medicines (he stresses, "including headache medicine"), machetes, and knives to trade. Under the seats and hanging off the sides of the truck were cages of all sizes he made by hand from palm wood. After fifteen days of traveling he would return home, the goods gone and the cages filled with large and small animals. In a year he would get hundreds of parrots, capuchin, tufted and howler monkeys, anteaters, currassows, and songbirds, like onoles and finches.

It took another eight days to dispense the animals. In a year, he would sell four to five hundred green-winged and scarlet macaws, another two hundred blue and gold macaws, five hundred Amazon parrots, and "hundreds and hundreds of songbirds." Matter-of-factly and without a sign of remorse, Lourival tells Munn that some songbirds and occasionally a large macaw would die.

Lourival was also a keen trapper who knew what he was doing was illegal. But Munn says judges in northeastern Brazil treat bird trapping like jaywalking, a minor offense. "Even if it went to court, it would have taken years to get prosecuted," says Munn.

Though parakeets, monkeys, blue-fronted Amazons, and conures were his bread and butter, Lourival expanded to include hyacinths, which had previously been seen outside of Brazil only rarely. "Here was the motherlode of hyacinths," says Munn. He describes Lourival as "more a rancher than a miner," because he always left just enough birds to make more babies but not enough to rebuild their numbers.

Lourival developed a relationship with a man named Carlinhos, the most notorious distributor of macaws in Brazil. He sold the birds nationally (Lourival says many were "consumed" in São Paulo and Rio de Janeiro) and overseas. Carlinhos took Lourival under his wing and treated him like an adopted son. He gave Lourival orders for parrots, which Lourival passed on to his suppliers. Between this man and other buyers Lourival had in the south, Lourival became the largest supplier of macaws in the country.

Munn says Lourival turned a lot of people into trappers to help fill his orders. Over the years, many families moved down from Campo Sales to work for him. In his heyday, Lourival had a network of one hundred suppliers in eleven counties. He had five primary climbers, but from 1985 to 1990, his most lucrative years for hyacinths, there were fifteen "daredevil" cliff climbers. Depending on the access, they would climb bare-chested down 150-foot cliffs or up 200 feet on hemp ropes to reach hyacinth nests.

They also trapped adult hyacinths, but those were caught on the ground. The men would lay out hardwood traps loaded with palm nuts with a hair-trigger door that would trap any bird that went in. Sometimes they would catch one of a pair. In one instance, Raimundo (who joined the discussion at this point) remembered how the mate of a caught bird stood by the cage for hours, waiting for her partner to come out. He had hoped to trap the second bird as well and watched for hours as the two birds called gently to each other and touched beaks through the bars. Finally at nightfall, when it was too dangerous for the mate to remain on the ground, he reluctantly flew off, calling out to his partner to follow. He flew overhead until he saw she wasn't coming. He returned at first light, searching frantically for her, but by then she was long gone.

Unlike his father, Lourival doesn't have costly vices, so the money he amassed was considerable. Much of it came from hyacinth trade because the rare birds were worth more than any other on the black market. "You can see his profits," says Munn. "You can figure the number of birds that were trapped to buy his color TV, land, and cars. You can figure it out— 'Fifty birds for this,' 'One hundred birds to buy that.' His is the house that hyacinths built."

By the time Munn arrived in 1994, the number of black macaws in the area had fallen below five hundred, the minimum needed for gene diversity and to maintain the health of the population. "I barely saved them," he says.

By then Lourival's buyer had gone to prison, and he had almost been caught himself. Still, Lourival was leery of Munn's strange proposal. "I thought it was very peculiar," he says. "It sounded like 'funny money' to be paid so well for doing so little, just to stop trapping."

The first land Munn bought was eighty-five hundred acres, which he describes as "peaks and valleys and rocky box canyons where the macaws nest and live and cool animals like pumas hang out." He got it for a good price—$7 an acre—and had to pay for only 65 percent of the property. He wasn't charged for the 35 percent that was rocky. "Anything you can't submit to a plow is considered worthless property, and that's what interested us most," he says. Two years later he bought another eighty-five hundred acres. The total seventeen thousand acres make up Hyacinth Cliffs Reserve. The next one thousand acres he purchased was Hyacinth Valley Reserve. Munn is now planning to add seven thousand acres of flat ground to the eighteen thousand he already has. All his Brazilian ecotourism endeavors are run by a nonprofit he formed called BioBrasil.

The first tests to see whether the hyacinths could be habituated to a particular spot with palm nuts were done in early 1995 and were working well by May of that year. Immediately after the initial positive results, Lourival informed all the suppliers on his route of his new occupation. "I told them that I was leaving that line of business, and that they shouldn't catch any more animals for me," he says.

It took almost two more years to be sure the other half of the equation, the tourists, would pan out, but Lourival didn't want to wait. His wife had been urging him for years to stop selling animals, and the work was weighing on his conscience. Now he says he believes no animal should be kept in a cage.

"Do you regret it?" I ask.

"I was doing something negative," he replies. "Now I'm doing something positive."

Johnson interrupts. He wants Munn to tell Lourival that he rescues parrots, that people buy them and throw them away, and that is what probably happened to the birds he caught and sold to wealthy Americans as pets.

Lourival can't believe it at first, but then says, "That's very sad. I'm very sorry to hear it."

By 1997, Munn, Lourival, and the others knew the plan would work when Bill Engler, the president of Kaytee Products, a large bird food company, visited and signed the company on as a patron of Hyacinth Valley. Since then Lourival, his family, and key climbers have all been employed by BioBrasil. (Munn figures out that Lourival is making 60 percent less money doing conservation work than he did poaching, and still he's stuck to it.) Lourival oversees his crew just as he always has, but now they are making a career of saving the same birds they spent years catching, caging, and selling. Previously they would stalk them; now they watch and monitor them. Instead of setting traps, they set out piaçava nuts. Instead of selling parrots, they sell tourists on how great they are.

Munn and Lourival make an interesting team. One had humble roots, was born poor, and was never educated; the other lived a privileged life and went to the best schools. One is a passionate talk-a-holic with moods that rise and fall suddenly; the other is even-tempered and speaks rarely, and then in a quiet voice. One adored birds and devoted his life to protecting them; the other spent most of his life destroying their lives. Lourival loved animals, but found the only way to be engaged with them and feed his family was to sell them. (Munn says many people who poach animals for a living here would be wildlife biologists in other countries.) Now, working together with their combined expertise, they are changing the face of conservation.

For Munn to work with poachers was controversial. The Brazilian government wasn't happy about it, feeling the men were basically getting rewarded for past offenses and might be "double dipping," as one parrot expert put it—getting paid by Munn to protect the birds and still poaching them on the side, only now with immunity. Many of Munn's peers were philosophically opposed to working with trappers. But Munn felt they were the best men for the job; they knew the parrots and their habits better than anyone, were in the loop on what other trappers were doing, and could oversee and protect the birds better than hired security. With Munn's good results and years of the hyacinth population growing— the ultimate test that the scheme works—many of his peers have come around.

Munn's personal style is also controversial. It is said he shows an open lack of respect for the countries he works in, though, as one colleague put it, "That criticism comes from people not noticing the blatant human rights and environmental violations those countries engage in." The same colleague said, "He doesn't respect anyone not working hard in the right direction," and he has no compunction about telling them so publicly. More than once, as an invited speaker for a gathering about parrot conservation, he has proceeded without hesitation to criticize his host's practices from the podium. When he addressed several hundred breeders at the annual convention of the American Federation of Aviculture, he showed the fundamental flaws in the argument that parrot breeders are the keepers of the gene pool, the Noah's Ark, for parrot species that are diminishing in the wild due to habitat destruction:

> I said the species of parrots you have were in trouble in the wild because their parents were taken to supply you with birds. The danger for those birds is not that their forest is cut out from under them, but rather the trade removes them from the forest before the forest is ever in any danger. None of the large macaws are going to go extinct in the wild now if we just stop the traffic. Those birds have one hundred years left in their habitat. Then I gave them a list of twenty-nine parrots they should have backup populations for—small parrots from the inner valleys of Colombia and Ecuador and the coastal forests of Brazil and the Caribbean islands.
>
> Most of them have no commercial value at all. They are not colorful, they don't talk very well and as a result they aren't traded because no one really likes to own them compared to the others. They have no friends because they're not worth anything in the trade. Once their habitat's gone, they're gone because there are no backup populations outside their forest. So I asked for a show of hands to see how many of the breeders present would be willing to devote time, space, and energy to breeding these unpopular, unsellable parrots. It was a deafening silence and it completely eviscerated their argument because the parrots that they should have a backup population for they don't have and they don't want to breed.

A generator battery has been found for Jean. She requested it to power lights she brought especially for this moment. She is going to photograph as many insects as she can by luring them to her with bright lights in an otherwise pitch-black night. The guys help her hook it up outside her cabin. One holds a flashlight. A slew of bugs are already dancing around its meager offering. I walk over and watch Jean diligently set up a large foldout photographic screen. When it's done, she plugs the generator into a large external camera light and flips the switch. A blazing blue-tinted light explodes into the darkness. Within seconds bugs migrate to the spot in a frenzy of light excitement. I quickly move a safe distance away and watch awestruck with the others as the horror movie *The Night of the Swarming Bugs* unfolds.

Soon thousands of insects form a cloud around her as she tries to photograph them. They are long-legged and flying, crawling up the generator, the screen, and her legs. Most I have not seen before in my life. Many have appendages I hope I will soon forget and are of a size that would seem an exaggeration to someone who hadn't seen them firsthand. They seem to be coming from miles around, but I fear this astounding number lives nearby, lurking in the darkness. They flutter and move eerily aglow against the sharp white tarp. Jean is full of glee; she couldn't be happier than to be standing in the middle of this melee. The moving cloud spills into her room. I yell out to suggest she close the door to avoid sleeping with them as well, but she yells back that it's no worry to her.

We drive about an hour west into the valley toward Hyacinth Cliffs Reserve, where we will spend the night. We are ambushed midway on the bumpy ride by giant dive-bombing grasshoppers. Their heads are so large they stare you in the eye when they land on you.

When we stop ducking the grasshoppers, we peer out onto a spectacular green vista of trees and shrubs, with a myriad of wildlife flying and roaming. There are red-legged seriemas, calling back and forth to one another, burrowing owls, great rheas, buff-necked ibis, and crab-eating foxes. We pass a meadow with about two dozen grazing cows. Munn says the farmers leave their cows unattended because there are no large predators to bother them. They graze on the grass and drink water from a nearby stream—a cow's dream life. But the dream will soon turn to a nightmare for all the animals here. Munn says 45 percent of this thirty-thousand-acre plateau is going to be clear-cut for agriculture this year.

The Hyacinth Cliffs lodge is similar to Hyacinth Valley in arrangement, but the lodge area is smaller and on top of rolling hills, overlooking another valley and more cliffs on the far side. The cliffs in the distance are reminiscent of the red plateaus of New Mexico, only these are covered in green trees and bushes.

The destination of the morning is a blind, similar to the one at Hyacinth Valley, but about a mile and a half from the reserve. Twenty minutes after our arrival, at just about sunrise, about a dozen hyacinths arrive and land in trees about fifteen feet away. It's a revelation to watch them in the wild and see their behavior—the antithesis of their lives in captivity. Here they travel in a flock and are always surrounded by their friends and family; birds in captivity are isolated and deprived of constant social stimulation. The wild birds forage in a complex, three-dimensional, changing environment, and their food takes great manipulation to retrieve. In captivity, they are handed the same foods every day (with an occasional treat), so they don't use any of those skills, and their environment is limited and inflexible. Here they fly, while in captivity they sit in the same spot all day.

Across the savanna on the far side is Salt Mountain. Munn estimates that the sandstone formations that define the mountain have been here for a billion years. "They are some of the oldest terrains in the world," he says.

Two miles farther on, his land is buffered by the newly designated Parnaiba River National Park. At 1.7 million acres, it is one-third the size of New Jersey. When it is completed, it will be the sixth largest park in Brazil and the largest outside the Amazon, with more *cerrado* habitat than any other. Munn's 17,000 acres encompass 1 percent of the total park area.

This has always been Munn's scheme, to have his reserve areas compounded by government parks with huge tracts of land forming habitat "fortresses." He spends time lobbying governments to designate parks near crucial habitat. In 1986, Munn drew the borders of a park the size of Connecticut on a napkin for the government of Peru. It became Tambopata National Reserve. Four years later, on another napkin, he outlined Madidi National Park, the size of New Jersey, and worked with the Bolivian government to see it designated. Madidi has tropical savannas at the foot of the Andes next to a 19,000-foot glacier elevation. "It is the jewel in the crown of the Bolivian park system," says Munn. "It has so many habitats, glacier and tropical, lowland savannas, cloud forest, and rain forest. There are more species protected there than in any park in the world. Colombia could have a park like it, but those areas are filled with cocaine dealers and ranchers."

Madidi backs up to Tambopata on the Bolivian side, forming one of the largest contiguous and continuous wildlife fortresses in the world. Munn has conservation projects with locals in the key perimeter or animal-rich areas of both Tambopata and Madidi, staffed with ecotourism employees to make sure animals aren't being poached. In this way, tens of thousand of animals, in addition to the parrots, are secure.

Some of the situations aren't as easy as these to set up, and can be rife with the problems South America is famous for. In Ecuador, oil is king. There are no prohibitions against exploratory drilling and putting up wells in national parks. Even though Munn bought land and has created a park, the government can sell the subsoil rights, making it hard for him to protect what is on the topsoil. "In Ecuador, the birds are very endangered, and every inch of the national parks in the Amazon are owned by ten oil company concessions," says Munn. "In Ecuador, 'national park' is synonymous with 'oil field.' The destruction of Amazon Indian cultures comes with the oil drilling because it brings prostitution, venereal disease, and alcohol problems. Those are the biggest harvests of oil companies. It's genocide in a velvet glove." Munn's Ecuadoran enterprise is in a ninety-two-square-mile park, which features giant otters and macaws at clay licks. It is cherished by the Indians who guard it, and have so far fended off any oil-company trespasses.

Munn faces problems here with the Parnaiba park. To complete the park, the government still needs to buy back much of the land from private owners who have had it for generations. Eminent domain doesn't apply here, and many of the owners don't want to sell. Those who do can often get more money per hectare from agricultural enterprises than they can from the government.

Munn points out that his reserve encompasses everything we can see, literally. He bought the valley and the cliff sides but not the top, because he didn't think he needed to. But he recently found out from Lourival that the ten thousand acres on top of the plateau are to be cleared this year to grow soy. A lot of the hyacinths' food sources will be killed off. Munn says that by the time this book is published, everything on top of the cliffs will be gone because of soy farming. The bigger tragedy is that the birds' habitat is being cleared to plant a crop that will feed cows, not people. The cows are being fed to make steaks and hamburgers, but the conversion rate is absurd: you can feed ten times more people with the soy than you can with the meat from the animals that eat it. It takes fifty-five square feet of forest to make a single hamburger.

Closer to the cliff face, we see smoke rising off the plateau. Fires have been set to clear the land for planting. The boom in agriculture is moving at light speed across rural areas. Munn estimates he has eight years left, at most, to buy significant parcels of land here, or it will all go under the plow. "It is like a battleship steaming north from Barreiras," he says. "We're screwed if we don't buy five hundred thousand to one million acres by then."

Munn can't afford to buy all the land needed, so he, like other conservationists, struggles to raise money. Sometimes he and his peers are pitted against one another for the limited funds available for a particular cause. Munn doesn't sling mud, but he says some in his field are threatened by what he does.

"People in conservation want to act as high priests; only they know how to administer funds and do tests," he says. "The priesthood becomes an end in itself, an elite group that can claim they are helping. They get into satellite analysis, small planes; they piss away money. It's like a doctor who never wants their patient to die, just to need constant care. What's threatening about what we do is, we make environments self-sustaining. They can pay for themselves with ecotourism and become hands-free after a while."

Because of his unconventional stand and financial independence, Munn has amassed a good number of enemies through the years, including some South American governments. "They consider me a 'risky gringo' because I have money," he says. "I can do what I want, and I don't have a job to lose. Bureaucracies grow up and they want to be fed forever. We're trying to empower local communities, which is an upward spiral. You don't have to scold or check in on local people, because they develop a love for this, they want to do it."

This was proven to Munn in Manu, Peru, where he has developed what is now an important conservation project and a lucrative ecotourism venture, encompassing five lodges, with parrots, tapirs, and monkeys. Munn says that here, as in Bolivia, the indigenous people seized the opportunity for the advancement these endeavors bring, and they have fun in the process.

We are almost at the cliff when we stop to see a pair of bat falcons sitting high atop the branches of a dead tree. Though they are black hooded like Batman, their name comes from the fact that they catch and eat bats at dusk. In all birds of prey, the male is smaller than the female, but with bat falcons it's most dramatic. She is 30 percent larger than he is. The male tries to mate, but she is keeping her eye on us. "Is she worried about us trespassing?" I ask Munn. "No," he says, "she thinks we're more or less like cows."

The cliffs are imposing up close. They are about nine hundred feet high, with a sheer face of ragged rock. A million years of erosion has provided nesting holes for the birds in the cliff faces, and this one is riddled with them; it looks as if artillery took aim and didn't stop. Unlike most nesting areas, here there are more holes than birds. Even so, birds covet the prime spots, and after they claim them will often come by, in the off season, to see that strangers haven't moved in. Munn says that anywhere there's a sheer drop on the face, you can likely find a nest. Those are the safest spots because few animals can crawl up and steal eggs there. The face in front of us, which Munn says is the most productive of all the cliffs, holds eight nests. Altogether there are ten pairs of hyacinths known to nest here, and five pairs of green-winged macaws nesting on the east side.

Lourival regularly did "baby harvests" in this same area. The trapping of hyacinths and other parrots by current poachers is still an issue, though not on Munn's land. One hundred miles north of us is an unprotected flock of hyacinths that Munn worries about, but raising money is hard, and he can't buy all the land needed to conserve the birds.

One can only hope he succeeds in protecting as many birds as possible. Seeing them here, it is apparent that this is the life they were meant to have—the lush open savanna, the temperate climate, flying free in an endlessly beautiful and challenging landscape, and sleeping under a blanket of stars.

The dozen or so birds we saw earlier in the blinds are in trees near the cliffs. As we get close, they become visibly alarmed. Their caws— "braaaat, braattt"—are deafeningly loud, and would likely keep away most predators. But their voices only ever drew humans to them, and it is no different now. As we move closer, they fly cross-hatching patterns above us. Their huge wings fan the air. Then in unison they hover like butterflies above a bush at the cliff plateau. They land and line up like weathervanes facing into the wind, cawing all the while. When none of this works, they fly down toward us, this time circling in, flying lower each time, until they are about thirty feet from our heads. All the while they are dramatically squawking a loud "rawww, rawww," wanting us to vacate the premises.

Munn and Lourival harmonize in a duet precisely mimicking the hyacinths' calls. The birds, perplexed, fly lower to see what bird on the ground is summoning them with an alarm call. Finally we relent. I'm glad, for the birds are so stressed now.

It's two hours farther north to Green Wing Valley—so remote that the dirt road we're on turns to sand for the last half hour of the drive. Green Wing Valley is also the home of Marino ("Mauro") Gomes de Oliveira and his family. In 2000, Lourival told Munn about Mauro. He said one of his former trappers had green-winged macaws on his property. Though Lourival had never seen the birds forage on the ground there, Mauro had been working to habituate them to humans for a year in the hope Munn would enlist him for ecotourism so he, too, could stop trapping the birds.

Munn went to see Mauro and was impressed. He had the vibrant red, blue, and green birds landing to eat piaçava nuts just as the hyacinths were doing. "What else have you got here?" Munn asked. "Got any mammals?" Mauro responded, "I've got monkeys that crack nuts."

The brown capuchin monkeys Mauro described are tied with chimpanzees as the first nonhuman primates known to use tools. Here their tools consist of igneous rocks weighing up to five pounds. (The monkeys themselves weigh about twelve pounds.) They carry the rocks from deposits hundreds of yards away to special coffee-table-sized anvil rocks made out of soft sandstone. Theirs is among the most complex use of tools in the world by a nonhuman primate, and is equaled only by hammer-and-anvil behavior of chimpanzees recorded on the Ivory Coast.

Munn says he thought it was too good to be true, and there was a hitch: it wasn't known if the monkeys could be habituated like the parrots to be at the anvil rocks at certain times of day.

Munn offered a "monkey prize" of three thousand dollars to whoever could get the primates do their nutcracking five days in a row. Raimundo teamed with Mauro (others tried as well), and the two prevailed after many months of methodical work. They watched the capuchins for weeks, learning their habits, and then lured them with bananas and cane. Soon the monkeys were showing up to crack nuts in the morning and afternoon without provisions. *National Geographic* and *BBC Wildlife* magazines and

TV shows from around the world run feature stories about the monkeys, but we are among only a few hundred people who have come to this very remote place, the outback of the outback, to see them in person.

Mauro's land is in a beautiful clearing adjacent to a mountainside. The flora is dense, and different from that at Hyacinth Valley; overall, it is more lush. Munn says forty different species of trees can be found in a square mile at Hyacinth Valley; seventy species live here.

Generations of Mauro's and his wife's families were born in this valley. Between them they have seventeen relatives within twenty square miles. The couple has seven young children. Their house is a small one-story structure with a flat roof and an attached pen that holds some sheep. Munn calls them "dirt poor." Until Munn enlisted them to work with him, they had no electricity. Now a generator produces electricity for a few hours at night, installed to upgrade the location both for visitors and to meet the family's daily needs. It's the same with the free-standing bathroom, which has a flush toilet and shower. The seven of us will share it while we're here.

After the drive we all hang out in the *pilapa*, which is furnished with hammocks, benches, and a dining table. This place lacks the open space of Hyacinth Valley, and the temperature, which we guess to be about ninety degrees, is sweltering with the humidity.

Mauro and one of his young sons walk over to us. The son has an armadillo cradled upside down in his arms. I take a photo, then feel guilty; the animal is terrified. Armadillos are considered a delicacy, and Mauro often hunts them with his dog. They try to run into the ground, but once the dog locates the holes, he digs then out. "They're known to be very tasty," says Munn. "This one would go into a pot if we weren't here." Mauro promises to release the kicking creature.

Today we are here for the premiere of the new two-hundred-foot-long walkway and blind at the monkey-sighting area. Munn is very excited about it. It's a stone's throw from Mauro's house, up a path through a small canyon. When we arrive, the monkeys are hard at work trying to crack the same hard nuts the macaws eat. There are five, three on different slabs of rock, knocking away at nuts. One slab holds two monkeys—an older one showing a younger how to do it. On another rock a monkey sits, watching and combing his hair with his fingers.

They are all very precise in their work. They tap the nut, then shake it next to their ear to hear whether the seed makes the right sound. If not, it's not worth the effort of cracking it. Just as we would, they use both their small hands to lift the giant hammer rock above their head and bring it thundering down with all their might. One uses his tail as a third hand to coil around a nearby tree trunk for balance. One is using an unusually large hammer rock, and Marc jokes that he is using the armadillo to crack the nuts.

We are all trained now to be silent but for the camera shutter snaps. As soon as we produce one of these alien sounds, the capuchins stop and look in our direction.

I walk out to stretch and find two monkeys looking at me as I leave the tunnel. They're closer than when I was in the blind. When I return, two more are sitting in a tree right above me. They call and run to each other, then jump on the thatch tunnel and follow me as I walk back to the blind. I mention this to the others, but they think nothing of it until one of the monkeys looks in at us through the peephole. The others join him. Now we're on exhibit. Munn is summoned and realizes the pointlessness of the blinds. Everyone goes out and starts walking around with the monkeys. The monkeys go back to work, unfazed. They don't mind that we're here. Munn tells us it took six months for the monkeys to accept the blind and not get spooked by noises coming out of the openings. Now they don't even mind that people are walking around. I wonder whether habituating these animals to humans compromises them. Munn states his position clearly. He isn't interested in making them pets or teaching them tricks. The food they're given is what they would naturally find and eat in this environment. If there is some small compromise in getting them used to seeing people—and it's only a small number of visitors at any one time—so be it. If people can't see them, they cannot be protected, and that's just the fact of it. If he cannot offer a wildlife experience, then there will be no ecotourism, because that's what people pay money for. And if there is no ecotourism, the locals will be forced by poverty to again trap and eat or sell these animals. Instead of being free and protected, with minor gawking and camera clicking from humans every once in a while, they'll end up isolated in small cages for the rest of their lives or on a dinner plate. Given the reality of the situation, Munn feels this least interfering trade-off is most equitable, and the monkeys don't seem to mind either. Plus, he says providing food doesn't change their natural behavior; it just intensifies it and makes them happy in the process.

That afternoon we drive about twenty minutes down a dirt road to see the green-winged macaws. Their natural range runs from eastern Panama south across northern South America east of the Andes into Bolivia, Brazil, and Paraguay. Like the hyacinths, green-wings eat the hardest nuts in the world, and in some places, such as Peru, they consume toxic seeds that are neutralized by ingested clay. Here the birds eat piaçava nuts, as do the hyacinths.

We're in the blind, waiting for birds to arrive. The nuts Raimundo and Mauro have laid out are waiting in a large pile in front of us.

Finally, two green-wings are slightly visible through the trees. Tentatively, they begin to descend from the sky, like colorful Japanese fans waving in the wind. They are all red from head to mid-back, with a green band that crosses wing to wing, followed by dark and royal blue bands, then red in a wide swath across their tail, which ends in a royal blue tip. They are so colorful with the sun on them that they look like firecrackers going off when they fly away.

We find they are very skittish.

"What do you think?" asks Jean.

"About what?" I reply, a little curtly.

"Anything," she says.

"I think they're unpredictable, and we can't expect them to perform for us," I respond.

"You're right," she says. "It's a privilege to see them at all."

A breeze rustles the trees and comes through to us, bringing a little relief from the heat. A pair of birds and their baby are sighted. We're told the baby fledged in December, but the parents are still feeding him at nine months old. In the States, the baby would have been in a pet shop and sold to a customer by the time it was six months—sold, confused, and forced to eat on its own or starve. I tell Munn. He says the foods humans feed them are so soft, it probably works out best for them to eat on their own; their beaks are designed to crack enormously hard things, and in captivity they hardly get to do so.

On the way back to the lodge the truck has a problem, and we wait by the side of the road for one of the guys to return with another vehicle. A giant, strangely shaped bees' nest hangs low on a nearby tree. These are stingless bees, the opposite of killer bees. A few fly over to chase us away. Without stingers, their primary line of offense is to wrap themselves in our hair to annoy us.

Just when we're laughing about the harmless bees, Munn hears a swarm of killer bees buzzing nearby. "How do you know?" I ask. "I was attacked by them three times," he says. "Once that happens, it's a sound you never forget." One incident was a close call with death. Munn saw the hive, and the bees saw him. "They sting first, ask questions later, and call in the cavalry as soon as they take off," he says. He ran, and the whole hive followed. He dove into cactus scrubs, getting caught on their spines, with the bees chasing him. It was close to the edge of a one-hundred-foot drop. In all, he got stung only three times. But that wasn't his only brush with death. At seventeen, on a bird-watching trip in Tanzania, Africa, he was infected with malaria and almost died. The same thing happened to Munn twice more, at ages twenty-eight and thirty-five, while in city hotels in Peru, all from lack of mosquito netting. He tells me it's easier to avoid malaria in remote areas, like where we are now, because to transmit the disease the mosquitoes must constantly be infected again by human carriers. There must be a critical mass of contagion to keep the mosquitoes infected, which you find only in populated areas.

Munn tells us about the honeyguide, an African bird that lures people to bee hives by beckoning them with its bent tail. It does this so the humans or honey badgers they lure will deal with the bees, leaving the bird to eat the leftover wax. At first I think Munn is making some kind of ornithological joke, but it turns out to be true.

The bee stories get even better. Lourival and Raimundo make killer bee honey. They retrieve the honey by lighting a smoke pot at one end of the bee hive; then Lourival puts his arm elbow deep into the midst of the frenzied killer bees and searches around for the large queen bee. When he finds her, he pulls her out, and the other bees follow, leaving the honey behind. "Why don't they sting?" I ask. "If your house is on fire, you don't think about the neighbor who set it to steal your TV," Munn tells me. But he admits Lourival and Raimundo have balls "the size of a wrecking ball."

Mauro, always quiet, has said little up to now. When I ask about his life as a trapper, though, he becomes animated as he recalls the past. He says he did it for for fifteen years and became known as the "King of the Green-wings." He trapped bellbirds, toco toucans, parakeets, coveted songbirds, and some monkeys, but hadn't gone after green-wings until he worked for Lourival.

He started in 1982, trapping scaly-headed pionus parrots and red-bellied macaws. With the latter he would hit forty-five to fifty-five nests and get sixty to seventy "red babies" a year. He would have gotten more, but some were inaccessible. He also raided the low nests of blue-fronted Amazons. He stole all the babies he could get, kept a few, and sold the rest. The parents would fly back and forth eight to ten feet away, scream-ing. "They wanted to attack us but felt we were too dangerous," Mauro says. He and Raimundo, his partner in poaching, would scare them off. When he started poaching green-wing babies, the parents were braver and would snap at him, but they never got their babies back.

Mauro would get orders from Lourival for a number of birds. He would get paid sixty dollars for a green-winged baby, seventeen dollars for a blue-fronted Amazon, and ten dollars for parakeets (not budgies but larger birds like the yellow-chevroned parakeets), which he says didn't bring a good price. For years he, too, fed his family on the backs of parrots.

Nestling season was from the end of September through December. Mauro would leave his home at 4:00 a.m. with ten liters of water, a bag, and a flashlight. He left early because of the heat. More than once when he left later, babies overheated and died in his bag on his return. By then the sun was high in the sky and the temperature had hit 100 degrees Fahrenheit.

If the nests were near, he would be finished by 5:30 a.m., when it was still cool enough to carry the babies in the bag. For some nests the two would walk twenty miles and stay overnight. On these long jaunts, the two men often ran out of water. "Those were long, terrible days," says Mauro.

They would scale thousand-foot cliffs by climbing from the bottom, hand over hand, fifty to eighty feet, then tying a hemp rope. They had only two hundred feet of rope. If they had access from the top, the two had a special method they'd designed to get the babies out of the deep cliff holes by lowering two ropes and a lasso. Mauro would use a long pole with the lasso at the end to grab the baby. Or he would break the rock and go in headfirst with a flashlight. If the babies in the nest were very young, three or four days old, the mother wouldn't leave them. She would stay sitting on top of them, and the male would come and feed them all. But by the time they were fifteen to twenty days old, she would go and find food with the male, making it easier to get the young. "At that age they are very little and they won't run into the back of the cave for safety," Mauro says of the deep caves their parents chose for the purpose. "They'll flip on their backs to try and kick you."

Often the parents would return as Mauro and Raimundo were in the act and start screaming. Mauro said taking the babies always left him very sad, and he felt bad taking the young when he saw the parents react, but it was the only way to feed his family.

Some of the babies they took were forty days old, some less than twenty, which was "too young," but Mauro had quotas when he worked for Lourival, so he had to take them. Plus a few of the nests were low and accessible, and other trappers might grab the babies first, or a predator might get them. The quota on green-wings was five babies at a time, but he normally did at least three nests, taking all the babies he found.

I ask what made him change his mind about trapping. He describes the pivotal moment that heralded the end of his trapping career. He becomes visibly upset as he recounts it:

> I took two babies out of the same nest. They were in the bag on my back. They were very young. As I walked, I heard clearly someone say, "Arara, arara" over and over, which means "macaw" in Portuguese. I thought I was going to be arrested. I looked around to see who was saying it, but there was no one. And they were too young to speak like that. Still, they said it very clearly, and I realized it was coming from inside the bag. They were saying, "We aren't nothing. We are parrots. Don't take us from our parents." They were charged with making me feel particularly bad. They were speaking for all the babies that had suffered at my hands. It weighed on my conscience terribly. It started eating away at me.

Within a year Mauro had stopped poaching. Munn says that when Lourival set up the introduction, he said, "You've got to meet this guy and hire him. He's wanted to get out of this business since he started. He always said it was 'dirty, unfair and mean.'"

Mauro and his family have worked with Munn for four years. In his best years poaching, Mauro would clear five thousand dollars. Working for Munn, he and Raimundo clear three thousand dollars a year, 40 percent less. Mauro says it's worth it. "We don't have to worry about being on the wrong side of the law or going to prison," he says. "We sleep better. Life is much more relaxing now. And my wife is earning, too. It makes the family dynamic better."

Mauro says that in these last years with Munn, he's become extremely sensitive to the beauty of the animals and the issues of protecting wildlife in ways he hadn't thought about before. He's also passing on the change by teaching his children how to view animals. And not only his children are benefiting. Local school classes come to see the monkeys and the macaws, and he talks about helping them think differently about wildlife. He's becoming famous in the county for his work. He has also been able to get accredited for homeschooling, so he can teach his children—the nearest school is too far.

Mauro's wife prepares another great meal for us, and afterward Johnson shows Munn, on Munn's laptop computer, footage of some his and Cullity's previous ecotrips. Johnson doesn't have medical insurance, but he took out a second mortgage on his house to fund the expenses of these trips (though Cullity covers most of the costs) as well as the work the two are doing in Guyana with the Amerindians who trap and sell parrots as a primary source of income. Of the latter, Johnson says there is a noticeable difference in the number of green-winged and scarlet macaws being sighted since the two have started their project there.

But the situation is still perilous for parrots in Guyana. "Parrots are being pulled out the jungles," Johnson says. "The future of Guyana's jungles and wild bird populations really depends on establishing ecotourism while ninety percent of primary virgin forest is still intact." A photo taken in Chiapas, Mexico, appears on the computer screen. The two had been there just a week before coming here. There's lush foliage, a river, some swimming otters, and some nice footage of Amazon parrots. Munn comments and asks questions about the macaws they saw there. He's approving of their trip and says Tropical Nature has contacts everywhere and would happily have provided a guide into areas where they had a hard time finding good locals to show them.

Just then the scene cuts to an interesting traditional festival with a salsa band and Mexican women dressed in brightly colored, fluffed skirts for the occasion. "This won't hold my interest," says Munn without a moment's hesitation. That's about as long as his patience holds for cultural fluff. He can talk without taking a breath for fifteen minutes, but will cut you off in thirty seconds if what you say is not compelling to him. If it isn't helping the world, its wildlife, and the environment, it's of zero interest to Munn. Johnson quickly fast-forwards to more animals.

The next morning a few of us drive up to the Santa Marta Mountains. Land off the main road has just been illegally cleared. Munn says it was done in the middle of a lot, so IBAMA (the enforcement arm of the Brazilian Ministry of the Environment) wouldn't find it.

Lourival finds the field easily. It is only twenty minutes from town and forty minutes from Munn's Hyacinth Valley. The fence posts are made of fallen trees. We walk onto a thousand acres of habitat, razed to the ground. The devastation is dramatic. Munn says the felling of two thousand trees, palm stands, bushes, and all the rest of the habitat that formerly stood here was accomplished by two tractors with a heavy metal blade on a chain dragged between them. The surrounding seventy-five hundred acres will soon be cleared as well.

We all look on silently. It is a terrible sight, and a humbling experience to see human destruction firsthand. What had stood here was ancient forest, and still it had no way to hold a claim on its roots. Now you could see across the rubble for half a mile. The sun blazed down, and there was not a single spot of shade as a wild wind swept across the vast tract of destruction.

Munn points us to the destroyed stands of piaçava nuts. They were already hard enough for the birds to find, so this is a real loss to them. Thinking of birds, I realize there are none here. After a clear-cut, nothing moves; there's not a bird to be heard. It's a dead area eerily bordered by standing forest that now looks strange against the bare land.

"Now it doesn't look as horrendous as it will in September or October, when they have piles of burning trees," says Munn. After that they'll grow rice for two to three years to diminish the iron toxicity in the soil. Then the soy will be planted.

I ask why he and Lourival don't report this clearing, since it was done illegally. "Courts tend to favor progress," Munn replies. Here clearing land is still synonymous with progress, and the government is powerless over clear-cutting in remote areas it can't possibly monitor. By the time officials find out, if they do, bribes have been paid, and there's no culprit to be caught. "For as many smart people as there are in conservation, there are ten times as many smarter than them on the business side who are figuring out how to take the habitat down," says Munn.

"Given the choices to leave the habitat or cut it down, humans will pick the worst one every time," says Johnson. "How hopeless is this that, despite regulations and laws, it's cleared illegally? Charlie has got his work cut out for him. If you can't move people to save hyacinths and their land, what can you move them to save?"

But Munn blames himself for this. "There were four million acres for sale at seven dollars an acre. Now it's thirteen dollars an acre—and that's on top of Hyacinth Cliffs! There was nothing stopping us from buying a million or two million acres full of animals, but I was too slow and incompetent in raising the money."

He is now ready to buy land adjacent to Hyacinth Valley that would make the trip from Barreiras a three-to-four-hour ride instead of a five-to-six-hour journey. But he might have to fight the agribusiness moguls for it. "We'll soon find out if a battleship is about to crush our dinghy or turn us into a tugboat," Munn says.

The next morning at three we head to the main road to get on buses back to the airport. On the way we stop to pick up an elderly man hitching a ride. I ask him (via Munn) what he knows about the hyacinths. He says he remembers seeing large flocks of the birds flying in the sky when he was young, sometime in the 1930s. He's not sure of the year he was born, but he thinks he was about ten. "They were more beautiful than any other bird," he tells Munn. He says a few people came to these parts to catch them even then. "Back then connoisseur collectors were vying for them," says Munn. "Hyacinths were like Fabergé eggs."

Once on the bus, we move along the asphalt at a good clip. With a new awareness of the land as habitat, it is hard not to realize that a nice paved road like this puts many species out of business and undermines their ecosystems.

While the others head back to the United States, Munn, Paulina, and I will fly to the state of Bahia and the coastal city of Salvador. There we will drive inland, seeking the last of the rarest macaws left in the wild: the Lear's.

Chapter Eleven

The Journey Continues to the Rarest Macaws in the World, Lear's and Spix's

While there are several thousand wild hyacinths left in their natural habitat in Brazil, there are believed to be only six hundred Lear's macaws. In the same genus as the hyacinths, they, too, are large macaws, all blue with patches of deep yellow on their cheeks and teardrop-shaped spots that wrap around their eyes.

On our trip from Barreiras we fly over Petrolina, north of Salvador, where an even more threatened bird once lived. The Spix's macaws, the most endangered of all parrots, were hunted to extinction in the wild. Sixty or so exist in captive breeding programs whose goal is to keep the birds from disappearing from the planet. I will try to see them when I return to São Paulo, though it's unlikely. The protocol is strict, and officials at the Brazilian embassy, who said they would put in a request for me when I was in Los Angeles, never did, so the zoo doesn't even know I'll be coming to São Paulo.

From an original population of ten or twenty thousand, by 1800 there were only two hundred Spixes left in the wild. There are records of captive Spixes in Paris around 1912. In the late 1980s, the last wild Spix's was called "the loneliest bird in the world." He flew around the area looking for another of his kind after his parents, the last wild pair, had been caught and he was left on his own. After a while he was seen flying with a female Illiger's macaw. A previously captured Spix's female was obtained by the Brazilian government and was released to rejoin him in 1994, in the hope that the two would mate and keep the species alive in the wild. It almost worked. They found each other and were seen flying together until she disappeared. A local reported seeing her dead near a power line, ostensibly having flown into it at night. After a sighting in 2000, the lone male was never seen again.

It is almost as if the Spix's existed only to be collected. For more than two hundred years, not a single one had a chance at life without persecution. Like anything, the smaller the supply, the more coveted the item. Wealthy collectors who want the rarest parrot species will pay exorbitant prices to get the birds illegally, further endangering them in the wild. This was the case with the Spix's. There were never enough of them for the average person to have as a pet; the price was always too high.

The Brazilian government maintains it never gave permission for a single one to leave the country. Yet all but a few are in private hands outside Brazil. Called "bird barons," private collectors now control the future of some species whose numbers have dwindled in the wild. "I've almost never met a bird collector who wasn't willing to bend the rules or look the other way to get some more birds or new species of birds or a different species of bird or a sexier species of bird," says Munn. "And the smuggler's justification is, 'Their native habitat is being destroyed. I'm taking these birds so they're in a safe place.'"

The thirty-seat propeller plane flying us to Salvador is filled with businessmen. I walk down the short aisle. Almost to the last, the fold-down tables hold open laptops with spreadsheets on their screens. The passengers are all doing agribusiness.

I start a conversation with a thirtyish man sitting in Munn's row. His name is Roberto. Formerly an agricultural investment banker with Citibank, he's now a consultant for international cotton growers. He says most of the passengers are either scouting investments or representing companies wanting to expand. It's a boom market for agribusiness. "Everyone is buying land and raking in the money," he says.

We're headed for the state of Bahia, which is adjacent to Piaui. It's the size of France and has a predictable rainy season every year. The most important thing for cotton is that it doesn't get too much rain at harvest time. "The soil here isn't great, but you can treat it with fertilizers, and the combination of soil and environment produces cotton fiber that is one of the best in the world," says Roberto.

He represents three large cotton producers. On this trip he's looking at their desired land locations and helping them secure funding for their projects from banks. "I have more work than I can handle," he tells me. He says 50 percent of cotton grown on newly converted land is already in production, bringing in revenues of more than $500 million a year.

He says it's getting competitive, with more producers and a lot of investment money coming into the market. "There's an enormous amount of land to exploit, and the government doesn't charge tax if you're exporting," he says. "There are low interest rates, which are key, and they can export raw product, which increases production.

"We're competing with China," he says proudly.

I ask him about soy. He says soybeans are expected to have growth over the next ten years and that Mato Grosso, to the other side of Piaui going west, is now primary for production. Soon cotton and soy will live where parrots once did.

Salvador is on the southern coast of Bahia. It has a population of almost five million people, and the largest concentration of black people in the New World. The city's African influence is still present in ritual worship and schools that teach capoeira, a unique African form of ritualistic fighting. The main point of entry to Brazil for early colonialists in the 1600s, it was the country's capital for two hundred years and the nation's busiest port until 1815. Now it is the state capital. The city lies between green tropical hills and broad beaches along the bay of Todos Santos. The city was designed to have court buildings, administration offices, and residences on the hills overlooking the sea, with the port facilities, forts, docks, and warehouses on the beaches. This arrangement has remained until this day, leaving the city a mix of five-hundred-year-old buildings and modern structures.

Green-winged macaws used to live in the Atlantic forest, *mata Atlantica,* along the coastal perimeter of Salvador. The forest has an estimated twenty thousand species of plants, and two hundred species of endemic birds. It was originally twice the size of Texas. Much of it was clear-cut for sugar and coffee plantations. Now only 7 percent remains, and only 2 percent of it is protected. The rest suffers from illegal logging, clearcutting for agriculture, and grazing, which threatens the survival of the remaining biodiversity. Eight species of parrot are found only in the *mata Atlantica*, and four—the red-tailed Amazon, the red-browed Amazon, the vinaceous Amazon, and the brown-backed parrotlet—are now endangered. If the remaining forest were protected, Munn would like to reintroduce green-wings to their former home there.

The day after our arrival in Salvador de Bahia we head inland with Pedro and Rita Lima. Munn calls Pedro, a veterinarian and aviculturalist, "a fist in a velvet glove, a subversive." He is famous in Brazil as a hero of the people because he's outspoken in his fight for the environment. He's often interviewed on television and often featured with birds. "People living near Lima have a real problem," says Rita. "He's always stopping something."

Lima is also known as the "bird-banding king." He bands birds in every free moment, which amounts to every day of the year. There are famous stories of his banding escapades. Lima's favorite way to celebrate his wedding anniversary is to drag Rita out to band birds. He did the same with his three grown children every year at Christmas and New Year's during their youth. Rita says the family has long complained that they are slaves to his obsession, but Lima remains undaunted, and his obsession has produced some valuable results for the study of ornithology. For example, he discovered that roseate terns had migrated five thousand miles to get from his wetlands to New York's Long Island Sound. Until then no one knew where they wintered. Some ornithologists didn't believe it until Lima banded some of the terns, and they showed up on Long Island. He has been working with U.S. tern biologists to track the birds ever since.

He has also reintroduced to the wild both recently captured and wild-caught birds that were kept captive for a period of time afterward. So far he has repatriated ten thousand birds of 140 different species. All are banded, and many are monitored. Munn applauds his work. "He's the one person south of the Mississippi who knows about a huge variety of birds and has the only real bird rehab in the New World."

Lima's income comes from work with a large chemical company (he jokes that he's its resident ecologist) called Cetrel, which funds his research and rehab. It benefits from the good publicity for his work (except for the many times he does something controversial), and he gets funding for his real mission, to help birds.

All trafficked birds that are captured by authorities in Bahia are brought to Lima to rehab. "People think this area is a wildlife department store," he says of traffickers. Lima gets the birds back to "fighting weight" and then releases them in their natural habitats. He has taken sparrow hawks from the egg to five years old, taught them to hunt in the wild, and then released them. Now they're doing well, he says.

His staff makes nests out of PVC pipe, which they can lower to check on the babies in tree hole nests to make sure the repatriated birds are caring for them properly. That can be a problem for orphans who didn't have role models when they were growing up. So far they have done fine, with a few exceptions.

When reintroducing birds, Lima sets up food stations in the area of the release so the birds have a place they can come back to for nutritious meals until they can fend for themselves. Then they don't come back anymore. Lima's staff also rigs food dishes on pulleys to deliver food to the tops of trees.

Lima tells a funny story of a reintroduced "household" Amazon that learned some bad language in captivity. Now it is heard cursing loudly in Portuguese from the forest canopy. Given that he successfully repatriated a pet bird, I ask why most rereleases don't work. "They're half-assed," he says, because neither time nor money is invested, and some of the parrots' basic characteristics are not taken into account. One is the birds' social nature. Lima has found that to have a successful rerelease, a bird must have been raised with siblings or other companions. If they are removed from the nest and individually hand-raised, it's almost impossible. He doesn't know why that's the case, but he's found it to be so in the many failures he's had.

One of his great successes was introducing a dozen golden-headed conures to the coastal forest, the appropriate habitat for this small, noisy green bird with a red and gold cap and red belly, whose numbers are diminishing in all its range areas. Where Lima introduced a few, the population is now up to eighty.

As we enter the inland countryside, black vultures take their place on the roadside. A dozen of the huge birds hop up and down, fighting over garbage. Munn says vultures here serve the same function as seagulls in the United States: Brazil doesn't have gulls to eat garbage, it has vultures.

Licuri palm trees begin to dot the landscape along the way. Munn points them out, making a mental note of their number. These dense, small palms are the singular food source in the Lear's macaw's diet. They are considered pest plants, so no one stops cattle from trampling them. Many are killed before they mature, which takes between four and six years, and grow large enough to fend off encroachers. Here as in Piaui, both the palms and the birds are in short supply. The licuris we see are surrounded by development, so Munn speculates about having the locals collect the nuts and sell them to him if this land deal works out.

The Barreiras Valley, where the Lear's macaws are reported to live, is so remote that we need a local guide to navigate the labyrinth of roads to it. No one in our group has been there, though others, such as Jamie Gilardi from the World Parrot Trust, have and have sent Munn photos. It is rumored that twenty to eighty of the rare birds are seen in the morning and afternoon like clockwork.

Over the previous year Munn had discussions with José Ze Grande, a landowning patriarch in this valley who wanted to sell his 625 acres, more than half the valley, encompassing the cliffs and Lear's nests, for $10,000. Ze Grande wanted to see the birds protected after he died and thought his children, who all lived elsewhere, wouldn't care to live here, but he died a week before they were to complete the transaction. Munn says Ze Grande's children are now holding the land ransom because they figure he is a "gringo with lots of money." Now they want $100,000 for it. Munn's plan to get around their asking price is to act as if he doesn't care and is looking to buy land from one of the other property holders.

Lima has contracted Carlinhos, a former trapper (not the same one Lourival worked for), to take us to the valley. We are to meet him here in a square next to the road that leads into it.

Already in the square is a shady-looking character named Zelito, an infamous criminal and one of the biggest trappers in Bahia. He was arrested a week earlier for poaching six Lear's babies. He says he doesn't trap anymore, but doesn't deny he was caught with the birds. Rita says Zelito is despicable because he has no conscience. He is arrested over and over, pays a fine, and goes back to trapping endangered birds.

Lima starts yelling at Zelito that he's a liar for saying he doesn't trap. Zelito says he was set up and didn't know the birds were wild. An argument ensues. Zelito says he was innocent of trapping the baby birds, even though he's photographed with them in newspaper clippings he passes around.

Just then Carlinhos pulls up on a motorcycle just across the square. Sitting astride the motorcycle, Carlinhos is Mr. Macho, with an outfit to match his attitude—a cutoff jeans shirt with a hyacinth macaw patch sewn on, an Italian stallion T-shirt, and a black leather jacket over both, even in this hundred-degree heat. On his head is a black cowboy hat with a band of silver coins around the crown, which masks half of his strong, sculptured face and gray-blue eyes. He smiles a lot to show off his gold-capped front tooth. But all this machismo is undermined by a high-pitched, squeaky voice.

Carlinhos says we can easily lose Zelito and his group (who may want to follow Munn and Lima) if we take back roads to the road that leads to the cliffs. The tall corn turns into a maze, and there's no map. Without a guide like him, Carlinhos says, it'll be impossible for them to find us.

In no time we are dodging wandering goats and donkeys on rough and muddy roads.

I ask Lima how he knew that Zelito had trapped the six Lear's macaws. He says that when he called Carlinhos to arrange this trip, Carlinhos told him what Zelito was up to. Carlinhos had once worked for Zelito, who was trying to recruit him back into the life. After Lima hung up with Carlinhos, he called the police and got Zelito arrested. Carlinhos doesn't speak English, and I'm figuring he'd be none too thrilled to hear all this, because if Zelito finds out who told on him, he'll be none too happy either.

This all feels like a Brazilian western—goats, donkeys, good guys and bad, saints, thieves, and a great ransom of flying gold in the cliffs.

We pass through some tiny villages with a few unpaved streets lined with two-story row houses, of the same design as the ones on the main road but smaller. The streets each lead to farmland alternating with dry tropical forest called *caatinga*. Now is the dry season. In El Niño years, the drought can be "crushing," according to Munn. It drives people out of the area and to the slums of big cities like São Paulo and Rio.

The embankment along the roadway becomes so high on both sides that it is soon impossible to see over it. There are no signs or posts, and every turn looks like the one before it. It seems to me as if we're going in circles. This is the maze Carlinhos was referring to. Carlinhos says he used to trap parrots here, so he knows this route like the back of his hand. But then he asks Lima to pull over so he can look over the embankment to get his bearings. Not a great sign.

Carlinhos learned how to trap nearly a decade earlier from Zelito, who wore a camouflage outfit and cap and told Carlinhos he was an official environmentalist who was just taking the baby birds to document and photograph them, and he would make sure they were returned to their nests afterward. Carlinhos asked whether he would get in trouble taking the babies. Zelito said not to worry, because the government approved of his work and he would handle any problems with local enforcement, given his official connections.

Carlinhos figured this was a great little job and started trapping in December 1998. It was usually a two-day operation. He would walk four hours (twelve miles uphill in sand) to a nesting spot on the land of a man named Otavio, who would shoot Lear's macaws for fun. Then he would climb the cliffs to get to an active nest. On his first foray, he got three babies right away. They were four or five weeks old; their eyes were open, but they had few feathers. He got 150 reals (about $25) each for birds worth between five and six figures on the open market. Carlinhos thought it was so much money that that was all he could think about while the six parent birds flew around over his head, screaming at him.

When Lima set up Zelito to be busted by government officials, Carlinhos was out of a job. By then he knew so much about Lear's macaws that IBAMA officials came to him for help locating the birds so they could monitor them. For a while he was on their payroll.

Lima is lighting another cigarette with his previous one when Carlinhos finishes telling me about his past as a trapper. Munn confides to me that he is worried about losing Lima, a longtime chain smoker, to cigarettes. His voice has a smoker's rasp, and he coughs heavily. He sounds as if he is on his way to emphysema. But Lima can't seem to quit for long, though he's tried numerous times. "Without him so much is lost," says Munn. "He's irreplaceable."

Carlinhos appears lost and says we need to backtrack. But we can't turn around here; the road is far too narrow. We go farther in the same direction and come to a wide spot under a tree, but a cow sitting there is in no mood to move. She only grudgingly gets up when Lima inches next to her.

It looks as if mules and cows formed the "road" we are driving on. More a well-worn path than a road, it is trodden into the now familiar rust-colored sandstone soil. We left the farmland behind a while back; here it's all *caatinga* around us. We have not seen another soul or sign of civilization in more than an hour, and I worry that Carlinhos might not find our way out of here. It's late afternoon, and heavy clouds threaten rain. The sun will set soon. Once it gets dark, there will be nothing to see but whatever is in front of our headlights.

Finally we turn a corner and arrive at a precipice, and the Barreiras Valley reveals itself below, a lush oasis bounded by sandstone cliffs. Munn looks through his binoculars and points out the nesting holes in the bordering cliffs. Licuri palms abound, surrounded by trees, rolling meadow, and powder sand. This is the habitat recipe for Lear's macaws. The cliffs border the valley about a half mile apart. Beyond this valley is a vast expanse of mountainous landscape that extends to the horizon. It is strikingly quiet.

In addition to Lear's, Munn says an estimated eighty nests of blue-fronted Amazons, more than one hundred nests of blue-crowned conures and Illiger's macaws, and a population of tufted-eared marmosets also live here. "They're still catching plenty of blue-fronted Amazons nesting in the cliffs here," he says. "If we buy this valley, it'll put an end to that."

It starts raining, but it doesn't cool down; it just gets more humid. The narrow decline into the valley is rocky and treacherous, even more so now that it's wet. Whether the truck will make it down the winding crevasse is questionable. If the tires fall into the trenches on either side, we might not be able to back out. I play it safe and walk down with Rita. Munn drives with Carlinhos and Lima outside, guiding the front and back, respectively. Munn alternates from side to side, trying to avoid the deep gaps. At some points he veers dangerously close to the cliff edge and can't right himself. It's painful to watch, and it wouldn't surprise me if we got stuck here for the night or worse.

Inching along, and slipping in places, Munn finally makes it down. After a collective deep exhale we venture to a small farm to the north, opposite Ze Grande's.

Munn's strategy is to buy the land of Ze Grande's neighbors and give his heirs the impression he's not interested in their land anymore. They know nothing about Lear's macaws and have no idea how much land he wants to buy altogether. He thinks they'll get nervous that he's not interested, and greedy when they see their neighbors making money. Then they'll come back to him with a lower price for their acres, which are what he really needs: he has to own their cliffs to protect the birds.

We come to the front of a small ramshackle cottage that looks as if it's out of the Old West. A thin donkey wearing a saddle is tethered to a post on the front lawn. It's the saddest creature I have ever seen.

The family comes out on the small veranda. There's an elderly grandfather and his farmhand; his daughter-in-law; and her children, a boy about seven and a girl about five. Munn and Lima introduce us and ask about the land. The grandfather answers all the questions.

He says his family has lived here for more than one hundred years. The house looks to be that old. It is the color of the cliffs and made of sandstone bricks covered in a layer of sandstone plaster, cracking in many places. I look around. The valley probably looks the same as it did when their relatives arrived, and they are living under the same conditions. The grandfather tells Munn the house has no running water or electricity. He says they carry drinking water from a small pond nearby. But when the summer comes, it dries up, and then they depend on the little rain-water they can gather. It's the only other way for them to obtain water for miles.

Munn asks about the birds. The old man points to a tree. "There were about five sitting there earlier, but they flew off," he says. Munn doesn't think they'll come back this late in the day; they've probably flown to their roosts. I think it's a shame not to see them after such a long trip, but Munn seems fine with it—the birds this man describes are most definitely Lear's macaws.

Rita asks about the children. Their mother, who is about twenty years old, says they cannot attend school because it is too far away, and the only means of transport is the single donkey used for farming.

On the way back Munn is very excited about the land. I'm somewhat surprised, because it is so inaccessible. That's not a deterrent to him; it's just par for the course with rare birds, which are found only in remote and isolated locations. He says that if it works out for him to get some of this land, he'll do tests over the next two months to see whether the massive king vultures can be baited for ecotourism like the hyacinths are. He also wants to know how many macaws and little monkeys are here, and what kind of other bird species populate the surrounding forest. "It could be extraordinary bird-watching," he says.

Munn starts calculating out loud. He figures that if he can bring eight hundred people a year here, with four or five people on salary, it will cost less than ten thousand dollars a year to run the operation. "But you didn't see any Lear's," I remind him. "No," he says, "but I saw the future, like seeing baby sequoias." It's a fitting simile. Like sequoias, Lear's macaws are one of the great wonders of the natural world, and like a forest of baby sequoias, the potential of this valley just needs nurturing. "It's a dream come true if I can make it happen," he says gleefully.

On the way back to town, Lima suggests we stop at the bird market near Salvador. There are usually parrots for sale. Selling native wildlife is illegal, so the sellers are all on the perimeter of the market, ready to flee if the authorities come. No parrots are visible, but a variety of songbirds sit in tiny wooden boxes. It's a cacophony of sound as they sing tragically to be released.

We return to the truck depressed, but Lima is still optimistic. "It is completely possible to change people's minds," he says. "Dove breeders were killing falcons until I wrote an article showing that falcons were part of the natural chain, and they weed out the sick doves." Lima says that after the piece ran, he got letters from dove breeders thanking him and saying they had never thought of it that way before.

Lima is especially proud of some of the animal welfare programs he's instituted at Cetrel. He says Brazilians keep pets as a matter of course, and the number-one pet in their homes is a wild bird. "Fifteen years ago this was true of the five hundred workers here. Now not a single employee has one as a pet," he says with a big smile.

Lima has found ways every day over the last fifteen years to reinforce to his coworkers the idea that captivity is bad for wildlife. "The most important thing with conservation is to get the public on board," he says. "You can do the best scientific work, but without the public it's just elegant scientific articles about something in the environment that is about to be all gone."

Lima says even long-standing cultural ideas about animals, such as Brazilians' superstitious fear of snakes, can be altered. Local people would go out of their way to drive back and forth over a snake if they saw one on the road, because they thought they were evil and carried transmittable diseases. Eight years ago Lima started a program to educate people about snakes, and now the practice of killing them has almost completely stopped in the areas where his programs are in place.

Back in Salvador, I prepare to leave for São Paulo. This time spent with Munn has been illuminating, yet he remains an enigmatic figure. I realize that in some ways the most important thing about him is also the most apparent: a nine-year-old child can love something, but to have this level of passion and sustain it for a lifetime is remarkable, at the least. Birds aren't just a passion of Munn's life; they are profoundly with him, a part of his primary family. They were there before his friends and lovers, his wives and children, and will likely be there in his psyche when all else fades.

Some say one man can't change the world, but Munn proves them wrong almost every day.

The São Paulo zoo's directors, chief executive officer Paulo Bressan and administrative director Joao Cruz, have agreed to meet with me on short notice, but it's only a first step. It's still highly unlikely that I will be able to see the Spixes. All requests are to be approved in advance by an international committee that includes members in the Canary Islands and the Philippines. It normally takes weeks to get permission, if it is granted at all, because the risk to the birds (which are guarded like the gold at Fort Knox) is too great.

Munn is angry about the government's lack of action to save the Spixes while there was still a chance to do so in the 1980s. He says he didn't have people on the ground then, or he would have done so. It's one reason he's so passionately determined to save the Lear's and hyacinths. "There's no excuse," he says. "They dropped the ball on those birds. They were asleep at the switch. The Spixes should not have died. Now the birds that are left are like the living dead." He says it's unlikely they'll be able to bring the species back in large enough numbers from the remaining birds, and even if they breed well, there will never be enough of them to risk reintroduction to the wild.

I meet with the senior staff in the zoo's conference room. They are polite but quiet. I'm expected to plead my case. I can see by their expression that they hear it all the time: people trying to talk their way into seeing the Spixes. It's understandable that the zoo denies most requests. What's in it for them? And there's certainly nothing in it for the birds. It only stresses them when strangers enter their area. That's why the same people care for them every day.

Finally I tell them it's okay if I can't see them, that I will be happy to ask them some questions.

We talk about Presley, the Spix's who arrived here after making news worldwide when he was discovered living in a Colorado living room in 2001. For twenty-five years, while his species was being wiped out, he was kept as a pet. He was smuggled out of Brazil to Czechoslovakia, then to England and then to the United States. The woman who kept Presley for all those years was sold him by the smuggler, an acquaintance of hers, as a blue-morph Patagonian conure. The smuggler was worried about being caught and figured the bird would remain anonymous in her living room. The woman later discovered Presley's pedigree, but still didn't report his existence for two and half decades. When her Amazon died and Presley, who was bonded to the bird, went into mourning and his health started to decline, the owner called a local veterinary office. Mickey Muck, a parrot enthusiast, fortuitously for Presley, took the call. Muck knew well about the Spixes' plight and recognized the bird in a photo for what he was. But getting the bird repatriated to Brazil took time and the concerted effort of a consortium of individuals and organizations interested in saving the species.

Muck immediately contacted the World Parrot Trust, which coordinated efforts with her, IBAMA, USFWS, and Presley's owner. The last would not reveal her identity or whereabouts until she had a guarantee in writing from USFWS that she would not be arrested for having the bird.

Some of Presley's tissue was cultured and put on ice for possible cloning for conservation purpose in the future (if needed, and if the procedure is ever possible for parrots; as of this writing, scientists are still working on cloning a chicken).

In the process it was discovered that Spixes aren't actually macaws. They are more closely related to conures than to the large macaws they have long been associated with.

When Muck took custody, Presley suffered from serious health problems. He had been fed a nutritionally poor diet of pellets for decades, and the lack of fruits, vegetables, nuts, and other nutritionally rich foods had caused physical ailments. Additionally, his feet were warped from standing flat on perches too wide for his toes to grip, and his body muscles had atrophied from lack of exercise, so he had trouble even holding himself upright for long periods (most parrots can stand legs locked for hours, or to sleep all night). Muck spent months rehabbing the suffering bird to build up his strength and make him healthy enough to endure the twenty-hour flight to Brazil. Muck and a USFWS agent flew with Presley to Miami, where he was handed off to an IBAMA representative.

All the Spixes except those in the zoo (and even some of them, like Presley) were smuggled out of the country for the pet trade. To recover them, the Brazilian government granted amnesty to whoever had them, wherever they were, in the hope they would come forward and relinquish the birds. This is a big issue for many conservationists, including Munn, who never supported amnesty and says the Brazilian government should have confiscated the birds in sting operations with Interpol. "They should have broken down doors and gotten them and made it illegal to have them anywhere in the world," he says.

Instead, only a few people with birds came forward, and there's still no knowing how many others have never been reported. An international committee was formed, with the participation of some of the people who had bought the birds illegally. The committee was formed in the Philippines because a large collection of Spix's resides there, but the birds are being kept all over the world. A sheik in Qatar personally owns the largest number of them (fifty-eight), and is running his own breeding program. In 2003, an exchange of birds took place between the Philippines and Loro Parque, a zoo in the Canary Islands. The zoo is the largest bird-breeding facility in the world, and its founder owned Spixes. Bressan isn't upset about the birds being spread out across the globe. "It's not safe to have them all in one place," he says. "It's best to share the responsibility."

Parrots International, a U.S.-based parrot conservation organization, learned that the last-known Spix's nesting area, the Gangorra farm south of Curaça, Brazil, which included the last known Spix's tree hole nest, was available for purchase. In February 2007, a thousand acres (five hundred hectares) was purchased with the idea of reintroducing the birds to their historical home in the future. Now, if the birds' numbers do increase and the day comes when they can return to the wild, they could return to their original home.

Here in São Paulo there are seven Spixes, including Presley. The zoo is hoping Presley will reproduce, but so far he's not shown interest in the female living in the cage next door. "Though historically we didn't have a breeding commitment, we are very committed to captive breeding them now," says Bressan. "But even with a small number, you can do it wrong."

One of the complexities is designing the right kind of nest. It's hard to know what shape the birds prefer, large or small, tall or deep. It's a crapshoot with high stakes. "If we make a mistake, it's a one hundred percent mistake, because they won't breed," says Cruz, a pathologist who was previously a veterinarian with the Washington National Zoo. Sadly, they all agree it is highly unlikely they can produce enough birds and rehabilitate them to be reintroduced into nature successfully.

I tell them about Lima's rehab. They hadn't heard about him, and they're impressed. He would be the guy to do it, I suggest.

"There's still ongoing traffic in Lears," says Cruz. "It's a crime people didn't learn with the Spixes. We need funds to educate. IBAMA is trying to convince people in the area not to shoot them, but there are too many out to get them and too few to protect them." They tell me that three weeks ago IBAMA confiscated six Lear's babies and brought them to the zoo. I tell them that three days earlier, I met the man who stole them.

Cruz says the areas the birds live in need to be appropriated, the land needs to be bought, the local people worked with, and the areas guarded by law enforcement to protect them. "If a local or international organiza-tion wants to buy the land, it's good," says Cruz. "It's not going to be a success if they buy the land and give it to IBAMA. They have no budget for personnel to maintain it or for equipment."

Budget is a problem here, too. There's no outside funding for the Spixes' care, and it's a burden for the zoo to bear all the costs, which are huge—a special feeding consultant, three biologists, three caretakers, and a nutritionist, not to mention all the security costs.

I think they agreed to meet me because American attention could lead to more funding. "In the U.S., fund-raising is big and popular," says Bressan. "Here there is no institution related to conservation; any money we could get in donations would go straight to the birds for their comfort."

It's getting late, the sun is setting out the conference room window, and as we rise to leave, I lose hope of seeing the birds. Bressan turns to me and says, "Come, we'd better hurry. Once the light goes, you won't be able to see them."

I smile and my heart races when I hear those words.

"There are six billion people in the world, and only a few have ever laid eyes on them, and only a few ever will," says Luiz Roberto Francisco ("Berto"), a consultant brought in to advise on the Spixes, as we all walk over. I nod in agreement and turn to Bressan. "How did you feel when you first saw them?" I ask. "Humbled," he says. "We are protect-ing diamonds."

As we reach the birds' compound, I find I had been sitting just forty yards from the Spixes the whole time. The walls are high and protected by barbed wire along the perimeter. Seven security cameras monitor them twenty-four hours a day, and guards are posted full-time at the front.

We see the Lear's macaws first. All paired up in large cages, they squawk loudly as we enter. One says, "Arara, arara," over and over clear as a bell, and I'm instantly reminded of Mauro's baby parrots in the bag. It's uncanny.

The squawking instigates the Spixes, who also go into a tizzy as we enter. They don't know me and would never allow a stranger to be so close in the wild. A wisp of a bird and smaller than the Lear's, they are a delicate light blue, but not all one shade, more like clouds in a sunset of blue gradations. Seeing them brings a surge of emotion.

Their local name was the blue macaw, which is more apt than their given name (from Johann Baptist von Spix, the naturalist credited with discovering them). Their cages are big, but barren of enrichments other than perches and a nest box. Berto tells me it's too hard to keep them clean and retrieve the birds for routine medical exams and tests if there is greenery inside. One pair has started using their beaks to expand the intentionally small hole in the wooden nest box. It's a fortuitous sign that this might be the season they breed.

Presley is in the last cage in the last row, as he was the last to arrive. He runs to the bars and greets me excitedly, bopping up and down, when I say, "Hello, Presley. How are you?" It's been a long time since someone has spoken to him in English, and he warms to it immediately. His caretakers have overheard him speaking English to the bird in the next cage. I tell him how beautiful he is, and he lowers his head to be scratched through the bars. He is visibly upset when I leave and tries to get through the bars to come with me. He's still a pet and doesn't understand why he's been left all alone here. I tell him he has to stay and make more like him, but he's not consoled.

It's a bittersweet situation in Brazil today. There's more protection in place than ever before, but lone dedicated crusaders like Munn, or small groups, are the ones working the hardest. The government is not supporting their parrots as they should. They could preserve habitat the birds need by making it protected parkland, but the will to do so isn't there. Still, if there is awareness in the global community of their situation, and support for the parrots is generated around the world, Munn's vision for their safe future all over Brazil could be assured.

Chapter Twelve

Repercussions, Ramifications, and Solutions

In the 24 hours since this time yesterday, over 200,000 acres of rainforest have been destroyed in our world. Fully 13 million tons of toxic chemicals have been released into our environment. Over 45,000 people have died of starvation, 38,000 of them children. More than 130 plant or animal species have been driven to extinction by the actions of humans—the last time there was such a rapid loss of species was when the dinosaurs vanished. And all this just since yesterday.

—Thom Hartmann, *The Last Hours of Ancient Sunlight*

Perhaps the greatest tragedy of the parrot crisis is that it is an unnecessary result of affluent consumerism. Parrots are a luxury item, deprived of liberty purely for human amusement. No one needs to keep a parrot. Their plight is symptomatic of the attitude that all nonhuman beings are products free for the taking from the largest shopping mall of all: the earth. The carelessness with which we exploit everything living around us has resulted in the wholesale loss of species and destruction of the earth currently under way at human hands.

Instead of trying to be a part of the world's ecological systems, humans have systematically endeavored to "conquer nature," and these actions have brought us to the point of imperiling our own existence. To live, we must use some of what nature offers. But the human population, one species, is consuming more than the planet can replenish, and usurping the needs of all other species in the doing. We are the deadly predator of all other species, heading for a final collison with nature when we should be embracing it and all its diversity.

Many living things, such as parrots and the forests they live in, can never be restored once lost. As a result, according to Harvard biologist E. O. Wilson, an estimated 25 percent of all plant and animal species on the planet will gone in the next fifty years.

We need to share the earth with other species because we depend on many of them for our own survival. The stark truth is, if we disappeared tomorrow (and took all of our toxin-producing technology with us), the world would be better off by far. On the other hand, if all the other living species disappeared tomorrow, we would perish almost immediately. We depend on little-thought-of creatures like ocean plankton to produce 60 percent of the planet's oxygen. When it comes to parrots, we also have a moral obligation to protect them. "Parrots are as old as condors," says Brazilian parrot expert Carlos Yamashita. "It took millions of years for them to reach this form. They have lived in the areas they are in now for a million years, traveling only to accommodate habitat and temperature changes. Ethically we need to have respect for animals that have a very long history on this earth, because they carry our evolutionary history."

In a paper, Charles Hall of the State University of New York's College of Environmental Sciences concluded, "The most important problem facing wildlife management is the growing human population, its affluence and the concomitant requirement for resources to accommodate this growth."

In the late 1990s, Hall and three other scientists at SUNY conducted groundbreaking research on American affluence, overpopulation, and our impact on the environment. Colloquially called the "baby paper," it measured the environmental impact of the life of a child born in the United States. They calculated that

an American born in the 1990s would produce in a lifetime about one million kilograms of atmospheric wastes, ten million kilograms of liquid wastes, and one million kilograms of solid wastes. In addition, an American will consume seven hundred thousand kilograms of minerals and 24 billion BTU's of energy, which is equivalent to 4,000 barrels of oil. In a lifetime, an average American will eat 25,000 kilograms of major plant foods and 28,000 kilograms of animal products, provided in part by slaughtering 2,000 animals.

Fifty years ago, the American Dream—which promised that hard work entitled Americans to expensive vacations, bigger homes, "a chicken in every pot and a car in every garage"—might have been a valid aspiration. Now, when a single American's consumption ecologically equals that of fifty individuals who lived one hundred years ago, the American Dream has become the American Nightmare, according to ecological economist William Rees. He bases this idea on the Ecological Footprint Analysis (EFA), a groundbreaking system Rees created to measure the impact humans have on the earth's resources. The EFA has since been adopted by the United Nations and countries and organizations around the world. It turns out Americans have the most disastrous effect worldwide: we make up just 4.7 percent of the world's population, but consume 30 percent of the world's goods. Each American consumes as much grain as 5 Kenyans, and as much energy as 35 Indians, a whole village of Bangladeshis (150), and 500 Ethiopians. And we are devouring land and resources within and without our borders: a recent study by researchers at Rutgers University concluded that within forty years New Jersey will likely be the first state to reach "build-out," a point where the state's supply of developable land will be exhausted. How will protected parks and other areas that native birds and other creatures count on remain so when states reach development capacity, and there's no place for humans to build? Not everyone wants to live in the desert. Who will win: people or birds?

Rees and his colleague Mathis Wackernagel coauthored the groundbreaking book *The Ecological Footprint*. In it they determined how much usable land and resources there were on earth and divided that amount by the number of people—six billion—on the planet today. After excluding unusable areas such as the deep ocean and the tops of mountains, they found that each person was allotted about two "global hectares" (gha), or five acres of ecologically productive land and waterscape. But because we consume inordinately more than other countries, the ecological footprint of an average North American is twenty to thirty acres (eight to ten hectares). That is how much agricultural land one American uses for food, how much industrial land is required for production of clothing and other daily essentials, and the resources needed to dispose of waste products. If everyone lived at the affluence level of just an *average* American or Canadian, we would need four Planet Earths to survive. "How can we continue to promote a lifestyle that requires four times as much productive ecosystem per capita as is available on earth?" asks Rees. A Cree Indian proverb says, "Only when the last tree has died, the last river has been poisoned, and the last fish been caught will we realize we cannot eat money." So far we are proving it right.

Rees and Wackernagel's EFA results are dramatic, but the allotment of hectares in their EFA addresses only the needs of people—it does not include the environmental resources required to support the other twelve million species on earth. The EFA is telling us we need to dial back consumerism, in a country whose operating model requires spending to keep the economy afloat. But the state of the planet compels us to rewrite the American Dream and redefine personal prosperity. It is no longer ecologically appropriate to import granite countertops, replace perfectly good appliances with new ones, and have rain forests or other animal habitat felled to have exotic woods for our homes.

Only revolutionary lifestyle changes by citizens of the major industrialized countries can mitigate the impact of overpopulation on the environment, and this crucial information, for the most part, remains unaddressed while our impact on the earth takes its toll in everything we do and use in our normal lives.

Our current government and some scientists still espouse the idea that we won't have to make significant personal sacrifices to fix problems

such as global warming, the environmental crisis, and species extinction. They suggest, for example, that legislation restricting automotive
designs will cut emissions sufficiently, and that making polluting indus-
tries operate more sustainably will protect our water supply and other
natural resources. But because our unrelenting exploitation of the planet
is in every single act, from the toilet paper we use (in North America it is
likely to include ancient boreal forest trees) to the clothes and food we buy,
experts are predicting much more drastic scenarios. What they outline is
akin to the personal deprivation experienced during the Great Depression. It involves rationing and does not include SUVs, or McMansions,
or *bigger* anything. The same holds true for animal preservation. There
are no simple fixes. We will need to make pivotal changes in our cultural
attitudes toward parrots and animals in general to save them and their
habitats, and we will need to make these changes quickly. But even if we
do, China is rising as a major force in opposition.

Today, the average Chinese citizen has ten times the purchasing power
he or she had just a quarter century ago. At this rate, China will reach
the current level of affluence of the United States in about two decades,
and pass it in about three. Parrots and other animals will not survive the
onslaught of a billion people with enough money and inclination to buy
them as pets. In less than three years after it went into effect, the EU ban
on wild-bird imports (made permanent in July 2007) already had saved
the lives of 9.9 million birds (calculated by the 2 million birds imported
into the EU each year and a conservative factoring of 40 percent to 60
percent mortality rate in the trapping and transporting process to achieve
that number of live ones).

After hundreds of years of active importation, the incident inciting the
ban was not a growing consciousness among EU residents of the suffering
wreaked by and the tremendous losses involved in securing their pet birds;
it was primarily the human health concern of securing Europe's borders
against the threat of the H5N1 avian flu virus and other human-infectious
avian diseases. But it was also the culmination of years of pressure by a

coalition of more than 230 NGOs, led by the World Parrot Trust, Defenders of Wildlife, and Species Survival Network.

China, now the world's largest producer and exporter of budgerigars and canaries, doesn't have this history of imports. It also has none of the powerful national conservation groups of the EU or the United States to lobby for a ban, or any impetus to institute humane treatment for the hundreds of thousands of birds it is breeding and exporting now. In contrast, what China has is a rapidly growing, first-time consumerist-minded middle class that covets all things exotic. It took fifteen years for the EU, a group of countries mostly similar to the United States in culture and economic development, to implement legislation like the United States' WBCA. How much longer will it take China, or India, which also has a population of over a billion that is rapidly growing more affluent, to do so, left to its own devices? According to Kathy Mackinnon of the World Bank, who lived and worked in Asia for ten years, China is a giant vacuum cleaner for timber and wildlife that is already "eating everything down to the reptiles."

How to prevent loss of the remaining wild parrots? The Chinese (and Indians, too) covet American lifestyles—homes, food, clothes, and culture. It is therefore incumbent on us to be examples of conservation in practice. But it is hypocritical to try to impress these ideas on them while we are living so unsustainably ourselves.

Says Hall, "We hardly ever think about environmental destruction when we make our routine purchases, but the economic activity occasioned by our purchases is certainly behind much of the environmental destruction of the world." As a nation we must start practicing conscious consumerism.

Ironically, current research shows that happiness has not increased with consumption. The *2004 State of the World* by the Worldwatch Institute reported that one-third of Americans said they were "very happy." The same number said so in 1957, when Americans were only half as wealthy. Other research shows that the richer people get, the less happy they are.

"Affluence is violence" is the catchphrase Rees coined to describe our impact on the environment, and clearly that is the case when it comes to the dynamics of the parrot crisis. The international trade in parrots could end tomorrow if CITES stopped sanctioning it and uplisted all parrots to Appendix I, because it is clear that parrots cannot be traded sustainably in a global market. The domestic parrot trade would end if consumers everywhere were educated to understand that it is a form of animal abuse to keep a bird caged, and understand the long-term implications, for them and the parrot, of buying a pet that may outlive them by decades.

When public approval becomes public outrage, people will stop buying parrots. When it becomes unfashionable to keep a parrot, no one will *want* to keep one. These are not unreasonable, nor even unlikely, scenarios, but it all starts with the consumer; the end user, not poachers or trappers, drives the trade. When the demand stops, the trade stops, and only through the efforts of a concerned and proactive public can transformations like these be effected. Affluence can no longer equal luxury; it must equal responsibility.

To be responsible global citizens, we in the developed world must be role models for the rest of the world. With global warming and the man-driven demise of the natural environment becoming ever more imminent, it is apparent that our own considerations, human considerations, can no longer be of primary importance. Trees, wildlife, and the rest of biodiversity must have an equal seat at the table with humans for our world, as we know it, to survive.

From now on, when we, as individuals, cause the removal of something from nature, we must replace it in addition to buying it. When we buy something, we only pay the retailer, not the earth. For example: with every book you buy, paying your bookseller doesn't cover the actual cost of the book. There was also a primary cost to nature when the tree was felled to make it. Today in the United States, only 5 percent of trees are sustainably harvested; the rest are habitat lost to animal species. And an estimated 80 percent of U.S. printers (and virtually all the ones in China, where the majority of books are now being published) are buying

Indonesian rain forest paper made in Asia, because it is the cheapest, highest-quality stock that can be bought anywhere. Because virgin trees make the best paper, Indonesian rain forests are being rampantly felled to make books—the ones that fill Barnes & Noble and Borders and come in the mail from Amazon. Any of the thirty-six species of parrot on that island-nation living in those trees go down with them. And if you purchased a book online, you didn't even have to leave home to participate in their decimation.

Parrots are the canaries in the coal mine of the present-day ecological crisis. When you follow the parrot trail—from the relentless hunting that is decimating populations in the wild, to the rampant deforestation that is clearing their natural habitats—it leads to the decline and destruction not only of these treasured species but of other species still unknown to us, and eventually to our systematic destruction of the planet as we know it. The ironic thing is that the very actions we must take to protect parrots will save us in the doing. For example, deforestation destroys parrot habitat and promotes global warming. If we preserve forests for birds, we will also preserve oxygen-generating trees, which act as a carbon sink for carbon dioxide and help stave off global warming. When we help them, we are helping ourselves.

For everything we do, there is someone, some green organization, struggling to make it up to the earth. In the case of books, Eco-Libris (www.ecolibris.net) has already planted thousands of trees to replace those taken to make them. For just a dollar apiece, they will plant a tree in a developing country for every book you buy and each you already own.

Save a parrot's tree. Save ten. Without our help, without needed legislative protection and worldwide consciousness-raising on their behalf, parrots will be lost in short years to come.

It is fitting to end this book with this succinct summation from Wayne Pacelle, president of the Humane Society of the United States:

We are at an odd moment in history. There are more people in this country sensitized to animal protection issues than ever before. The Humane

Society of the United States alone has 8 million members, and in addition, there are more than 5,000 other groups devoted to animal protection.

At the same time, there are more animals being harmed than ever before—in industrial agriculture, research and testing, and the trade in wild animals. It is pitiful that our society still condones keeping millions of parrots and other wild birds as pets—wild animals that should be free to fly and instead are languishing in cages, with more being bred every day. It's an issue of supply and demand and it's also an issue of right and wrong. Animals suffer in confinement, and we have a moral obligation to spare them from needless suffering.

Every person can make a difference every day for animals by making compassionate choices in the marketplace: don't buy wild animals as pets, whether they are caught from the wild or bred in captivity. If we spare the life of just one animal, it's a 100% positive impact for that creature. If we can solve the larger bird trade problem, it will be 100% positive for all parrots and other wild birds in the U.S. and beyond our borders.

I believe we will look back in 50–75 years and say "How could we as a society countenance things like the decades long imprisonment of extraordinarily intelligent animals like parrots?"

Acknowledgments

For this work, which took more than two and a half years to research and write, I amassed thousands of documents and conducted several hundred interviews with leading scientists, environmentalists, paleontologists, ecological economists, conservationists, global warming experts, federal law enforcement officers, animal control officers, avian researchers, avian rescuers, veterinarians, breeders, pet bird owners, bird clubs, pet bird industry executives and employees, sanctuaries and welfare organizations, legislators, and officials with the Convention on International Trade in Endangered Species of Wild Fauna and Flora (CITES), and other sources in the United States and around the world.

There are too many to be thanked here, but thanks they have nonetheless, as do the many I came in contact with peripherally who helped with research, obtaining photos, and other key elements needed to produce this book.

Much appreciation for continuing support from friends, colleagues, and particular interview subjects that have stayed in touch over the long haul to publication. They are listed only in the order that their names came to mind, and my thanks go equally to the scores not mentioned—you were all instrumental to the book or my writing of it: Frank Clifford—I still miss writing for you, and if you hadn't championed my parrot-trade story to the *Los Angeles Times* magazine, it's unlikely this book would be here today; Taryn Poole; Michele Kuraner; Marvin Davis; Ronnie Gunnerson; Jody Merritt; Karyn Taylor; the Venerable Reverend Dr. Karuna

Dharma; the Reverend Vajra Karuna; Victor Bumbalo; Lynn Sipe (and for all the fabulous research info you generated for me, a very special thanks); Charles Munn and his crew in Brazil; Lourival Lima, his wife Antonia, brother Francisco, and brothers-in-law Raimundo and Edivan Nobres, and Cid Simões and Paola Segura; Jamie Gilardi at the World Parrot Trust (a special thanks to you for all the photos and information, research, and fascinating, if sometimes heated, dialogue); Samuel Jojola of U.S. Fish and Wildlife Law Enforcement; thanks for fact-checking chapter seven go to Nancy Clum, a new friend and colleague; Laureen Mitchell; Henry and Donna Wiencek; Vincent Bond of U.S./I.C.E.; John Brooks of U.S. Fish and Wildlife; Lawrence Hawkins, U.S. Department of Agriculture; Jacques Gauthier at Yale University; Aaron Sanger of Forest Ethics; the marvelous Gay Bradshaw (thank you for everything and all the inspiration you continue to bring my way); Richard Brooks of Greenpeace; Beci Carr; Cara Templeton and the lorikeets of the Aquarium of the Pacific; Michael Schindlinger for his sharp eye and fantastic knowledge base of parrots and the animal world; Christiana MacKnight; Hugh Choi; Steve and Paula Fitzsimmons; Pat Baltozer; Denise Kelly; Eileen McCarthy; Aimee Morgana and N'Kisi; gratitude to Irene Pepperberg and our lost Alex, who changed the world with their work; Benny Gallaway of the American Federation of Aviculture; Phoebe and the other breeders who gave me interviews; Chester Gipson and Jerry D. DePoyster at the U.S. Department of Agriculture; Tracy Bennett, DVM; Attila Molnar, DVM; Wayne Pacelle; Beverly Kaskey; Kathy Bauch and everyone at the Humane Society of the United States; everyone involved with *Here, There and Everywhere* (that book and this one are linked by subject; the only difference is age range); Dr. Jane Goodall; Rosemary Low; Nigel Collar; and all those who have written about parrots before me and helped my work by doing so.

To my excellent agent, Jandy Nelson of Manus & Associates Literary Agency: you were right, writing and researching this book was a life-changing experience—though I now think getting it to this point was just the beginning.

Major thanks to friend, colleague, and excellent editor Randy McCarthy, who worked tirelessly editing this book for me.

Special thanks to Marc Johnson and Karen Windsor of Foster Parrots Sanctuary, who were open and forthcoming about their work—the trials and tribulations of caring for hundreds of parrots every day—and their unwavering support of this endeavor as it continued. Marc, now you can stop holding your breath.

And to all the avian rescuers across the country who devote their lives to the thankless job of caring for unwanted, needy parrots: thank you. There is a special place in heaven for the work you do.

Last but most important, to all the pet parrots and those stuck in the pet trade that made this book necessary—those neglected and abused, and the millions who never knew the love of their parents—you are not forgotten. You are always in my thoughts, and my heart goes out to you wherever you are suffering at our hands.

Author's Note

The vast majority of the books published in the United States today are not environmentally friendly. The paper used to produce this book contains 20 percent postconsumer waste.

It's important that we all realize that the cost of a book is more than the money paid for it in a bookstore. There is also a cost to the environment. A tree is a living thing. To show respect for our planet it is only right to replace a life where one is taken, and to repay the earth for what we use. You can do this for your copy of *Of Parrots and People*.

Eco-Libris is an environmentally conscious business whose mission is to green up the book industry and plant trees in developing countries to compensate for the ones killed unsustainably for books. Its goal is to plant a tree for every book you buy, and for every one you already own.

For just one dollar you can have a tree planted for *Of Parrots and People*. Do so by going to www.ecolibris.net/parrots/.

As an ecoresponsible citizen of the earth, you will have done something to replenish deforested areas and help the planet thrive. And you will have helped make the book you hold fully green.

Thank you,
Mira Tweti

Index

PHOTOGRAPH CREDITS